Challeng
Rights in
America

Challenges of Human Rights in Latin America:

Minutes of the Fourth Conference of Fundamental Rights

Edited by

César Landa

Cambridge Scholars Publishing

Challenges of Human Rights in Latin America:
Minutes of the Fourth Conference of Fundamental Rights

Edited by César Landa

This book first published 2019. The present binding first published 2021.

Cambridge Scholars Publishing

Lady Stephenson Library, Newcastle upon Tyne, NE6 2PA, UK

British Library Cataloguing in Publication Data
A catalogue record for this book is available from the British Library

ISBN (10): 1-5275-7252-8
ISBN (13): 978-1-5275-7252-2

TABLE OF CONTENTS

Thematic Table 9: Constitutionalization of Law

PREFACE

Since the beginning of the 21st century, the affirmation of the constitutional democratic model in Latin America finds challenges still unresolved on the validity and effectiveness of fundamental rights, and the necessary balance between the powers of the State. The first product is the transfer of the public economy to private groups and public burdens to the citizens, and; the second, has been characterized by the open confrontation of presidentialism with parliamentarism.

The constant economic growth in the region in recent decades, due largely to the long period of the rise in international prices of renewable and non-renewable natural resources, which is the main source of wealth in the region, has been created in sectors of the population not only vulnerable, social and political instability due to the lack of redistribution of wealth, through the old and new rights, and governmental corruption.

Also, the balance and control between the powers has not been achieved satisfactorily, nor has governmental stability; on the contrary, until the 1980s, the political practice was, in the majority of countries, conflict between the government and the opposition, which is not always resolved through democratic elections, but through military coups and even civilians against the President of turn. The collapse of the rule of law by appealing to the doctrine of necessity and urgency, was the way to resolve conflicts between the government and the opposition during the XIX-XX centuries.

However, with the end of the military governments in Latin America, on the one hand, democracy is protected by limiting political rights against the threats of terrorism and prosecution, and, on the other hand, the dismissal or forced resignation of many Presidents has been a parliamentary practice in a presidential political regime in Latin America. In particular, the impeachment of the President apparently has become a new practice to solve the serious political conflicts between the government and the opposition.

So, the strengthening and development of this model of the constitutional state are a common challenge for the Latin American region, which has been characterized by historical problems of legal and political instability, and by the need to carry out structural reforms to make the equitable distribution of power and wealth among all citizens.

Moreover, it can be noted that the role of the constitution is not only justice, but also, the Inter-American Court of Human Rights is placed at the heart of the issues of the new constitutional State, to the extent that their work if it is legal in nature is becoming a new pipeline instance and a legal resolution of major issues on human rights with all the dangers of judicial activism and the problems for democratic legitimacy.

In this scenario is the development of the IV Latin American Conference on Fundamental Rights (Lima, 11-13 October), under the auspices of the Rule of Law Program for Latin America of the Konrad Adenauer Foundation, in which the members of the Inter-American Network of Fundamental Rights and Democracy (RED-IDD) have discussed the political rights and the consolidation of democracy, political judgment, the plurality of information and media concentration, due process in the judicial protection of individual rights, new technologies and fundamental rights, the State's fight against corruption, the control of constitutionality and conventionality control; new fundamental rights; and the constitutionalization of law, which are published in this volume, which would not have been possible without the valuable contribution of María-Fernanda Caparó.

We consider, that the Latin American conferences on Fundamental Rights have been consolidated through the academic bridge that has been formed between professors of Constitutional Law of Brazil, Peru, Chile, Colombia, Mexico and Argentina. This will lead to the affirmation not only of the exchange but the construction of constitutional ideas of their own; through the development of research on the problems that beset the democracy and fundamental rights of our constitutional states in Latin America.

César Landa, May 2018

THEMATIC TABLE 1: POLITICAL RIGHTS AND CONSOLIDATION OF THE LATIN AMERICAN DEMOCRACY

CONSTITUTIONAL LIMITS OF THE RIGHT TO RUN FOR OFFICE

CÉSAR LANDA*

I. Introduction

In the most recent elections in Peru (2016), there was a plethora of candidates—coming from nearly every political party—who had criminal records and/or pending criminal charges. Those who were successfully elected now have immunity and privileges against being investigated by district attorneys or charged in criminal proceedings, due to the fact that members of congress in Peru have legislative immunity. Indeed, in the 2016 congressional elections, there were 52 candidates with criminal records (Transparencia, 2016), a circumstance that serves to weaken our democracy by enabling persons involved in acts of corruption and members of criminal organizations engaged in drug trafficking and/or terrorist financing to infiltrate the constitutional state.

The fact that there was such a high number of candidates with pending criminal charges or convictions for the commission of certain crimes raises serious doubts regarding the transparency and quality of the candidates running for public office under our democratic model, as enshrined in the Constitution of 1993. The principle of democracy does not just mean electing representatives from among those candidates who run for office, on a plural basis, in elections. To earn its name as such, a representative democracy must presuppose that those representing us are citizens with respect for the principles that govern the representation of the general interest and the common good, as provided for in the Constitution and the law.

In view of this scenario and the public debate over electoral reform, it is essential that we analyze some of the proposed impediments to standing for office applicable to individuals with convictions upheld on appeal; those applicable to convicted individuals who have served their sentence; and those applicable to persons with pending criminal charges (when the district attorney has brought formal charges, but no judgment has been issued yet).

The Right to Political Participation

In the Peruvian constitutional model, the right to political participation has three facets that may be inferred from the constitutional body of law: 1. The facet pertaining to the right to vote and the right to run for public office (Section 2.19); 2. The facet pertaining to control over democratically elected authorities (removal, revocation, accountability), in accordance with Section 31 of the Constitution of 1993; and 3. The facet pertaining to mechanisms for direct participation in decision-making (referendums) or proposals of public interest (legislative initiatives and constitutional reform initiatives) recognized in Sections 31 and 206 of the Constitution; and indigenous peoples' right to prior consultation (Law 29785).

The presuppositions for the exercise of suffrage rights are set forth in both the Constitution and the law (Jurado Nacional de Elecciones, 2016),[1] thus making this a legally established right, although in an intermediate sense, since Sections 90 and 91 of the Constitution itself establish the requirements for and impediments to being congresspersons; and the requirements for being the president of the republic (Section 110 of the Constitution). In this presentation, we will not be touching on electoral problems involving candidates in regional and municipal elections, given the local particularities of these issues.

In the model of a constitutional democracy, the right to vote and to stand for public office is fundamental, given that our democracy is representative (Section 43 of the Constitution). The right to vote helps to bolster our democracy and civic responsibility, thus channeling and enforcing the principle of political pluralism, which is inseparable from the democratic model enshrined in our Constitution.

According to constitutional theory and jurisprudence, however, no right is absolute. This means that restrictions are admitted, provided they are reasonable and proportional. Under this system, all limits on the right to citizen participation are defined by the legislative branch. These limits typically involve aspects such as age, nationality, criminal convictions, and civic or mental capacity, among others, which will be analyzed below.

---

[1] See the Jurado Nacional de Elecciones (National Electoral Board). Compendio de Legislación Electoral 2016.

This right may also be limited, however, in the case of persons who commit certain crimes that seriously and directly violate the Constitution.[2]

II. Limits on the Right to Run for Public Office

In the Peruvian legal system, any constituent aged 18 or older is able, in principle, to exercise his or her right to be elected to a public position by popular vote. To exercise the right to vote, in turn, one must be registered with the electoral board. This provision is established in Section 30 of the Constitution of 1993.

Nevertheless, there is currently a public debate regarding the possibility of limiting participation: firstly, by a person with serious criminal charges pending, when no conviction has been issued but the criminal proceeding is underway; secondly, by an individual who has been found guilty and lost a first appeal, when all other possible remedies have not yet been exhausted; and thirdly, by establishing an impediment against standing for public office even after the convicted party has served his or her sentence.

To begin with, it must be noted that the Constitution and the law regulate two aspects pertaining to the right to run for public office: 1. Requirements for being a candidate; and 2. Impediments to being a candidate for a popularly elected position. Those limitations on the right to run for public office applicable to persons with pending criminal charges, those who have been convicted, and even those who have served out their sentence following a criminal conviction all fall within the scope of impediments to running for public office.

We must be careful to point out, on the other hand, that Section 33 of the Constitution establishes two of the grounds for the suspension of suffrage rights: prison sentences, and convictions involving a disqualification from exercising political rights. In principle, the content of this section of the Constitution makes it impossible to suspend the right to run for office in the case of individuals with pending criminal charges, as well as those whose conviction has not yet become *res judicata*. Nevertheless, it is necessary to interpret these provisions in keeping with the principle of practical concordance with the Constitution as a whole.

---

[2] With regard to this matter, Section 23.2 of the American Convention on Human Rights recognizes that the law may regulate the exercise of rights of citizen participation, including the right to vote and to be elected (active and passive suffrage).

In effect, if it were only possible to suspend political rights—specifically, the right to run for public office—through a judgment, then it could not be argued that Section 100 of the Constitution allows for political disqualification, both from remaining in public office and from exercising the right to run for public office during the disqualification period. Such disqualification, resulting from the commission of a constitutional violation, must be established by a legislative resolution (*resolución legislativa*) issued by Congress; that is, by virtue of a parliamentary document that is *not* a court judgment with the status of *res judicata*. This, too, is a matter of constitutional interpretation, of course, as well as requiring an assessment of the balance between two constitutionally legitimate rights.

The jurisprudence of the Peruvian Constitutional Court contains certain standards intended to protect the rights of candidates and citizens elected to positions by popular vote. Specifically, in the cases of Espino Espino (File No. 2366-2003-AA/TC, 2004) and Castillo Chirinos (File No. 2730-2006-PA/TC, 2006), the court noted the need for a final and binding conviction against the candidate and/or democratically elected authority in order to enforce any restrictions on running for office or to remove the authority from a popularly elected position.

Given that rights and freedoms must be interpreted in accordance with the conventions to which Peru is a party, as per the Fourth Final and Temporary Provision of the Constitution of 1993, it must be noted here that according to the standards of the Inter-American Court of Human Rights (IA Court of HR), suffrage rights *may* indeed be restricted. Thus, States can legitimately regulate political rights through formal laws, although any legal limitations on a political right such as suffrage must meet the prerequisites established by the principle of proportionality: legitimate purpose, necessity, and proportionality in the strict sense (**IA Court of HR, *Case of Castañeda Gutman vs. Mexico*, paragraph 149).**

In the Colombian legal system, for example, that country's Constitutional Court has rejected the application of jurisprudence derived from the case of López Mendoza vs. Venezuela, specifically stating that the mandate established by the IA Court of HR—with regard to the need for a final and binding conviction issued by a criminal judge as a prerequisite for the suspension of the right to run for public office—is applicable to Venezuela, since its constitution specifically establishes such a requirement; but that the same rule did not apply to Colombia, where the legal system recognizes the power to disqualify (suspend the suffrage rights of) even administrative authorities (Constitutional Court of Colombia, Judgment SU 712/13).

On the other hand, a measure limiting the rights of defendants with a guilty verdict upheld on appeal and/or who have not received any judgment whatsoever does not affect the principles of equality and non-discrimination. Specifically, while such persons may be prevented from standing for a popularly elected position, the reasons for which such a restriction has been imposed are not among the motives prohibited by the Constitution and the American Convention on Human Rights. Since this is a measure limiting fundamental rights, however, it must be duly founded and based on a proper rationale set forth by the legislative branch.

Generally speaking, States have a broad margin of appreciation when regulating their electoral systems and the rules applicable thereto, including rules involving restrictions and/or limitations on the right to run for public office. In principle, the margin of deference on electoral matters will only be limited in cases where the rights of certain disadvantaged groups are violated, or when the practices of a specific State run contrary to the other countries that form part of the Inter-American System of Human Rights, that is, when the State acts in violation of the consensus currently existing on electoral matters (IA Court of HR, *Case of Yatama vs. Nicaragua*, 2005).

III. Types of Crimes due to which the Right to Run for Public Office may be Restricted

In view of the foregoing arguments regarding the crisis faced by the democratic system in Peru, and given the legislative branch's power to freely establish election law, it becomes necessary to set forth a standard on the types of crimes that may be considered grounds for the suspension of the right to run for public office, applicable to those persons accused of serious crimes who have not yet received a final and binding judgment, or those who have already served the sentence issued against them and are supposed to have been rehabilitated.

In fact, the Peruvian legal system already contains provisions affecting the right to run for public office. However, these are not applied until *after* the election campaign, i.e., once the authority has already been sworn in to the popularly elected position. This concept of "vacancy" is, in a way, the *a posteriori* response established by the legal system in the event that an elected authority receives a final and binding criminal conviction.

On the other hand, although the principle of rehabilitation of those convicted of crimes supposes that once the citizen has served the respective sentence, he or she may once again exercise his/her rights, including the right to run for public office, the fact is that this principle appears to allow for some limitations. Indeed, it might be reasonable, in the case of certain crimes, to impose a restriction against running for a popularly elected position, especially if the aspirant has served a sentence for acts that, in and of themselves, violated the very structure and essence of the State.

It could thus be deemed legitimate for the legislative branch, on an exceptional basis, to develop limitations on the right to run for public office, based on certain supreme constitutional values that are essential to the democratic State under the constitutional rule of law—even when there is not yet a conviction with the status of *res judicata*, or when the convicted party has served his/her sentence and has been deemed rehabilitated.

Specifically, the right to run for public office could be restricted provided certain prerequisites are met (Espíndola, 331):

a) The crime must be established in the Constitution, and must warrant a punishment involving the suspension of political rights;
b) The provisional suspension of political rights must be suitable, useful, and necessary for safeguarding a constitutionally acceptable objective; and
c) The crime must involve probable cause of harm or a clear and present danger.

Specifically, it should be noted that the suspension of the right to run for public office—in cases with pending criminal charges, or where a conviction has been upheld on appeal but is not yet final and binding, or in cases where the convicted party has already served the sentence imposed—does not apply to the commission of just any crime, but only to those cases in which a truly serious crime has been committed, of the type the constituent power itself has included directly in the Constitution. As such, the relativization of the principle of the presumption of innocence and the principle of rehabilitation is permissible only in the case of the following constitutionalized crimes:

(i) Commission of the crime of terrorism (Sections 2-24-F and 140).

(ii) Commission of the crime of drug trafficking (Sections 2-24-F and 8).
(iii) Commission of the crime of corruption (Section 41).

Drug Trafficking Crimes

In the case of illegal drug trafficking, Section 8 of Peru's Constitution establishes the State's obligation to fight and punish this crime. The inclusion of the said crime in the Constitution makes sense in view of the risk it poses to the very effectiveness of the model of the State under the rule of law. On the subject, the Constitutional Court has declared the following:

> (…) this Court has had occasion to reiterate the nature of illegal drug trafficking—a crime that has been constitutionalized, and one subject to the highest degree of prosecution and punishment—and even the effects of this crime on the national economy. Thus, in the case at hand, the laundering of assets gained through illegal drug trafficking *undermines the legal economy and threatens the stability, security, and sovereignty of the State*. It went on to state that *illegal drug trafficking is an international criminal activity, the suppression of which demands urgent attention and the highest possible priority*; and that it *generates considerable financial returns and great fortunes that permit transnational criminal organizations to invade, contaminate, and corrupt the structures of public administration, along with legal, commercial, and financial activities, and all levels of society.* (File No. 0033-2007-PI/TC: 74)

As such, there are well-founded reasons to establish measures—as part of the criminal policy of the Peruvian State—that restrict the right to run for office among those persons found guilty of drug trafficking. Above all else, it must be borne in mind that this is a crime that serves to foster corruption and finance terrorism, consequently giving it the ability to lay siege to the very structure of the State, through candidates who inevitably make their way into legitimate political parties.[3]

---

[3] EL COMERCIO newspaper. "García returns US$ 5,000 that attorney Abanto contributed to his 2006 campaign, stressing that his administration is waging a forceful fight against drug trafficking." Edition dated Sunday, February 13, 2011. Likewise, presidential candidate Keiko Fujimori was accused in 2011 of having accepted US$ 10,000 from persons tied to drug trafficking. See LA REPUBLICA newspaper. "Keiko received $10,000 from family involved in money laundering proceedings." Edition dated Tuesday, February 22, 2011.

Indeed, the financing that political parties receive from drug trafficking is decisive in helping those who hold representative positions. Anyone backed by funds of illegal provenance does not represent the nation, however, but only the private interests of those involved in drug trafficking. This financing thus becomes a source of corruption and influence peddling, with negative consequences for ethics in public administration and the very health of a democracy (Castillo and Zovatto, 1998: XXIII).

Indeed, the Constitutional Court itself has noted that the existence and spread of drug trafficking affect different basic values and institutions in any social State based on the rule of law, such as the principles and rights to the dignity of the human person (Section 1), the family (Section 4), and social peace (Section 2, Subsection 22), among others (File No. 0020-2005-PI/TC: 118).

In comparative law, measures have also been taken with regard to the preventive control of drug trafficking. In Colombia, for example, Law 001 of 2009 establishes that those parties whose candidates have been convicted of crimes related to drug trafficking and similar deeds—regardless of whether they are actually chosen to fill popularly elected positions—shall lose their eligibility to present candidates for the following election. This example illustrates the seriousness with which narco-politics are taken in the said country, where even the political organizations themselves are punished.

Crime of Terrorism

The same argument can be applied to the case of terrorism or membership in an illegal armed group. It is of particular interest here to note that the Constitutional Court has proclaimed the Peruvian legal system to be a militant democracy. Specifically, it has stated that:

> (…) It should be noted here that the Constitution has enshrined two fundamental principles: one of a political and the other of a legal nature. The first is based on the people's sovereignty, by virtue of which they have opted for a militant democracy, which refuses to allow abuses in the exercise of rights to the detriment of the legal system; while the second is based on constitutional supremacy, by virtue of which the fundamental rights of those who attack the constitutional State under the rule of law and the social order may be reasonably and proportionally restricted. For such reasons, the Court finds that these two points of the claim must be dismissed. (File No. 0003-2005-PI/TC: 371)

The fact that Peru's democracy falls under this category means that it has the power to create and/or apply mechanisms with which to respond to antidemocratic parties or political organizations, or those whose purposes are illegal or run contrary to the model of a State under the rule of law.[4] Indeed, the concept of a militant democracy also enables the legislative branch to impose limits or restrictions on those individuals who have been convicted of or tried for crimes such as terrorism, this being one of the ways to defend the constitutional democratic model.

While the Political Parties Act (Law 28094) has established a legal mechanism to prevent organizations with concealed illegal purposes (such as terrorism) from forming political parties (Landa, 2012: 224),[5] there is also the possibility of establishing a mechanism to prevent the participation of those who have been convicted of or tried for crimes such as terrorism and have not expressed remorse, acting through parties or organizations that are legitimately registered and whose purposes do not formally run contrary to the concept of the constitutional State under the rule of law.

Indeed, the recently-passed Law 30353 creates a Registry of Civil Reparations Debtors, by virtue of which those persons who have been convicted for terrorism and corruption and who still have outstanding debts "shall be prohibited from performing any duties or holding any position, employment, contract, or commission of a public nature, nor may they run for or gain access to public positions by virtue of popular election." The fact of being a "debtor" does not seem sufficient reason—in view of the supreme values of the State—to restrict a person's right to run for public office. Rather, such limitations must be aimed at preventing the aforementioned constitutionalized crimes, when they are currently under investigation or subject to pending charges and/or a criminal conviction.

Crimes of Corruption

When it comes to crimes against State property, restrictions against running as a candidate are based on the fact that those individuals who

[4] In its Resolution No. 224-2011-ROP/JNE, the National Electoral Board denied an application for registration by the political party "Por amnistía y derechos fundamentales" ("For Amnesty and Fundamental Rights").

[5] See also Resolution No. 1147.2016-JNE, whereby the National Electoral Board rejected the registration of the political party Unidad y Defensa del Pueblo Peruano, a new version of MOVADEF.

hold senior public positions by virtue of popular election must, in fact, meet certain conditions, such as an adequate behavior that reflects transparency, efficiency, and honesty in the management of public affairs, so as to ensure compliance with the general interests of society as a whole.

Corruption is one of the gravest threats to the model of the social State under the rule of law. This threat brings with it perverse institutional and social consequences, resulting, for example, in a sector of voters who prefer candidates "who can steal, as long as they get work done." In this way, crimes of public corruption erode the democratic political system, the public economy, and the constitutional principles of transparency and honesty in the performance of public duties. More concretely, corruption results in a loss of citizens' trust in the model of the State under the rule of law, while also affecting the legitimacy of decision-making authorities, not only at the federal level, but also the regional and local levels.

Corruption likewise has an impact on the country's very economic development, reducing investments and diminishing efficiency and competition among companies active in the same sectors. Indeed, because of corruption, the economic resources necessary to modernize markets and goods are not invested. It is likewise necessary here to draw attention to the fact that crimes of corruption affect the State's ability to function with objectivity, legality, and efficiency (Constitutional Court of Colombia C-944-12).

The Peruvian legal system has implemented a constitutional reform declaring the non-applicability of statutory limitations to crimes of corruption committed by senior public officials (Law 30650), thus expanding upon Section 41 of the Constitution.[6] There is also the need to

[6] "FORTY-ONE: Those public officials and servants established by law, or those who administrate or manage the funds of the State or of bodies maintained thereby, shall file a declaration of assets and income upon taking possession of their positions, during the exercise thereof, and upon leaving the said positions. These declarations shall be published in the official gazette, in the form and under the conditions established by law.
When an official is presumed to be involved in a suspicious increase of net worth, the State Prosecutor's Office, acting on a complaint filed by a third party, or ex officio, may bring charges before the judicial branch. The law establishes the responsibility of public officials and servants, as well as the term during which they shall be disqualified from holding public office.
The term for the running of the statutes is doubled in those cases of crimes committed against the public administration or the property of the State, both for public officials and for private individuals.

respect international conventions on the fight against corruption, such as the Inter-American Convention against Corruption, which was ratified by Peru. This convention establishes that the States parties must adopt the necessary mechanisms to prevent, detect, punish, and eradicate corruption. The same convention also stresses the direct link between the strengthening of the democratic model and the need to fight all forms of corruption in the performance of public duties.

IV. Analysis of Proportionality in the three cases for the Relativization of the Principle of the Presumption of Innocence, Rehabilitation, and the Suspension of Suffrage Rights

The constitutionality of restricting the right to political participation (as an impediment to running as a candidate for a popularly elected position) due to a conviction upheld on appeal

As noted above, the restriction against being a candidate should be implemented in response to the commission of the three crimes of willful misconduct established in the Constitution—namely, drug trafficking, terrorism, and corruption—as discussed hereinabove. The first aspect to be analyzed here is the content of Section 33 of the Constitution of 1993, according to which political rights shall be suspended due to a sentence involving imprisonment or a sentence with disqualification from exercising political rights. As such, it is not necessarily essential for there to be a conviction imposing restrictions on the guilty party's personal freedom as a prerequisite for limiting his or her right to vote or to run for public office (active/passive suffrage).

With regard to both of these cases, it must be noted that the Constitution does not specifically establish whether the judgment must be final and binding, or to have attained the status of *res judicata*. This matter, however, may potentially lead to a conflict with the principle of the presumption of innocence. Thus, it becomes necessary to examine its proportionality, as follows:

The statute of limitations on the criminal action shall not run in the most serious cases, in accordance with the principle of legality."

a. Suitability

This step involves an analysis of the relationship between means and end, that is, *between the means adopted, through legislative intervention, and the end proposed by the legislative branch*. The means here are the restriction of the right to run for public office among convicted persons with a guilty verdict upheld on appeal for any constitutionalized crime involving imprisonment, even if this judgment has not yet been enforced. From my point of view, the conviction must also find that the crime was willfully committed as a prerequisite for the full application of this restriction.

The purpose of this measure is to promote a representative political system that meets the standards required by the democratic principle of the representation of the popular vote. Specifically, it seeks to guarantee the morality, transparency, efficiency, and proper functioning of the administration of public assets.

b. Necessity

In Peru, the political system is currently experiencing a crisis tied to the legitimacy of its representatives, a situation that poses a serious risk to the proper functioning of the country's democracy. There is no denying the influence of drug trafficking in the sphere of politics, for example, given the glut of candidates who have been convicted of this crime, but whose judgment has not yet been ruled final and binding. These reflections on crimes of drug trafficking also apply to other types of crimes deemed especially grave due to the legal rights violated, most notably crimes of terrorism and corruption.

In this case, the measure should be aimed at restricting—or, if one prefers, preventing—convicted persons from running for office (even when the sentence has not become *res judicata*), so long as the conviction has been upheld on appeal. The fact is that a decision to this effect would be a violation of the presumption of innocence. Nevertheless, it should be noted that the situation referred to in the question involves a second-instance sentence upholding the candidate's criminal responsibility, meaning that a presumption has been made with regard to the commission of a crime that warrants criminal punishment.

When faced with this matter, the legislative branch might decide not to establish any restrictions whatsoever, allowing the guilty candidate to stand for office and possibly even win an election. In the case of the

Peruvian Congress, this would lead to a procedure for their replacement by a substitute (Section 23 of the Regulations on the Congress of the Republic) in the event that the winning candidate was later convicted in the final instance. The question that needs to be asked here, however, is whether this possible restriction should prevail over the current situation, where—in practice—a candidate who has already been found guilty (when the ruling is not yet final and binding) stands for office, possibly wins the election, and is later declared guilty and forced to vacate his position.

The first option should also prevent the party or political movement from continuing to occupy the congressperson's vacant position, in view of the fact that the said organization allowed the candidate—who had already committed illegal acts that prove his inaptitude to hold a popularly elected position—to run for a position in an election. It is precisely the political parties that have a responsibility to select the candidates who will represent them. Therefore, they are also responsible for making sure that the political system has the most suitable representatives to safeguard the general interests of society.

In view of the foregoing, responsibility for this situation must not be analyzed in purely individual terms, but instead must be based on the candidate's membership of the political group he or she represents. It would thus appear more feasible to prevent a candidate from running for office at the start of the election process, as opposed to after being elected.

Mechanisms for *a posteriori* control fail to not explicitly establish or faithfully reflect the need to legitimize the democratic system starting from its very foundations upward—that is, to ensure that the representative aspect of the constitutional democratic model allows only those citizens who respect the law and the Constitution to participate. It thus becomes necessary to establish or assume that the suspension of the right to run for public office among those being tried for terrorism, illegal drug trafficking, and corruption is not a *conviction*, but rather a *precautionary measure* aimed at protecting the democratic order.

With regard to this matter, the Spanish legal system—in its Law 1/2003 (the act guaranteeing democracy in city councils and the safety of council members)—establishes that those individuals who have been found guilty and sentenced—even if that sentence is not yet final and binding—for crimes of rebellion, terrorism, or attacks on state institutions cannot run for popularly elected positions on city councils in Spain's autonomous communities.

The European Court of Human Rights has likewise ruled—in the case of Scoppola vs. Italy (No. 3)—that the voting rights of convicted prisoners (currently serving prison sentences) may be limited or suspended, given that such measures help prevent crime, enhance civic responsibility and respect for the rule of law, and guarantee the democratic regime itself.[7] To a certain extent, this criterion can also be considered in the case of guilty parties with a second-instance sentence, even if that sentence is not yet final and binding. Specifically, the Court has established that States have a broad margin of appreciation in electoral matters, especially with regard to the regimen applicable to those found guilty of certain crimes (*Case of Scoppola vs. Italy (No. 3)*, 2012, paragraph 90).

As such, it could be argued that the fact that a candidate has a second-instance sentence is equivalent to the requirement of plausibility that must be met when issuing a precautionary measure, given the threat posed to democracy by a candidate with a conviction upheld on appeal—even if it is not yet final and binding—who seeks to hold a popularly elected position.

It should be recalled here that in the Peruvian legal system, the Code of Criminal Procedure allows for precautionary measures such as preventive custody, without such measures violating the right to the presumption of innocence. In this regard, it has been pointed out that preventive custody does not affect the right to the presumption of innocence because it is not a punitive measure, strictly speaking (Peruvian Constitutional Court, File No. 1260-2002-HC/TC: 3).

Thus, the restrictions set forth in the bill under consideration are similar to a precautionary measure aimed at defending the democratic order. This measure seeks to protect the rights of the average citizen, along with other constitutionally protected rights, such as constitutional public order, legal certainty, and the proper functioning of justice, social peace, and democracy, which itself encompasses all of the foregoing (Ovejero, 2004: 141).

---

[7] The European Court of Human Rights has acknowledged that the suspension of the suffrage rights of convicted prisoners serving jail time may be a legitimate objective for preventing crime and enhancing civic responsibility and respect for the rule of law.

c. Proportionality in the Strict Sense

The principle of proportionality in the strict sense can be translated into the following statement: “The greater the degree to which one principle is not met or is affected, the more important it is to satisfy the other.” In this regard, it should be noted—in the case of individuals with a conviction upheld on appeal—that while the right to run for public office is restricted, this measure also fosters the legitimization of the representative political system, given that only those persons with a suitable profile—that is, those who not only possess technical knowledge, but also ethical principles—should hold the position of democratically elected authorities. Therefore, the measure is proportional.

The constitutionality of restricting the right to political participation (as an impediment to running for a popularly elected position) despite having completed rehabilitation

a. Suitability

The end sought here by the legislative branch is to defend and strengthen the democratic model by assuring the personal quality of those who wish to run for a popularly elected position. Specifically, what is being limited here is the right to run for public office and the principle of resocialization. The principle of resocialization is affected to some degree, in any event, although not its essence which remains untouched.

b. Necessity

The proposed measure is necessary, given that the principle of rehabilitation is not limited by establishing terms of disqualification that go beyond the completion of the criminal sentence imposed. Here, it must be noted that the relationship between rehabilitation and impediments to being a candidate for a popularly elected position is not strictly one of necessity. The fact that a person convicted of a crime has completed his or her sentence does not prevent the legislative branch from deeming this individual fully rehabilitated for reinsertion into society, but not necessarily fit to manage public affairs by holding a popularly elected position (Constitutional Court of Colombia C-652-03).

It is necessary, however, to establish a period of disqualification as an impediment to running for a popularly elected public position. In other words, this restriction cannot be indefinite. In the Peruvian legal system, one reference point can be found in the disqualification imposed following impeachment. According to Section 100 of the Constitution, this disqualification has a maximum term of ten years. This does not mean, however, that the legislative branch is not necessarily required to establish this same period as a limitation, given that constitutional offenses differ from the commission of criminal offenses involving willful misconduct. If we were to propose a time limit, left up to the discretion of the legislative branch, it would be two-thirds of the sentence, without exceeding the total prison sentence served, given that in such a case the accessory sanction or punishment would end up being more severe, in some ways, than the prison sentence itself.

In regards to whether the suspension of suffrage rights should be temporary or permanent, note must be made that under Law 29444, teachers found guilty of terrorism, corruption, or sexual assault are barred from sitting examinations for public sector teaching positions, some even permanently. In this case, it could be said that the right to access a public position has been restricted under equal conditions. However, because education is a right and an essential public service, the Constitution has established that it must be imparted in accordance with constitutional principles and the purposes of the corresponding educational institution (Section 14). Thus, an examination of proportionality shows that this latter purpose (that of the respective institution) legitimizes the restriction of the right to access a public position among teachers convicted of terrorism.

In the case of political representation at the national level, special note should be made of the particular nature of the right to run for public office, given that a candidate who is ultimately elected must represent the interests of the nation or region where he was elected, as well as seeking the general interest of the public, in accordance with the principles enshrined in the Constitution. It may thus be legitimately argued that political representation can only be exercised by persons who have been proven to meet the respective profile and who conduct themselves ethically, in accordance with the Constitution and the principles of democracy.

In any event, a person who aspires to a public position under equal conditions may fully develop and realize him/herself in other spaces or spheres in which the criminal conviction for the especially serious crimes he/she has committed is not decisive in impeding him/her from engaging in the *res publica*.

It is useful here, however, to look at a comparative legal analysis when determining the level of consensus existing among States regarding the restriction of the right to run for public office. In any event, if there is a limit to the measure restricting the right to run for public office, it would have to be tied to the principle of resocialization inherent to the sentence. While a temporary limitation is admitted for those convicts who have served a sentence for one of the aforementioned crimes, an absolute limitation might ultimately violate the essence of the principle in question.

With regard to this matter, there is a discussion in North American theory about whether the limitation of the plaintiffs' right to run for public office is, in fact, admissible under the social contract theory. The truth of the matter is that while there is some justification for limiting the suffrage rights of those who have committed crimes so serious that they have affected the very notion of the social pact on which the model of the constitutional State has been built, such limitation cannot be absolute (Levine, 2009, 193). Indeed, there are also other arguments that lead us to the conclusion that suffrage rights may only be limited on a temporary basis.

Among other reasons, Levine argues that the idea that an ex-convict will contaminate the democratic process cannot be partially admitted in the legal system, without in fact assuming that the ex-convict is completely incapacitated, as if all other citizens were superior to him. Likewise, a sanction such as perpetual disqualification would mean that the model of the constitutional state is guided by the parameters of retribution as punishment for the commission of a crime, but lifetime disenfranchisement is neither an inhibitor—nor, if one prefers, a mechanism for preventing the commission of crimes—and it most certainly does not rehabilitate the prisoner. On the contrary, it has more negative effects, even going so far as to affect the very principle of equality (Cosgove, 2003: 157)

c. Proportionality in the Strict Sense

As far as proportionality in the strict sense, it should be noted that this measure, too, has been adopted in legal systems such as that of Colombia. Section 122 of the Colombian Constitution, along with that country's criminal laws, has established that the political disenfranchisement of those convicted for the crimes constitutionalized in Peru is legitimately constitutional.[8] This measure helps to strengthen democracy by ensuring

[8] Conviction for the commission of a crime against the public administration—with imprisonment. Conviction for the commission of crimes against State

the efficiency, transparency, and honesty of the representative democratic system itself.

Going into further depth on the comparative experience, some countries have established the suspension of the right to run for public office even after the sentence has been served. One illustrative case is that of *Zdanoka vs. Latvia*. In this case, the European Court of Human Rights analyzed the situation of a candidate running for a seat in the Latvian Parliament, who was prevented from running due to her ties to the Communist Party. In 1991, the Communist Party had tried to promote multiple coups aimed at bringing Latvia back into what had been—up until 1990—the Soviet Union. As a consequence of these coup attempts, Latvia declared the Communist Party illegal and passed laws under which anyone who had actively participated in the parties (among them, the Communist Party) that formed part of the coup attempt in 1991 was barred from running for election or being elected to the Parliament or city councils (ECHR, *Case of Zdanoka vs. Latvia*, 2006)

In its decision, the Grand Chamber of the ECHR stated that this measure was admissible in a context such as Latvia's, where democracy had been established after many decades, following the dissolution of the Soviet Union. In effect, by ruling that democracy formed part of the European model or public order, the court admitted that it was legitimate to restrict the right of certain individuals to run for public office, if this measure succeeded in preserving democracy (*Case of Zdanoka vs. Latvia*, 2006).[9] As such, it deemed Latvia to be in a better position than the Court itself to define and assess the country's political context. This, in turn, legitimized Latvia to restrict certain citizens' suffrage rights, based on their membership of a prohibited political organization (*Case of Zdanoka vs.*

---

property. Conviction for the commission of crimes related to illegal armed groups, crimes against humanity, or drug trafficking.

[9] In order to guarantee the stability and effectiveness of a democratic system, the State may be obligated to take specific measures to protect itself. Thus, with regard to the demand for political loyalty imposed upon public functionaries, the Court recognized the legitimacy of the concept of a "democracy capable of defending itself" (§§ 51 and 59). It has also been found that pluralism and democracy are rooted in a commitment that requires various concessions by individuals, who must sometimes be prepared to limit some of their freedoms in order to guarantee the greater stability of the country as a whole. ECHR. Case of Zdanoka vs. Latvia, 2006.

Latvia, 2006).[10] Nevertheless, the European Court noted that it was necessary to establish a limit on the application of such prohibitive measures, based on the context and situation of each country, as well as the assertion of the democratic model itself. Indeed, the ECHR pointed out that the law in question—although it did not affect suffrage rights—needed to be continually reviewed, and even amended in the near future.

Based on this case, it can be argued that the right to rehabilitation, too, is relative, and may take a back seat to the need to ensure the permanence and stability of the democratic model, which in turn guarantees the full effectiveness of fundamental rights such as the right to equality, to non-discrimination, and to the dignity of the human person. As such, it is admissible and strictly proportional to limit the right to run for public office by those who have served a sentence for the constitutionalized crimes of terrorism, drug trafficking, and corruption.

The constitutionality of restricting the right to political participation (as an impediment to running for a popularly elected position) due to the commission of any type of willful wrongdoing

Here, we are dealing with a case in which the person who aspires to a popularly elected position has not yet been convicted, but currently has charges pending for the crimes mentioned in the first section. It thus becomes necessary to establish a proportionality test to determine whether or not the measure is constitutional.

a. Suitability

The end sought by the law via the aforementioned measure is to ensure that the legislative branch is able to defend and strengthen the democratic model by assuring the personal quality of those running for popularly elected positions. What is specifically being limited here is the right to run

---

[10] The Court accepts that, in the case at hand, the national authorities of the State of Latvia, its members of parliament and judges, are in a better position to evaluate the difficulties involved in establishing and guaranteeing the democratic order. The said authorities must evaluate the needs of their society and those of its new democratic institutions. As such, they must periodically review the measure or law restricting the suffrage rights. In 2000, the Constitutional Court argued that, due to historical and political circumstances, the restriction was neither arbitrary nor disproportional, since—as of the year of the decision—it had only been nine (9) years since the attempted coups d'état.

for public office and the principle of the presumption of innocence. As such, this is a legitimate end, given that representative democracy is a basic principle recognized in Sections 43 and 45 of the Constitution of 1993. On the other hand, it should be recalled that the Peruvian political model is a militant democracy. It is thus necessarily bound to respect fundamental rights and other essential principles, such as that of transparency, etc.

b. Necessity

In the case under analysis, one alternative to the suspension of the right to run for public office—as a consequence of criminal proceedings brought against the aspirant to a popularly elected position for any of the crimes discussed herein—is to require that the individual has a conviction upheld on appeal, even if it is not yet final and binding. This, however, would mean ruling out the suspension of the alleged criminal's right to run for public office.

Another alternative would be to make this information public through the one-stop window (Law 30322),[11] which ought also to be an obligation for all those who wish to run for public office. Political parties likewise ought to establish a filter for naming their candidates for public positions. In any case, if the accused has been found guilty of a willful offense such as drug trafficking, terrorism, or corruption, among others, vacancy proceedings should be initiated. This leaves us, however, with the problem of whether the position vacated due to the aforementioned crimes should then be occupied by a substitute member from the same political party or movement, either at the regional or local level.

Nevertheless, the proposed measure does not necessarily involve a prior control mechanism regarding the quality of the candidates who wish to run for a popularly elected position. To the contrary, it allows the representative democratic model to lose its legitimacy and begin to deteriorate. It is therefore constitutional to suspend accused parties who have not yet been convicted, provided the district attorney has formally brought charges before a criminal judge.

In such a case, the suspension of the alleged criminal's right to run for public office does not necessarily affect the right to the presumption of innocence in an unreasonable or disproportionate manner. Indeed, Ríos

[11] Law 30322 needs to be amended, since it does not include criminal proceedings currently underway among the information to which political parties have access.

Vega has noted that if the right to the "presumption of innocence were absolute, it would be impossible to request search warrants, orders for arrest, tap telephones, etc." (Ríos, 2010: 331).

c. Proportionality in the Strict Sense

The degree to which the presumption of innocence goes unsatisfied is greater in a context where the electoral process has been seriously compromised by candidates with criminal proceedings for constitutionalized crimes, in order to rectify the quality of the nation's representatives, rather than allow accused parties without a final and binding conviction to abuse the law. In Italy, for example, the law establishes that accused individuals who have recognized ties to the Mafia are subject to a precautionary measure restricting or suspending their right to run for public office. In the case of Labita vs. Italy, the European Court of Human Rights ruled that when it comes to the electoral sphere and/or matters, States have a wide margin of appreciation to curtail or establish restrictions on suffrage rights (*Case of Labita vs. Italy*, paragraph 201).[12]

The European Court found that the suspension of suffrage rights pursues a legitimate aim of the State when there is evidence that the persons whose rights are being suspended have ties to the Mafia (*Case of Labita vs. Italy*, paragraph 203).[13] While it is admissible to limit the rights of persons on trial for Mafia ties, however, in this specific case, the measure restricting suffrage rights was applied after the trial was over and the victim had been acquitted. For this reason, the ECHR declared that his suffrage rights had been violated. Note should be made, however, that the Court did not establish, *a priori*, that a measure of this kind—i.e., one suspending the suffrage rights of those standing trial—was necessarily a violation of the standards of the European human rights system (ECHR, *Case of Labita vs. Italy*, 2000).[14]

---

[12] In their internal legal systems, the Contracting States make subject the right to vote and the right to run for public office to conditions that are not, in principle, precluded under Article 3 [of Protocol No. 1]. They have a wide margin of appreciation in this sphere (…), but it is for the Court to determine in the last resort whether (…) the conditions are imposed in pursuit of a legitimate aim.

[13] The Court has no doubt that temporarily suspending the voting rights of persons against whom there is evidence of Mafia membership pursues a legitimate aim.

[14] In this connection, the Court considers that it is legitimate for preventive measures, including special supervision, to be taken against persons suspected of being members of the Mafia, even prior to conviction, as they are intended to

Likewise, Section 38, Subsection 2 of the Mexican Constitution establishes that citizens' rights are suspended "when they are being tried in a criminal proceeding for a crime warranting corporal punishment, to be applied as from the date of the formal order for imprisonment." With regard to this matter, it has been noted that the application of the said constitutional section as grounds for the suspension of suffrage rights, in their active (right to vote) and passive (right to run for public office) aspects, shall depend on each specific situation, or rather, on a proposal for application based on an intermediate thesis. This does not always lead to a suspension of suffrage rights, given that this measure depends on the nature of the crime and the danger or the possible effects that the exercise of the said rights may cause to the State under the rule of law.

V. Conclusions

Representative democracy in Peru is going through a period of crisis, given the numerous candidates who have pending criminal charges and/or criminal and civil convictions that cast doubt upon their legitimacy and suitability to hold popularly elected positions. In this regard, the State has the legitimate power to establish a series of measures to help strengthen the representative democratic model, which is one of the pillars of the Peruvian Constitution.

One measure for protecting the democratic model is to limit the right to run for public office, so that citizens may effectively exercise their right to vote by casting votes for constitutionally suitable candidates. This is an obligation of the State, which may be inferred from the constitutionally protected essence of this aspect of suffrage rights, as seen from an objective standpoint. In other words, the electorate has the right to elect candidates whose public and/or private lives have not led to legal accusations against them.

---

prevent crimes being committed. Furthermore, an acquittal does not necessarily deprive such measures of all foundation, as concrete evidence gathered at trial, though insufficient to secure a conviction, may nonetheless justify reasonable fears that the person concerned may in the future commit criminal offences. In the instant case, the decision to put the applicant under special supervision was taken on 10 May 1993, at a time when there effectively existed some evidence that he was a member of the Mafia, but the measure was not put into effect until 19 November 1994, after his acquittal by the Trapani District Court (see paragraphs 63 and 69 above).

For such purpose, the standards of international human rights law hold that States have a wide margin of deference or appreciation in electoral matters. Consequently, the rule by which a final and binding conviction is a legitimizing element or necessary prerequisite for the suspension of suffrage rights is in fact relative in nature. Therefore, the Peruvian State may apply its own criteria or treatment in limiting suffrage rights, providing it acts proportionally and reasonably.

In those cases where there is not yet a final and binding conviction (where the accused has a conviction upheld on appeal, or no judgment has been issued at all), or in those cases where the sentence has already been served, the limitation of the right to run for public office is not unconstitutional when imposed on an exceptional basis. It should be noted here that the suspension of this right is applicable in cases of the commission of the constitutionalized crimes (involving willful wrongdoing) of corruption, terrorism, or drug trafficking.

The right to run for public office may be limited even when there is no final and binding conviction against the accused. Specifically, the principle of presumption of innocence is relative when faced with the need to guarantee the stability of militant democracy as a fundamental principle of the constitutional State. In such cases, the limitation acts as a type of precautionary measure, whether a conviction has been upheld on appeal (although it has not yet become *res judicata*) or the accused has not yet been sentenced, but has pending criminal charges.

It is likewise constitutional to restrict the right to run for public office by convicted individuals who have served the criminal punishment imposed upon them, especially if they have committed crimes that pose a latent threat to the militant democracy that is so necessary for the strengthening of the constitutional State; but also, in view of the fact that candidates must have a morally suitable profile that allows them to represent their constituents and the interests of the nation. Nevertheless, the suspension of suffrage rights must only be temporary, since, to the contrary, this would violate the very basis of the constitutional model, which rests upon the principle of rehabilitation, and not of retribution.

Bibliography

CASTILLO, Pilar del, and ZOVATTO, Daniel (1998). *La Financiación de la Política en Iberoamérica.* Instituto Interamericano de Derechos Humanos-Centro de Asesoría y Promoción Electoral, p. XXIII.

CONSTITUTIONAL COURT OF COLOMBIA (2003). Judgment C-652-03. 5 August.

CONSTITUTIONAL COURT OF COLOMBIA (2012). Judgment C-944-12. 14 November.

CONSTITUTIONAL COURT OF COLOMBIA (2013). Judgment SU712/13. 17 October.

COSGOVE, John. "Four New Arguments against the Constitutionality of Felony Disenfranchisement." In *Thomas Jefferson Law Review,* pp. 157-202.

ESPÍNDOLA MORALES, Luis. "El derecho al sufragio del presunto delincuente. El Caso Facundo." Toluca, Estado de México, Tribunal Electoral del Poder Judicial de la Federación, p. 331. Available at http://www.juridicas.unam.mx/publica/librev/rev/juselec/cont/27/dtr/dtr12.pd. Retrieved on 24 August 2017.

EUROPEAN COURT OF HUMAN RIGHTS (2012). *Case of Scoppola (3) vs. Italy.*

EUROPEAN COURT OF HUMAN RIGHTS (2006). *Case of Zdanoka vs. Latvia.*

EUROPEAN COURT OF HUMAN RIGHTS (2004). *Case of Labita vs. Italy.*

INTER-AMERICAN COURT OF HUMAN RIGHTS (2005). *Case of Yatama vs. Nicaragua.* Preliminary Exceptions, Merits, Reparations, and Costs. Judgment dated 23 June.

INTER-AMERICAN COURT OF HUMAN RIGHTS (2008). *Case of Castañeda Gutman vs. Mexico.* Preliminary Exceptions, Merits, Reparations, and Costs. Series C, No. 184, paragraph 149. Judgment dated 6 August 2008.

LANDA, César (2012). "Los partidos políticos y sus límites en el régimen democrático peruano: el caso MOVADEF." In *Elecciones* Vol. 11, No. 12, January-December. Lima: ONPE, pp. 195-233.

LEVINE, Eli (2009). "Does the Social Contract Justify Felony Disenfranchisement?" In *Jurisprudence Review,* Washington University, pp. 1993-224.

OVEJERO PUENTE, Ana (2004). *Régimen constitucional del derecho a la presunción de inocencia.* Juris Doctor (J.D.) thesis paper, Getafe.

PERUVIAN NATIONAL ELECTORAL BOARD (2016). *Compendio de Legislación Electoral 2016. Sistematización de leyes y reglamentos en materia electoral.* Lima.

PERUVIAN CONSTITUTIONAL COURT (2002). File No. 1260-2002-HC/TC. Judgment dated 9 July 2002.

PERUVIAN CONSTITUTIONAL COURT (2003). File No. 2366-2003-AA/TC. Judgment dated 6 April 2004.

PERUVIAN CONSTITUTIONAL COURT (2005). File No. 0020-2005-PI/TC. Judgment dated 27 September 2005.

PERUVIAN CONSTITUTIONAL COURT. File No. 0003-2005-PI/TC. Judgment dated 9 August 2006.

PERUVIAN CONSTITUTIONAL COURT. File No. 2730-2006-PA/TC. Judgment dated 21 July 2006.

PERUVIAN CONSTITUTIONAL COURT. File No. 0033-2007-PI/TC. Judgment dated 25 September 2009.

RÍOS VEGA, Luis (2010). "El derecho al sufragio del presunto delincuente (caso Facundo)." In *Revista del Tribunal Electoral del Poder Judicial de la Federación*, Vol. 1, No. 6, Cuarta época.

TRANSPARENCIA (2016). Updated information on candidates running for Congress. http://elecciones2016.transparencia.org.pe/verita/797/informacinactualizadasobrecandidatos-al-congreso. Retrieved on 10 August 2017.

THE PERUVIAN STATE OF CONSTITUTIONAL EMERGENCY IN THE LIGHT OF INTERNATIONAL LAW OF HUMAN RIGHTS: THREE RELEVANT ASPECTS

ABRAHAM SILES VALLEJOS[1]

I. Introduction

The purpose of this article is to examine the principles and norms of International Human Rights Law (IHRL) that are relevant to Peru in terms of constitutional emergency states.[2]

The work focuses on the two international human rights treaties, of a general nature, which are in force in Peru and which contain regulations on the state's power to declare a state of emergency and suspend certain international obligations for the protection of human rights for the duration of the crisis situation.

Such treaties are, on the one hand, the American Convention on Human Rights (ACHR), adopted on November 22, 1969, in force since July 18, 1978; and, on the other hand, the International Covenant on Civil and Political Rights (ICCPR), adopted on December 16, 1966, in force since March 23, 1976. Both international instruments—the first, of an American regional scope, celebrated in the framework of the Organization of American States (OAS); and the second, of universal scope, celebrated at

---

[1] Professor of Constitutional Law at the Pontifical Catholic University of Peru, coordinator of the Research Group on Constitutional Law and Fundamental Rights (GIDCYDEF), general editor of the journal *Derecho PUCP*.

[2] I thank my colleagues in the Research Group on Constitutional Law and Fundamental Rights (GIDCYDEF) for their comments to improve a preliminary version of this chapter.

the level of the United Nations Organization (UN)—entered into force for Peru on the same day, on July 28, 1978.[3]

Although the creation of the IHRL as a "legal and political phenomenon" is relatively recent, since it dates back only to the post-World War II period,[4] it is not possible to doubt its current importance.[5] From the point of view of positive Constitutional Law, the Peruvian Fundamental Charter contains "opening clauses" toward international law. First, the Fourth of the Final and Transitional Provisions (IV FTP) must be taken into account, in virtue of which the Universal Declaration of Human Rights (UDHR) and the international treaties and agreements on this same matter (human rights), ratified by Peru, are a hermeneutical guideline for the application of the provisions on rights and freedoms contained in the Constitution.

In this sense, the Constitutional Court, in jurisprudence that can be considered already established, has affirmed that the public authorities are obliged to incorporate in the constitutional rights, through an interpretative exercise, the protection granted by international human rights treaties, indicating that there is a "Substantial nuclear identity shared by

---

[3] On the date of adoption and entry into force of the ACHR and the ICCPR, see Novak, Fabián and Salmón, Elizabeth, *Las obligaciones internacionales del Perú en materia de derechos Humanos*, Lima, PUCP, 2000, pp. 233 and 173.

[4] See Gross, Oren and Ní Aoláin, Fionnuala, *Law in Times of Crisis. Emergency Powers in Theory and Practice*, Cambridge, Cambridge University Press, 2006, p. 247.

[5] Giuseppe de Vergottini considers that the internationalization of human rights after the end of the Second World War has produced a relevant process of "circularity of constitutional models", since the distinctive values of the liberal and socialist constitutions were embodied in international instruments of human rights approved after the victory of the allied powers over Nazi Germany and the other Axis powers, and this in turn has conditioned the preparation of the new constitutional texts, which are thus influenced by the IHRL. See Vergottini, Giuseppe, Las transiciones constitucionales: desarrollo y crisis del constitucionalismo a finales del siglo XX, Bogotá, Universidad Externado de Colombia, 2002, p. 19 (my translation). For his part, Antonio Cançado Trindade observes that the recent transformations in the world, such as those that have followed the fall of the Berlin Wall, "have generated, at the same time, a new constitutionalism as well as an opening to the internationalization of the protection of human rights». See Cançado Trindade, Antonio, El Derecho Internacional de los Derechos Humanos en el siglo XXI, Barcelona/Buenos Aires/México, D.F./Santiago de Chile, Editorial Jurídica de Chile, 2001, p. 271 (my translation).

constitutionalism and the international system for the protection of human rights", which is based on the value of the dignity of the human person.[6]

Secondly, the human rights treaties signed by the Peruvian State and in force are part of national law, as stipulated in Article 55 of the Constitution. And its legal status is constitutional, as established by means of interpretation by the Constitutional Court, based on the IV FTP and Articles 55, 3, 57 and 205 of the Charter.[7]

Consequently, both the hermeneutic value of international instruments and the legal nature and constitutional status of human rights treaties make it necessary to determine the scope of the IHRL's regulations with regard to the state of emergency provided for in article 137.1 of the Peruvian Constitution.

To undertake the task, there must be consideration of what is indicated by Scott Sheeran, for whom states of emergency are currently "one of the most serious challenges to the implementation of International Human Rights Law (IHRL),"[8] as well as the views of Criddle and Fox-Decent, for whom "at the heart" of the IHRL "lies a practical challenge intertwined with a theoretical problem", namely, the practical challenge of the massive and systematic violations of human rights that are often occurring during emergencies, and the theoretical problem expressed in the question of "in what sense are human rights rights if they are subject to derogation during emergencies?"[9]

Having stated the above, it can be said that the general objective of this article is to establish in what way and to what extent the supranational human rights order in force for Peru complements the regulations of the Peruvian Constitution regarding the state of emergency. As will be seen in the following pages, in certain cases there are appreciable differences

---

[6] See STC 2730-2006-PA/TC (Castillo Chirinos case), dated July 21, 2006, paragraph 9.

[7] See STC 0025-2005-PI/TC and 0026-2005-PI/TC (case PROFA 2), dated April 25, 2006, paragraphs 25-34. See also Hakansson, Carlos, *Curso de Derecho Constitucional*, Lima, Palestra, 2009, pp. 234-235; Salmón, Elizabeth, *Curso de Derecho Internacional Público*, Lima, PUCP, 2014, pp. 284-287.

[8] See Sheeran, Scott, "Reconceptualizing States of Emergency under International Human Rights Law: Theory, Legal Doctrine, and Politics," in *Michigan Journal of International Law*, vol. 34, num. 3, 2013, p. 491.

[9] See Criddle, Evan and Fox-Decent, Evan, "Human Rights, Emergencies, and the Rule of Law," in *Human Rights Quarterly*, vol. 34, 2012, p. 40.

between what is foreseen in the Fundamental Charter and what is enshrined in the ACHR and the ICCPR, which must be addressed in this investigation.

However, the article will focus on three specific issues, which are judged to be of particular importance. They are: (i) a panoramic view of the evolution of the instruments of the IHRL in matters of states of exception, in particular with regard to the difference between clauses of repeal or suspension and clauses restricting human rights; (ii) the subject legitimated for the proclamation of the emergency; and (iii) the situations that enable the declaration/maintenance of the state of exception, as well as the adoption of specific measures aimed at conjuring up crises.

These remain some topics to be developed in a subsequent investigation: the impact of the emergency on human rights, as regards both "non-derogable" rights and rights that may be suspended; and guarantees or constitutional processes during the state of emergency.

II. A Brief Overview of the Evolution of the Instruments of the IACHR Regarding States Of Exception

Without any intention of exhaustiveness, it is convenient to make a quick review of the general evolution of the instruments of the IHRL with regard to states of exception. This summary overview will provide elements of the historical context that are necessary to adequately understand not only the evolution of the IHRL in the subject matter of this article, but especially certain influences and normative loans made between the different international protection systems of human rights.

The same can be said, in particular, of the question concerning the difference between clauses of restriction and clauses of derogation or suspension of rights, a matter of theoretical importance, but also practical, that even a basic idea of the historical perspective helps to better understand, and that should be taken up when studying in a future article on the human rights regime during the state of emergency.

As is known, the first human rights instruments approved by the international community at the end of the Second World War were the Declarations of American regional scope and of universal scope. In effect, the American Declaration of the Rights and Duties of Man (ADRDM) was adopted by the IX International American Conference, held in Bogotá (Colombia), on May 2, 1948, and entered into force on that same date;

whereas the UDHR was approved by the General Assembly of the United Nations, meeting in Paris (France), on December 1, 1948, the date on which it also began its validity.[10]

The truth is that neither the American Declaration nor the Universal Declaration contains provisions that regulate the state of emergency and that contemplate the possibility of repealing or suspending certain obligations of International Law on human rights as a means to face extreme emergencies that threaten the life of the nation or the State.

Both instruments contain only general clauses limiting or restricting rights. Thus, article XXVIII of the ADRDM, whose epigraph reads "Scope of human rights", stipulates that "the rights of each man are limited by the rights of others, by the security of all and by the just demands of general well-being and of democratic development ". In turn, article 29 of the UDHR, together with mentioning the existence of the duties of every person toward the community, indicates the only permissible limitations established by law in order to ensure the rights of others and satisfy "the just demands of morality, public order and general well-being in a democratic society".

After this initial stage, there comes a period in which general human rights treaties are approved, both universal in scope (United Nations system) and regional in scope (European and American systems). The first legally binding instrument is the Convention for the Protection of Human Rights and Fundamental Freedoms or the European Convention on Human Rights (ECHR), which was opened for signature on November 4, 1950 and entered into force on September 3, 1953.[11] The European Convention dedicates its article 15 to regulate the "derogation in time of emergency", incorporating for the first time in an instrument of the IHRL a clause of derogation or suspension of human rights facing existential crises that hover over the continuity of the national life or state.

The next international treaty, in chronological order of approval, was the aforementioned ICCPR—adopted, as indicated, in 1966, and entered into force ten years later—, belonging to the universal system of the United

---

[10] On the date of adoption and entry into force of the DADDH and the UDHR, see Novak, Fabián and Salmón, Elizabeth, Las obligaciones internacionales del Perú en materia de derechos Humanos, op.cit., pp. 221 and 161.

[11] See Fitzpatrick, Joan, *Human Rights in Crisis. The International System for Protecting Rights during States of Emergency*, Philadelphia, University of Pennsylvania Press, 1994, p. 52 (note 6).

Nations, which likewise enshrines a regime of derogation or suspension of human rights in situations of extreme crisis (article 4). It should be noted, however, that the drafting process of the Pact occurred in a manner that was partially concurrent with the elaboration of the European Convention, so that some crossings and mutual influences could have taken place. Be that as it may, it must be remarked, as Anna-Lena Svensson-McCarthy does, that during the preparatory work for the ICCPR the discussion on Article 4 was for some time "closely linked to the question of limitations in general."[12]

The third international treaty, in order of approval, was the ACHR, already referred to—approved in 1969, entered into force in 1978, as has been said—, which also includes a clause of suspension of human rights in situations of serious emergency (article 27).

As can be seen, in this second phase of the development of international human rights instruments, which goes from the year of 1950 to the end of the 1970s, the international community adopts treaties of universal and regional scope (in Europe and the Americas) which, together with their binding nature in terms of International Law, consider insufficient the general clauses that enable the restriction of rights, and stipulate, rather, additional clauses of derogation or suspension of rights in situations of existential crisis.

Despite the evolution recorded in the first two stages referred to in this section—which led from non-binding Declarations that contained only general clauses of restriction of rights (ADRDM and UDHR) to international treaties, of mandatory legal force, which included special provisions on derogation or suspension of rights in emergencies (ECHR, ICCPR and ACHR)—, since the 1980s until recently, the situation has become more complex because there is no longer a clear and unique evolutionary line.

On the contrary, the African Charter on Human and People's Rights (ACHPR), known as the Banjul Charter, which was adopted by the Organization of African Unity on June 27, 1981 and entered into force on October 21, 1986, does not contemplate the states of exception or authorize the repeal or suspension of the rights enshrined in the new regional instrument, including only several provisions that allow

---

[12] See Svensson McCarthy, Anna-Lena, *The International Law of Human Rights and States of Exception*, The Hague; Boston, London, Martinus Nijhoff Publishers, 1998, p. 200.

restrictions of rights with amplitude and enshrining a strong conception of duties.[13]

Even closer in time, and returning to the scope of old Europe, the Charter of Fundamental Rights of the European Union (CFREU), which was proclaimed by the European Parliament, the Council of the European Union and the European Commission on December 7, 2000, in Nice (France), the state of exception does not regulate either and only establishes general clauses limiting rights (articles 52-54).

Something different happens, however, in the case of the most recent regional instrument of all, namely, the Arab Charter of Human Rights (AChHR). Approved by the League of Arab States on May 22, 2004, it entered into force on March 15, 2008, and regulates the state of exception in article 4.

Therefore, in this third stage of the evolution of the instruments of the IHRL—from the 1980s to date—we have a remarkable heterogeneity in the IHRL regulations on states of emergency. Both the ACHPR and the CFREU have returned to the suppression of the clauses of derogation or suspension of human rights, to rely again on mere clauses limiting or restricting rights. However, the AChHR, the last regional instrument to be approved and enter into force, dismisses such models and adheres to the tradition established in the ECHR and followed by the ICCPR and the ACHR, which authorizes the most stringent interventions on human rights in cases of states of exception.

III. The Subject Legitimized for the Proclamation of the Emergency

In a previous article I have defended that, regarding the proclamation (and maintenance) of the state of emergency, the model assumed by the Peruvian Constitution of 1993 is that of the "auto-investiture."[14] This

[13] See Criddle, Evan and Fox-Decent, Evan, "Human Rights, Emergencies, and the Rule of Law", *op. cit.*, p. 46. For a critique of the "Business as Usual Model" that apparently distinguishes the African Charter, but that in practice admits adaptations through interpretative modalities, see Gross, Oren and Ní Aoláin, Fionnuala, *Law in Times of Crisis. Emergency Powers in Theory and Practice*, *op. cit.*, pp. 252-255.

[14] See Siles, Abraham, "Problemática constitucional del estado de emergencia en el Perú: algunas cuestiones fundamentales", en *Estudios Constitucionales*, Año 15, N° 2, 2017, pp. 141-144.

means that the body legitimized to declare the existence of an extreme crisis, which eventually merits the assumption of extraordinary powers and the suspension of certain fundamental rights, is the Executive Branch, as article 137 of the current Charter in effect provides when delegating in the President of the Republic, with the agreement of the Council of Ministers, the power to introduce one of the two constitutional exception regimes (the state of emergency and the state of siege).

It is interesting now, as an extension and complement, to highlight the perspective of the IHRL on this matter. And, as for the competent authority for the proclamation of the emergency, both article 27 of the ACHR and article 4 of the ICCPR refer in general to the "State Party", so that it corresponds to the domestic legal systems of each State—in the first place, to the constitutional texts—to determine which will be the specific body that will receive this legal capacity.

As Claudio Grossman points out, from the perspective of International Law, they have the capacity to represent a State party—for example, under a treaty such as the ACHR: those authorities whose actions may give rise to the international responsibility of that State, that is, the Executive Power, the Legislative Power and the Judicial Power.[15] It is clear, then, that the election of the Peruvian constituent is fully compatible with the International Human Rights Law applicable in the country, insofar as it is the executive authority to whom the Fundamental Charter grants this attribution.

More relevant, however, is the role that should be assigned to the other organs of public power, and, in what matters in this section, especially to Parliament, in accordance with the IHRL. And it is that they are the principle of the separation of powers and the clause of the democratic state, enshrined in both applicable treaties (the ACHR and the ICCPR), which determine that the Legislative Power is called to play a leading role in the establishment of the exceptional regime.

Indeed, even when the declaration of the state of emergency gives rise to a strong concentration of powers in the hands of the Executive, this does not mean that the other powers of the State are annulled and the rule of law and the corresponding principle of legality are suppressed, as well as the

[15] See Grossman, Claudio, "Algunas consideraciones sobre el régimen de situaciones de excepción bajo la Convención Americana sobre Derechos Humanos", in AA.VV., *Derechos Humanos en las Américas. Homenaje a la Memoria de Carlos A. Dunshee de Abranches*, Washington DC, CIDH, 1984, p. 123.

protection of the fundamental rights. On the contrary, the real possibility of committing serious violations of human rights during the emergency necessitates the role of counterweight and controller under the other powers of the State, which must operate from the first moment (that is, from the proclamation of the emergency).

Hence, the Inter-American Court of Human Rights (IACtHR), in its very important Advisory Opinion 8, entitled "The Habeas Corpus under Suspension of Guarantees", issued on January 30, 1987, had the opportunity to emphasize that, impeded as is to "ignore the abuses" to which it may give rise, and in fact has given in the hemisphere the application of unjustified exception measures, it is its duty to note that "the suspension of guarantees cannot be separated from the 'effective exercise of representative democracy' referred to in Article 3 of the OAS Charter" and that it "lacks all legitimacy when used to attempt against the democratic system..."[16]

Later, in this same pronouncement, the Inter-American Court establishes the following guiding principles:

> The guarantees being suspended, some of the legal limits of the action of the public power may be different from those in force under normal conditions, but they should not be considered non-existent and, consequently, it cannot be understood that the government is invested with absolute powers beyond the conditions under which such exceptional legality is authorized. As the Court has already pointed out on another occasion, the principle of legality, democratic institutions and the rule of law are inseparable. (See "The expression 'laws' in Article 30 of the American Convention on Human Rights, Advisory Opinion OC- 6/86 of May 9, 1986. Series A No. 6, paragraph 32".)[17]

Moreover, even before the adoption of the ACHR, the Inter-American Commission on Human Rights (IACHR), in an important public statement, issued on April 16, 1968, had highlighted these same values in relation to the protection of human rights in cases of the "suspension of constitutional guarantees" or the "state of siege". On that occasion, the Inter-American Commission stated that for the proclamation of emergency to be compatible with the "democratic representative government regime", an indispensable condition is required, among others, that "it does not entail the restriction of the rule of law or the constitutional norms, nor the

---

[16] See Corte, I. D. H., Opinión Consultiva 8, «El Hábeas Corpus bajo Suspensión de Garantías», del 30 de enero de 1987, paragraph 20 (my translation).
[17] *Ibid.*, paragraph 24 (my translation).

alteration of the Powers of the State or the operation of the means of control."[18]

And even earlier, in 1966, the Final Report of the Special Rapporteur appointed by the IACHR to study the states of exception in the American hemisphere—which constituted an important precedent in preparing the Draft and the final text of the CADH, helping to make sense of its provisions[19]—said that, among the various alternatives related to the "competent body" to declare the emergency, that which consisted in a self-investiture of the Executive without any participation of the Parliament should be ruled out.[20]

Consequently, Dr. Martins considered that it was appropriate for the Executive to decree the suspension, but immediately submitting to the national representation the adopted measures, in such a way that it was the Congress of the Republic that decided whether the said measures had to be maintained or if they should cease or be modified.[21]

Thus, it can be concluded that according to the Inter-American Human Rights System (IAHRS), there is no absolutist regime derived from the extraordinary powers that the Government assumes as a result of the establishment of the state of emergency, but there must be respect, even in situations of extreme crisis, for the limits of power set by the principle of

---

[18] See IACHR, "Resolución sobre la Protección de los Derechos Humanos frente a la Suspensión de las Garantías Constitucionales o Estado de Sitio", emitida el 16 de mayo de 1968, en CIDH, *Informe sobre la Labor Desarrollada durante el Decimoctavo Período de Sesiones (1-17 de abril de 1968)*, Washington DC, Secretaría General de la OEA, 24 de julio de 1968, pp. 46-48 [documento OEA Ser.L/V/II.19, Doc. 30 (Spanish), paragraph 79] (my translation).

[19] Several authors have pointed out the influence of the Report of Rapporteur Martins in the elaboration of the ACHR. See Norris, Robert and Reiton, Paula, "The Suspension of Guarantees: A Comparative Analysis of the American Convention on Human Rights and the Constitutions of the States Parties," in *American University Law Review*, Vol. 30, No. 1, 1980, pp. 192-193; Grossman, Claudio, "Algunas consideraciones sobre el régimen de situaciones de excepción bajo la Convención Americana sobre Derechos Humanos", *op. cit.*, p. 123.

[20] See Martins, Daniel Hugo, "La Protección de los Derechos Humanos frente a la Suspensión de las Garantías Constitucionales o Estado de Sitio", en Secretaría General de la OEA, *La Organización de los Estados Americanos y los Derechos Humanos. Actividades de la Comisión Interamericana de Derechos Humanos 1960-1967*, Washington DC, 1972, p. 140 (documento OEA/Ser.L/V/II.15 Doc. 12, October 11, 1966).

[21] *Ibid.*, p. 142.

legality, the rule of law and democratic institutions, including the means of control, all of which form an inseparable unit.[22]

It is understood then, that for Claudio Grossman the scope of article 27 of the ACHR, as regards the extent of the powers conferred to the body in charge of conjuring the emergency and the role of the Legislature as a control body, should be read in harmony with article 29 of the same American Convention, referring to the "norms of interpretation". And this last provision stipulates that none of the clauses of the treaty must be interpreted in the sense of "excluding other rights and guarantees that are inherent to the human being or that *derive from the representative democratic form of government*" (emphasis added). According to Grossman,

> in the 'representative democratic forms of government' the legislature is normally given an important role in the declaration of emergency, either because of the need for prior authorization or confirmation of a previous statement by the executive when it has not been possible that the parliament meets to consider such a declaration.[23]

In the Universal System of Human Rights too, the democratic principle and the principle of separation of powers play in favor of an active role of Parliament in the balance of and control over the Executive that assumes extraordinary powers before an existential threat. This can be inferred from the requirement, provided only in the ICCPR (not in the ACHR), regarding the need to proclaim the emergency. As is known, the United Nations Pact requires that the extraordinary situation that endangers the life of the nation "has been officially proclaimed" (article 4.1 ICCPR).

That is why, in General Comment N° 29, entitled "Emergency States (Article 4)", the Human Rights Committee, the Covenant control body, has indicated that the proclamation "is essential for the maintenance of the principles of legality and rule of law when they are most needed."[24] For his part, the United Nations Special Rapporteur on States of Emergency, Leandro Despouy, in his Final Report, issued after twelve years of work, together with mentioning that the proclamation constitutes a measure of

---

[22] See also Gross, Oren and Ní Aoláin, Fionnuala, *Law in Times of Crisis. Emergency Powers in Theory and Practice*, *op. cit.*, p. 292.

[23] See Grossman, Claudio, "Algunas consideraciones sobre el régimen de situaciones de excepción bajo la Convención Americana sobre Derechos Humanos", *op. cit.*, p. 124 (my translation).

[24] See Comité de Derechos Humanos, Observación General N° 29, «Estados de emergencia (artículo 4)», del 24 de julio de 2001, párrafo 2 (documento ONU CCPR/C/21/Rev. 1/Add. 11, del 31 de agosto de 2001) (my translation).

publicity, which is "inherent in the Republican form of government" and that tends to "avoid *de facto* states of emergency", considers that it "also points to the appreciation of the competent national authority to make the decision."[25] Later in the same Report, the United Nations Rapporteur deplores the pernicious effects of diminishing until eventually the role of Parliament as a means of controlling extraordinary powers disappears, warning that, in certain cases, deviations from the canonical model enshrined in the ICCPR can lead to "the substitution of the principle of separation of powers for the hierarchy of them, in favor of the Executive and this, in turn, in some cases, is subordinated to military power."[26]

As a result of the review made, it can be concluded that the applicable IHRL in Peru regarding states of emergency requires the State to adopt the rules and procedures that are necessary so that, by virtue of the democratic principle and the principle of separation of powers, the Congress of the Republic has a relevant role in the balance and control of the extraordinary powers assumed by the Executive by its own decision when declaring a state of emergency.

This controlling role is very important and must be carried out from the moment of the self-investiture of the President of the Republic. Unfortunately, as I have stated in a previous article, this does not occur in Peru, since neither the Regulations of the Congress nor other regulatory bodies provide for the necessary mechanisms to do so.[27] Nor has the national representation enshrined a practice that, despite the regulatory deficiencies, imposes such control, as in fact it could have happened.

The role of the Constitutional Court, in its turn, has also been modest, although it has stated that under a state of emergency there must be

---

[25] See Despouy, Leandro, *Los derechos humanos y los estados de excepción*, México, IIJ-UNAM, 1999, p. 26 (my translation).

[26] *Ibid.*, pp. 67 and 69 (my translation). The Report of Nicole Questiaux also noted the existence of characteristics by virtue of which the concept of separation of powers was replaced by the "hierarchy of powers", placing even at the top of the Executive a civil authority that, despite retaining some prerogatives, could be subordinated to military power. See Questiaux, Nicole, *Study of the Implications for Human Rights of Recent Developments Concerning Situations Known as States of Siege or Emergency* (Document ONU E/CN.4/Sub. 2/1982/15, released on July 27, 1982). See also Fitzpatrick, Joan, *Human Rights in Crisis. The International System for Protecting Rights During States of Emergency*, *op. cit.*, p. 35.

[27] See Siles, Abraham, "Problemática constitucional del estado de emergencia en el Perú: algunas cuestiones fundamentales", *op. cit.*, pp. 133-134.

political controls under Parliament, "so that the principles of accountability and political responsibility are met."[28] Moreover, the supreme interpreter of the Fundamental Charter has argued that the institution of the state of emergency has evolved to achieve respect for the "principle of balance of powers", so that the declaration of the emergency must have a "foundation (political-legal)" that enables a "progressive system of accountability", which should not be limited to the jurisdictional scope, but include the parliamentary action.[29]

IV. The Causes of the State of Emergency in light of the Human Rights Treaties

In the aforementioned article, I developed the argument according to which the applicable IHRL in Peru helps to determine, by means of interpretation, that the grounds provided in Article 137.1 of the Constitution for the declaration of a state of emergency—the "case of disturbance of peace or internal order, catastrophe or serious circumstances"—must always be understood as qualified by the requirement to affect "the life of the Nation", also provided for in the said constitutional clause.[30]

It is worth saying that I used the ACHR and the ICCPR, as well as their jurisprudential and doctrinal developments, to defend the thesis that, even in situations of internal disturbances, riots, violent action as a result of popular protests, as well as in the event of disasters caused by nature or with human intervention (earthquakes, floods, mudslides, fires, industrial accidents, etc.), it is necessary to overcome a certain threshold of seriousness—there must be, in reality, an "existential threat"—in order to proclaim the emergency and assume the corresponding extraordinary powers aimed at conjuring it.

On this occasion, I will reinforce the argument by recourse to the preparatory work of the American Convention and the International Covenant, which confirms that the correct interpretation is the one that has been chosen. For this, however, it is necessary to start from the enabling

---

[28] See STC 017-2003-AI/TC, de 16 de marzo de 2004, paragraph 18.i (my translation); STC 00022-2011-PI/TC, de 8 de julio de 2015, paragraph 351 (my translation).

[29] See STC 00002-2008-AI, de 9 de septiembre de 2009, paragraph 21 (my translation).

[30] See Siles, Abraham, "Problemática constitucional del estado de emergencia en el Perú: algunas cuestiones fundamentales", *op. cit.*, pp. 145-152.

normative causes stipulated in the applicable international treaties. The ACHR provides for "a case of war, a public danger or another emergency that threatens the independence or security of the State Party" (article 27.1), while the ICCPR contemplates "exceptional situations that endanger the life of the nation" (article 4.1).

The question then arises about how to harmonize these different normative texts. Are there different thresholds of demand between one international treaty and the other? Are there any between both international instruments and the Peruvian Constitution? Even more precisely, it is worth asking whether the ACHR is more permissive than the ICCPR, as well as whether the Peruvian Basic Charter is more permissive than both treaties.

Thomas Buergenthal has drawn attention to the fact that a first assessment of the "wording" of article 27.1 of the ACHR shows it as "substantially different" from the ICCPR, as well as from the ECHR, so that such differences could be understood as indicating that these last two instruments "envisage emergencies of a greater magnitude" than those contemplated in the American Convention.[31]

However, as has already been anticipated, the preparatory work for the Pact of San José and the ICCPR allows us to arrive at a different conclusion, in the sense that the differences in the meaning and scope of the regulation are not so broad,[32] but rather, on the contrary, they converge on the interpretative construction of a threshold of emergency severity that is essentially the same in the ACHR and in the ICCPR, as well as in the ECHR (which, incidentally, served as inspiration for the writers of article 27 of the American Regional Convention).[33]

---

[31] See Buergenthal, Thomas, "The American and European Conventions on Human Rights: Similarities and Differences", in *American University Law Review*, Vol. 30, 1980-1981, p. 165 (note 32). See also O'Donnell, Daniel, *Protección Internacional de los Derechos Humanos*, Lima, Comisión Andina de Juristas, segunda edición, 1989, p. 398; Provost, René, *International Human Rights and Humanitarian Law*, Cambridge, Cambridge University Press, 2004, p. 272.

[32] See O'Donnell, Daniel, «Legitimidad de los estados de excepción, a la luz de los instrumentos de derechos humanos», en *Derecho*, Vol. 38, Lima, PUCP, 1984, p. 204.

[33] See the speech of the delegate of Brazil, Dr. Carlos Dunshee de Abranches, in the debate held in Committee I of the Inter-American Specialized Conference on Human Rights, which approved the Pact of San José, en Secretaría General de la OEA, *Conferencia Especializada Interamericana sobre Derechos Humanos: Actas y Documentos (7-22 de noviembre de 1969)*, Washington DC, OEA, s/f, p. 264.

The first thing that should be noted is that the Report presented by Dr. Martins as part of the activities of the IACHR in 1966, when dealing with "the cause" that enables the emergency, along with rejecting terms of excessive "generality" and "very weak limitations" of the extraordinary powers, considered as adequate the clause "When the security of the State so requires", insofar as it refers only to "serious cases in which the integrity or existence of the three constituent elements of the State: population, territory, legal order."[34]

The Rapporteur of the IACHR added that the expression favored by him included "exclusively" the following situations:

(i) A current or imminent danger to the existence of the people as a nation.
(ii) For the survival of the State as a sovereign and independent political entity.
(iii) For the integrity of the territory.
(iv) To comply with the current Political Constitution.
(v) For the exercise of legitimate powers by the constitutional authorities.
(vi) A serious and imminent danger of profound disturbance of social peace, public order, which endangers the internal security of the State.[35]

These considerations about the special gravity required for a State to go to the institution of the "suspension of guarantees" or "state of siege" were then adopted specifically by the IACHR when studying the suspension clause (article 19) of the Draft Convention on Human Rights for the Americas written by the Inter-American Council of Jurists (IACJ) and the Projects of Uruguay and Chile. In this regard, the IACHR referred to the Martins Report in the following terms:

> With regard to article 19 of the IACJ Project and the corresponding texts of the Projects of Uruguay and Chile, the Commission may suggest to the Council of the Organization [of the OAS] that it take into consideration the corresponding part of the Second Report entitled 'The Protection of

---

See also O'Donnell, Daniel, *Protección Internacional de los Derechos Humanos*, *op. cit.*, p. 398.

[34] See Martins, Daniel Hugo, «La Protección de los Derechos Humanos frente a la Suspensión de las Garantías Constitucionales o Estado de Sitio», *op. cit.*, p. 141 (my translation).

[35] *Ibid.*

Human Rights Faced with the Suspension of Constitutional Guarantees or State of Siege', prepared by Dr. Daniel Hugo Martins, Member of the Commission.[36]

Later, in the aforementioned Resolution issued by the IACHR in April 1968, the Inter-American Commission confirmed the criterion of the severity necessary to declare the state of emergency, considering that for its compatibility with the governmental regime of "representative democracy" it is essential that the "suspension of guarantees" be adopted "in case of war or other serious public emergency that endangers the life of the Nation or the security of the State."[37]

As can be seen, the Resolution chose wording that is similar to that established in article 15.1 of the ECHR and, without the express mention of war, in article 4.1 of the ICCPR, since it refers to one (other) "emergency" public "that endangers, in a serious way", the life of the Nation", while adding to this the risk for "the security of the State". Beyond the peculiarities and nuances, it is clear that, based on the special studies conducted and the institutional experience with the states of exception in the hemisphere, the IACHR is of the opinion that the threat posed by the emergency must be of a large scale.

This criterion was embodied in the "Proposed Draft American Convention on the Protection of Human Rights", which, on behalf of the OAS Council, was prepared by the IACHR at its Nineteenth Session (Extraordinary), held in July 1968. Indeed, in article 24 of the Draft Bill it was stipulated that "in case of war or other emergency that threatens the independence or security of the State Party", the latter could adopt provisions for the suspension of its human rights obligations.[38]

---

[36] See CIDH, *Informe sobre la Labor Desarrollada durante el Decimocuarto Período de Sesiones (3-21 de octubre de 1966)*, Washington DC, Secretaría General de la OEA, 30 de diciembre de 1966, p. 18 (documento OEA Ser.L/V/II.15, Doc. 29 (español), párrafo 56).

[37] See CIDH, «Resolución sobre la Protección de los Derechos Humanos frente a la Suspensión de las Garantías Constitucionales o Estado de Sitio», emitida el 16 de mayo de 1968, en CIDH, *Informe sobre la Labor Desarrollada durante el Decimoctavo Período de Sesiones (1-17 de abril de 1968)*, *op. cit.*, p. 47 [documento OEA Ser.L/V/II.19, Doc. 30 (español), párrafo 79] (my translation).

[38] See CIDH, *Informe sobre la Labor Desarrollada durante el Decimonoveno Período de Sesiones (Extraordinario) (1-11 de julio de 1968)*, Washington DC, Secretaría General de la OEA, 30 de diciembre de 1966, p. 51 (documento OEA

The text thus followed closely the drafting of the Resolution adopted by the IACHR in April 1968, for which it had to depart from the proposal originally formulated as a Working Document by the Secretariat of the IACHR, which referred, rather—taking into account the recent model established by the ICCPR, then already approved, although not yet in force—"to exceptional situations that endanger the life of the nation and whose existence has been officially proclaimed."[39]

The text of the Draft Bill prepared by the IACHR was the one used at the San José Conference that adopted the ACHR, to which the representatives gathered in the Costa Rican capital only added the "public danger" assumption. Although this is a very broad and vague expression, the preparatory work shows that the intention of the drafters was to allow the inclusion of cases of natural disasters, without political characteristics, as the delegate of El Salvador, author of the proposal finally accepted at the Plenary of the Conference.

Without doubt, then, the preparatory work of the ACHR shows an evolutionary route that confirms that the enabling emergency of the state of emergency and the consequent assumption of extraordinary powers, including the possibility of decreeing the suspension of certain human rights, must be of a considerable entity. In the light of these preparatory works, it is clear that the wording finally enshrined in the ACHR cannot be understood as looser or less demanding than the counterpart instruments of European or universal scope.

Moreover, as noted by authors such as Robert Norris and Paula Reiton, Claudio Grossman and Joan Fitzpatrick, the initial proposals of the ICJ and Uruguay and Chile allowed the "suspension of guarantees" under the indefinite formula of "exceptional situations", which, in the projects of the South American countries mentioned, had to be determined by each State unilaterally.[40] The IACHR, however, criticized this plan early on and

---

Ser.L/V/II.19, Doc. 51 (español), de 18 de diciembre de 1968, párrafo 57) (my translation).

[39] *Ibid.*, p. 50 (párrafo 57) (my translation).

[40] See Norris, Robert and Reiton, Paula, «The Suspension of Guarantees: A Comparative Analysis of the American Convention on Human Rights and the Constitutions of the States Parties», *op. cit.*, pp. 191-192; Grossman, Claudio, «Algunas consideraciones sobre el régimen de situaciones de excepción bajo la Convención Americana sobre Derechos Humanos», *op. cit.*, p. 125; Fitzpatrick, Joan, *Human Rights in Crisis. The International System for Protecting Rights During States of Emergency*, *op. cit.*, p. 58.

exercised a strong leadership that leads, through a process not free of ups and downs, to finally enshrine conventional provisions whose threshold of severity has to be judged as similar to that in force in the ICCPR, which, as has been said, is also similar to the European instrument.

An additional element to consider, of undoubted theoretical and practical relevance, is that, as Claudio Grossman has pointed out, the inclusion of the clause on "State security" as a condition that enables the declaration of emergency requires considering in relation to the various provisions that, by enshrining private rights, admit ordinary restrictions, different from the suspension, which must be applied in situations of constitutional normality, hence the subsidiary or residual nature of the system of derogation or suspension of guarantees.[41]

Of course, this verification refers us to the theoretical question of the difference between suspension or derogation and the restriction of rights, which should be addressed in a future article.

With regard to the preparatory work for the ICCPR, we cannot now undertake a reconstruction of the main milestones of the process. We will only point out that, according to the most authoritative doctrine, the requirement of a threat to the life of the nation, a formula similar in its essential features to that adopted in article 15 of the ECHR, prepared in conjunction with article 4 of the ICCPR, must be understood as referring to events of significant magnitude that consist of the four elements defined by European jurisprudence and that have become widely consensual, to be stated within the scope of the universal system of the United Nations and also in the American system: the "public emergency" "must be (i) present or imminent, (ii) exceptional, (iii) involve the entire population, and (iv) constitute "a threat to the organized life of society"."[42]

---

[41] See Grossman, Claudio, «Algunas consideraciones sobre el régimen de situaciones de excepción bajo la Convención Americana sobre Derechos Humanos», *op. cit.*, pp. 125-126.

[42] See Criddle, Evan and Fox-Decent, Evan, «Human Rights, Emergencies, and the Rule of Law», *op. cit.*, p. 61. For a reconstruction of the drafting process of Article 4 of the IDCP, see in particular Svensson McCarthy, Anna-Lena, *The International Law of Human Rights and States of Exception*, *op. cit.*, pp. 199-217; and Fitzpatrick, Joan, *Human Rights in Crisis. The International System for Protecting Rights During States of Emergency*, *op. cit.*, pp. 52-54. See also Despouy, Leandro, *Los derechos humanos y los estados de excepción*, México, IIJ-UNAM, 1999, pp. 34-38. For the reception of European jurisprudence on states of exception, in the American system, see O'Donnell, Daniel, «Legitimidad de los estados de

From what has been said in this section, it can be concluded that the preparatory work of the ACHR and the ICCPR corroborates, as a correct interpretation, that which requires of the three grounds provided in article 137.1 of the Peruvian Constitution for the declaration of the state of emergency such a threshold of seriousness, which requires in each case that the life of the Nation be affected. This is a mandate that is imposed by the applicable IHRL in the country, in a manner complementary to that enshrined in the Peruvian Fundamental Charter.

Bibliography

BUERGENTHAL, Thomas (1980-81). "The American and European Conventions on Human Rights: Similarities and Differences." *American University Law Review*, Vol. 30, pp. 155-166.

CANÇADO TRINDADE, Antonio (2001). *El Derecho Internacional de los Derechos Humanos en el siglo XXI.* Barcelona/Buenos Aires/México, D. F./Santiago de Chile, Editorial Jurídica de Chile.

COMISIÓN INTERAMERICANA DE DERECHOS HUMANOS (CIDH). «Resolución sobre la Protección de los Derechos Humanos frente a la Suspensión de las Garantías Constitucionales o Estado de Sitio», emitida el 16 de mayo de 1968, en CIDH, *Informe sobre la Labor Desarrollada durante el Decimoctavo Período de Sesiones (1-17 de abril de 1968)*, Washington DC, Secretaría General de la OEA, 24 de julio de 1968, pp. 46-48 [documento OEA Ser.L/V/II.19, Doc. 30 (español), párrafo 79].

«Informe sobre la Labor Desarrollada durante el Decimonoveno Período de Sesiones (Extraordinario) (1-11 de julio de 1968), Washington DC, Secretaría General de la OEA, 30 de diciembre de 1966 (documento OEA Ser.L/V/II.19, Doc. 51 (español), de 18 de diciembre de 1968).

«Informe sobre la Labor Desarrollada durante el Decimocuarto Período de Sesiones (3-21 de octubre de 1966), Washington DC, Secretaría General de la OEA, 30 de diciembre de 1966 (documento OEA Ser.L/V/II.15, Doc. 29 (español)).

COMITÉ DE DERECHOS HUMANOS, *Observación General N° 29, «Estados de emergencia (artículo 4)»*, del 24 de julio de 2001 (documento ONU CCPR/C/21/Rev. 1/Add. 11, del 31 de agosto de 2001).

---

excepción, a la luz de los instrumentos de derechos humanos», op. cit., pp. 203-209; O'Donnell, Daniel, *Protección Internacional de los Derechos Humanos*, *op. cit.*, pp. 400-403; see also Corte I. D. H., Sentencia del caso Zambrano Vélez y otros vs. Ecuador, del 4 de julio de 207, párrafo 46.

CORTE INTERAMERICANA DE DERECHOS HUMANOS (Corte IDH), *Opinión Consultiva 8, «El Hábeas Corpus bajo Suspensión de Garantías»*, del 30 de enero de 1987.

CRIDDLE, Evan and FOX-DECENT, Evan (2012). «Human Rights, Emergencies, and the Rule of Law», in *Human Rights Quarterly*, vol. 34, pp. 39-87.

DESPOUY, Leandro (1999). *Los derechos humanos y los estados de excepción*. Mexico: IIJ-UNAM.

FITZPATRICK, Joan (1994). *Human Rights in Crisis. The International System for Protecting Rights During States of Emergency*. Philadelphia: University of Pennsylvania Press.

GROSS, Oren and NÍ AOLÁIN, Fionnuala (2006). *Law in Times of Crisis. Emergency Powers in Theory and Practice*. Cambridge: Cambridge University Press.

GROSSMAN, Claudio (1984). «Algunas consideraciones sobre el régimen de situaciones de excepción bajo la Convención Americana sobre Derechos Humanos», en AA.VV., *Derechos Humanos en las Américas. Homenaje a la Memoria de Carlos A. Dunshee de Abranches*. Washington DC: CIDH, pp. 121-134.

HAKANSSON, Carlos (2009). *Curso de Derecho Constitucional*. Lima: Palestra.

MARTINS, Daniel Hugo (1972). «La Protección de los Derechos Humanos frente a la Suspensión de las Garantías Constitucionales o Estado de Sitio», en Secretaría General de la OEA, *La Organización de los Estados Americanos y los Derechos Humanos. Actividades de la Comisión Interamericana de Derechos Humanos 1960-1967*. Washington DC, pp. 122-154 (documento OEA/Ser.L/V/II.15 Doc. 12, del 11 de octubre de 1966).

NORRIS, Robert and REITON, Paula (1980). "The Suspension of Guarantees: A Comparative Analysis of the American Convention on Human Rights and the Constitutions of the States Parties." *American University Law Review*, Vol. 30, Num. 1, pp. 189-223.

NOVAK, Fabián and SALMÓN, Elizabeth (2000). *Las obligaciones internacionales del Perú en materia de derechos Humanos*. Lima: PUCP.

O'DONNELL, Daniel (1989). *Protección Internacional de los Derechos Humanos*. Lima: Comisión Andina de Juristas, segunda edición.

(1984). "Legitimidad de los estados de excepción, a la luz de los instrumentos de derechos humanos." *Derecho*, Vol. 38, Lima, PUCP, pp. 165-231.

PROVOST, René (2004). *International Human Rights and Humanitarian Law*. Cambridge: Cambridge University Press.

QUESTIAUX, Nicole. *Study of the Implications for Human Rights of Recent Developments Concerning Situations Known as States of Siege or Emergency* (Document ONU E/CN.4/Sub. 2/1982/15, released on July 27,1982).

SALMÓN, Elizabeth (2014). *Curso de Derecho Internacional Público*. Lima: PUCP.

SECRETARÍA GENERAL DE LA OEA, *Conferencia Especializada Interamericana sobre Derechos Humanos: Actas y Documentos (7-22 de noviembre de 1969)*, Washington DC, OEA, s/f.

SHEERAN, Scott (2013). "Reconceptualizing States of Emergency under International Human Rights Law: Theory, Legal Doctrine, and Politics." *Michigan Journal of International Law*, vol. 34, num. 3, pp. 491-557.

SILES, Abraham (2017). "Problemática constitucional del estado de emergencia en el Perú: algunas cuestiones fundamentales." *Estudios Constitucionales*, Año 15, N° 2, pp. 123-166.

SVENSSON MCCARTHY, Anna-Lena (1998). *The International Law of Human Rights and States of Exception*, The Hague, Boston, London: Martinus Nijhof Publishers.

VERGOTTINI, Giuseppe (2002). *Las transiciones constitucionales: desarrollo y crisis del constitucionalismo a finales del siglo XX*. Bogotá: Universidad Externado de Colombia.

THEMATIC TABLE 2: IMPEACHMENT AND FAIR TRIAL

Dialogue between Jurisdictions and Legal Security in the Effectiveness of Human Rights Treaties in Brazilian Jurisdiction

Eduardo Biacchi Gomes[1]
and Daniella Pinheiro Lameira[2]

I. Introduction

With post-war 1945, a new world order was inaugurated regarding international law, this occurred with the very dimension of the individual's subjectivity to act—juridically—in an international society. In fact, when discussing the individual, as a subject of international law, it is worth mentioning that it is an exceptionality.

In the specific case, we talk about the hypotheses in which the individual has the capacity to sue against the States, in the case of human rights violations. In this sense, it is worth noting that the Federative Republic of

---

[1] Post Doctor in Cultural Studies from the Federal University of Rio de Janeiro, with studies at the University of Barcelona, PhD internship at PPGDH-PUCPR, PhD in Law from the Federal University of Paraná, Professor of International Law and Integration of UniBrasil, Undergraduation and Master, Full Professor of International Law PUC/PR, Adjunct Professor of International Law at Uninter and Collaborating Professor of the Master of the same institution. eduardobiacchigomes@gmail.com.

[2] Master in Constitutional Law from the Integrated Faculties of Brazil (UniBrasil). Specialist in Law from the School of the Judiciary of Paraná (EMAP). Specialist in Civil Law Lato Sensu from Cândido Mendes University/RJ. Professor at the International University Center (UNINTER). Professor at the Superior School of Law—ESA. Member of the American Laboratory of Comparative Constitutional Studies (LAECC). Member of the OAB/PR Ethics Court. Researcher at the Constitutional Law Research Center of UniBrasil. Member of Conpedi—National Council for Research and Post-Graduation in Law. Lawyer.

Brazil is part of the Inter-American System for the Protection of Human Rights, since it ratified the Pact of San José, Costa Rica, 1969, and the Clause of Jurisdiction of the Inter-American Court for the Protection of Human Rights.

Such a perspective, within the Inter-American System for the Protection of Human Rights, in this concrete case, expands the need for judges and jurisdictions to understand the law within a systemic view, in which there is no longer a classic division between domestic and international law, since it is within the jurisdictions of the states that it is possible to carry out the treaties and, concretely, human rights.

It is necessary to question, however, which constitutional mechanisms may exist to ensure the applicability of human rights treaties. In the Brazilian case, although we may speak improperly of the control of convention, as the said system does not exist in our legal system, even though in practice the judges use such a mechanism; the most used procedural instrument is the control of constitutionality, in its concentrated and diffuse modalities.

Within a true perspective of the dialogue between jurisdictions, it is increasingly necessary that the judiciary can properly interpret and apply human rights treaties as a way to seek legal security, both domestically and internationally.

This article has the purpose of pointing out other constitutional instruments that are perhaps more effective, to seek the protection and the effectuation of human rights within the Brazilian legal system, through the General Repercussion. To do so, based on a bibliographical and jurisprudential analysis, it is noted that the Federal Supreme Court's understanding is still timid, in the analysis of the General Repercussion cases involving human rights.

In the end, we will verify that it is increasingly necessary that the Federal Supreme Court, through existing Constitutional Actions and other more binding procedural instruments, such as Actions with a General Repercussion, ensures the application of human rights treaties broadly to protect legal relationships involving individuals.

II. The Question of the need for the Observance of Human Rights by the Brazilian Judiciary

For a better understanding and approach to the subject, we need to situate the reader in the current dimension of human rights and the need for their observance, at the international and national levels. It is worth mentioning, as a matter of curiosity, that the notion of Human Rights (not as we know them today), had already appeared in the Middle Ages in England, in important documents such as the Magna Carta Libertatum in 1215. In the Modern Age, great institutes of individual protection were the Petition of Right in 1628, Habeas Corpus in 1679, the Bill of Rights in 1689 and the Act of Settlement in 1701, which portrayed the importance of the subject to the English (Ramos, 2016: 33 and ss).

Afterwards, in the US, the Virginia Declaration of Rights in 1776 and the Constitution of the United States of America in 1787 also showed remarkable concern with the subject.

However, it was in the Contemporary Age, with the French Revolution and the Declaration of the Rights of Man and the Citizen, in 1789 that there was definitely the normative consecration of human rights (Liberté/Egalité/Fraternité). There were also important diplomas of the time, the constitutions arising from post-World War I, such as the Constitution of Weimar in 1919, the Soviet Constitution in 1918, and the Mexican Constitution of 1917 (the last with the ongoing war).

But it was the 1948 Universal Declaration of Human Rights which was the most important achievement of fundamental human rights at the international level, and from there many letters of rights came at the international level: the African Letter on Human and Peoples' Rights, the American Declaration of the Rights and Duties of Man, the Solemn Declaration of the World's Indigenous Peoples, and others (Ramos, 2016).

At the global level, with the creation of the United Nations (UN), the Global System for the Protection of Human Rights and its international norms were created, for instance, the Universal Declaration of Human Rights, 1948, the International Covenant on Civil and Political Rights, and the International Covenant on Economic, Social and Cultural Rights, both from 1966 (Ramos, 2016).

At the regional level, Regional Systems for the Protection of Human Rights have emerged, and in the case of the American continent, the Inter-

American System, which is part of the Organization of American States. The Inter-American System for the Protection of Human Rights has as its normative framework the Pact of San José, Costa Rica, 1969, and its structure is represented by the Inter-American Commission for the Protection of Human Rights and the Inter-American Court for the Protection of Human Rights. The last is the true interpreter of the Pact of San José (Ramos, 2016).

Internally, nothing is more correct than seeking an authentic interpretation of constitutional norms, which refer to human rights treaties. In this sense, it is worth highlighting the provisions of Paragraph 2 of the 5th Article of the Federal Constitution of 1988, which states that "the rights and guarantees expressed in this Constitution **do not exclude** others arising from treaties, agreements and international acts that the Federative Republic of Brazil is part of." Article 4 of the Federal Constitution of 1988 points to the need for the Federative Republic of Brazil, in relations with other States, to observe the principle of the dignity of the human person.

In his work on the subject, Norberto Bobbio (1992: 33) states that the evolution of human rights goes through three phases: the first phase is the one which affirms the rights of freedom; the second phase is called political rights; and finally, there is the third stage in which social rights are expressed, new demands are expressed, with new values such as "welfare and freedom through the State."

Since the democratization process of 1988, Brazil has ratified the main international treaties for the protection of human rights, such as: the Inter-American Convention to Prevent and Punish Torture and the Convention against Torture and Other Cruel, Inhuman or Degrading Treatment, both in 1989; the 1990 Convention on the Rights of the Child; the International Covenant on Civil and Political Rights, the International Covenant on Economic, Social and Cultural Rights, and the American Convention on Human Rights, all in 1992; the Convention Protocol to the American Convention on the Abolition of the Death Penalty in 1996, as well as the Protocol to the American Convention on Economic, Social and Cultural Rights (known as the Protocol of San Salvador) in 1996.

Coincidentally, or not, the same constitutional amendment which presented the certiorari to Brazilian law, brought, in addition to the institution of the CNJ (National Council of Justice), and the adoption of Binding Summaries by the STF, the new procedure for the ratification of the International Treaties of Human Rights in the country.

It is worth mentioning that with the advent of Constitutional Amendment 45/2004, which inserted paragraph 3 in article 5 of the Federal Constitution of 1988, the National Congress established a quorum for the approval of the human rights treaties. The quorum of three-fifths was double-voted in both houses, with the status of constitutional amendment (CF/88, article 5, 3rd paragraph).

With the appreciation of Extraordinary Appeal 349.703-1, the Federal Supreme Court understood the supra legal nature of the human rights treaties incorporated before the said Constitutional Amendment 45/2004, which has still been the subject of much criticism. Regardless of the obstacle created by the derived constituent, such amendment was not declared unconstitutional in any of its provisions.

The Brazilian Constitutional Court has been acting, in many instances, as guardian of the Brazilian Constitution, especially with regard to the protection of individual rights and guarantees. However, what sounds strange is the reason why such perspectives are not commonly analyzed from the point of view of the norms derived from the Human Rights Treaties of which Brazil is a part.

Looking back over the performance of the STF (Barroso; Osorio, 2016)[3] last year, it can be seen that extraordinary resources are a very rich source

---

[3] High-impact themes which were analyzed by the STF in 2015 through the recognition of a general repercussion on an extraordinary appeal involving fundamental and human rights: 1) Emergency works in prisons (RE 592.581, with general acknowledged repercussions, Rel. Min. Ricardo Lewandowski , judgment concluded on 08.13.2015) in which he began the trial of the controversial issue of the decriminalization of drugs possession for personal consumption, currently typified in article 28 of the Drug Law (Law 11.343/2006); 2) Social treatment of transsexuals (RE 845,779, with general repercussions recognized, Rel. Min. Luís Roberto Barroso, judgment not yet concluded); 3) Case not yet completed, RE 845.779, which discusses the right of transsexuals—one of the most marginalized minorities in society—to be treated socially in a way that is consistent with their gender identity; 3) Damage to prisoners (RE 580 252, with general acknowledged repercussions, Rel. Min. Teori Zavascki, judgment not yet concluded). A case which discusses the right of prisoners submitted to inhuman conditions of incarceration to obtain indemnification from the Public Power as moral damages; 4) The validity of the waiver clause in the incentive dispensation plan (RE 590.415, with general repercussion recognized, Rel. Min. Luís Roberto Barroso, judgment concluded on 04/30/2015). In a relevant decision in the labor law, the STF Plenary recognized, in a unanimous vote, the validity of a broad settlement clause of all the installments arising from the employment contract in the

of the STF's thinking evolution in the perspective of fundamental rights, and, in the same way, the said general repercussions analysis is also part of the aegis of international treaties.

III. Dialogue between Jurisdictions and Control of Conventionality

Therefore, the Federative Republic of Brazil, when ratifying a treaty and in the specific case of this article on tax matters by applying the principle *pacta sunt servanda,* has the duty and obligation to comply with it, otherwise it will be held responsible internationally. In addition, the Vienna Convention on the Law of Treaties itself, 1969, ensures the primacy of international law regarding the domestic law.

As the Federative Republic of Brazil is part of the Inter-American System for the Protection of Human Rights, it accepts the jurisdiction of the Court as mandatory. Pursuant to Articles 2 and 3 of the Pact of San José, Costa Rica, 1969, it was obliged to comply with the rights established in that treaty and to ensure its applicability within its legal system.

In this sense, the effectuation of the Human Rights listed in the Pact of San José of Costa Rica, stems from obligations assumed before the Inter-American System, and in the event of its violation, the State may be held responsible internationally.

Therefore, it is primarily for the Federative Republic of Brazil, especially through the Federal Supreme Court, to guarantee and ensure the effective fulfillment of the human rights listed in the Pact of San José of Costa Rica. Its utilization, primarily, must occur through constitutional actions.

Only in the event of omission by the Judiciary, or even the incorrect application of Human Rights Treaties, does the international responsibility of the State become possible provided the legal requirements are met.

Incentivized Exemption Plans (PDIs), provided that this item of Collective Bargaining Agreement and other instruments are signed by the employee; and 5) Investigative powers of the Public Prosecutor's Office (RE 593.727, Repr. Min. Cezar Peluso, Rel. For Min. Gilmar Mendes, judgment concluded on May 18th, 2015). The Court also concluded the awaited trial of the RE that discussed the investigative powers of the Public Prosecutor's Office, which had begun in June 2012. Retrieved from: <http://www.conjur.com.br/2015-dez-28/retrospectiva-2015-10-principais-decisoes-pauta-supremo>. Accessed on: 30 June 2016.

In this hypothesis, the Inter-American Court of Human Rights, which is in fact the authentic interpreter of the Pact of San José, may hold the State accountable for its failure to comply with Human Rights and *pacta sunt servanda.*[4]

Therefore, it is the Inter-American Court of Human Rights' duty to act in the jurisdiction of the Convention on Jurisdiction, in order to exercise its jurisdiction over the states, which have ratified the Pact of San José, Costa Rica, and have accepted its jurisdiction as mandatory.

Although the Inter-American Court of Human Rights has a preponderant function to seek the fulfillment of the rights listed in the Pact of San José, compliance with its decisions depends on an Act of the State itself. This means that many of its convictions are not fulfilled in their entirety or are still met in part.[5]

Hence, there is the need for the primary action of national courts in the application and observance of Human Rights. In this respect, we have the control of horizontal conventionality, in which it is the national jurisdiction itself, through its courts, which seeks the effectuation of international norms.

However, one of the great difficulties nowadays, especially in civil law systems, is the great number of actions within the Judiciary, including those that reach the Federal Supreme Court which makes difficult the effectuation of judicial protection, especially in relation to Human Rights. As a way of seeking to give greater effectiveness and celerity to the jurisdictional action, perhaps the procedural instrument of the General Repercussion may be an alternative.

IV. Effectuation of Human Rights Treaties: The General Repercussion

Regarding the application and observance of Human Rights Treaties, ratified by the Federative Republic of Brazil, it can be seen that even the

---

[4] Artigos 26 e 27 da Convenção de Viena sobre Direito dos Tratados, 1969.
[5] Para maiores detalhes acessar:
<http://www.corteidh.or.cr/cf/jurisprudencia2/casos_en_etapa_de_supervision.cfm>;
<http://www.corteidh.or.cr/index.php/es/casos-en-tramite-pendientes-de-emitirse-sentencia>;
<http://www.corteidh.or.cr/cf/jurisprudencia2/casos_en_etapa_de_supervision.cfm>. Acesso em: 27 ago. 2017.

position of the Federal Supreme Court is still timid. It should be noted that a great advance occurred, as previously mentioned, in the matter of the unfaithful depository.

Despite this reality, within a Democratic State of Law, it is necessary to use constitutional instruments which, decisively guarantee the effectuation of Human Rights Treaties within our legal system and which contribute to a faster solution to the jurisdictions.

In this sense, it is worth noting that constitutional control, concentrated or diffuse, is an extremely important constitutional instrument to guarantee the supremacy of the Constitution and, consequently, Human Rights. It is worth highlighting the provisions of article 102, paragraph 3 of the Federal Constitution of 1988, which conditions the demonstration of the General Repercussion, as a requirement for the admissibility of Extraordinary Remedies. Thus, if one of the functions of the General Repercussion is to avoid sending repetitive questions to the Federal Supreme Court, naturally the more the said judging body goes on to analyze the issues which involve Human Rights in order to apply the said Treaties and, on large issues, the greater the attribution to the effects of the General Repercussion, it is feasible to observe Human Rights, not only by the Constitutional Court, but by the courts of lower instances (Rocha, Jan./June 2010: 211-232).

According to Vilhena Vieira (2004: 195-207), this is the function of the General Repercussion:

> *The idea of giving the Supreme Court the power to choose—with a certain degree of discretion—the causes that it will judge is of the greatest importance. After all, the vast majority of cases, which reach the Court, have already passed the double degree of jurisdiction. Thus, the fundamental principle of the double degree of jurisdiction is already satisfied. In this sense, access to the jurisdiction of the STF, by means of an extraordinary appeal, would not be an absolute subjective right, in the sense that, if some objective conditions were satisfied, the STF would be obliged to know the appeal.*
>
> *It is interesting to note that in both the diffuse American model and the non-concentrated model exemplified by the German system, the Supreme Court and the Constitutional Court exercise enormous control over what they will judge. In the United States, of the nearly five thousand cases that reach the Court, only about one hundred receive attention annually. This selection takes place at the beginning of the judicial year. The criterion is the relevance of the case, and the Court is not obliged to offer any*

justification about its choices. In Germany, in turn, every citizen has the right to appeal to the court through the ***Verpssunjsbesehawerde****, a kind of popular constitutional appeal. The fact, however, is that the Court appreciates only about 1% of these appeals, with the other 99% being ignored by the Court on a number of arguments.*

(.....)

The adoption of a filtering mechanism will increase the authority of the STF, without thereby increasing its workload. On the other hand, it will also strengthen the lower jurisdictions, especially the Courts of Justice and the TRFs, which today are debased in their jurisdiction, functioning as judicial warehouses, since their decisions are invariably challenged before the STF and STJ.

Although the General Repercussion was introduced in our procedural system in 2004, through Constitutional Amendment 45, regarding human rights treaties, there are few cases analyzed by the Federal Supreme Court (Dantas, ago. 2017).

Moreover, in a recent survey carried out on the website of the Federal Supreme Court, in terms of sampling, in the years 2016 and 2017, it is rare to find issues analyzed by the Ministers, which deal with international law or even human rights.[6]

> **CONSTITUTIONAL RIGHT. EXTRAORDINARY REMEDY. PROHIBITION OF USE OF A RELIGIOUS HABIT COVERING THE HEAD OR PART OF THE FACE IN A PHOTOGRAPH OF A DOCUMENT OF QUALIFICATION AND CIVIL IDENTIFICATION. PRESENCE OF GENERAL REPERCUSSION.** 1. The contested decision recognized the right to use a religious habit in a photograph of a qualification and civil identification document, removing an administrative rule that prohibits the use of an item of clothing/accessory that covers part of the face or head in the photo. 2. It is a relevant constitutional question to determine whether it is possible, in the name of the right to freedom of belief and religion, to exclude an obligation imposed on everyone in relation to civil identification. 3. Recognized general repercussion. **(RE 859376 RG, Rel. Min. Roberto Barroso, j. em 29.06.2017, DJe-168 DIVULG 31.07.2017, PUBLIC 01.08.2017.)**

> **EXTRAORDINARY REMEDY. INTERNATIONAL ORGANIZATION. UNITED NATIONS ORGANIZATION. UN. UNITED NATIONS DEVELOPMENT PROGRAM—UNDP. CONVENTION ON PRIVILEGES AND IMMUNITIES OF THE UNITED NATIONS**

[6] Retrieved from: <www.stf.jus.br>. Accessed: 27 August, 2017.

DECREE 27.784/1950. CONVENTION ON PRIVILEGES AND IMMUNITIES OF THE UNITED NATIONS SPECIALIZED AGENCIES DECREE 52.288/1963. BASIC TECHNICAL ASSISTANCE AGREEMENT WITH THE UNITED NATIONS AND ITS SPECIALIZED AGENCIES DECREE 59.308/1966. *The impossibility of the international body to be sued in court, except in the case of express waiver of immunity from jurisdiction. Consolidated understanding in precedents of the Federal Supreme Court. Constitutional controversy with general repercussions. Reaffirmation of the jurisprudence of the Federal Supreme Court. Extraordinary Appeal Provided.* **(RE 1034840 RG, Rel. Min. Luiz Fux, j. em 01.06.2017, ELECTRONIC PROCESS. GENERAL REPERCUSSION—MERIT DJe-143 DIVULG 29.06.2017, PUBLIC 30.06.2017.)**

EXTRAORDINARY APPEAL WITH OFFENSE. GENERAL REPERCUSSION. HUMAN RIGHTS. INTERNATIONAL RIGHT. FOREIGN SOVEREIGN STATE. IMMUNITY OF JURISDICTION. KNOWLEDGE PROCESS. COMPETENCE. ACTS OF EMPIRE. ACTS OF MANAGEMENT. CRIME AGAINST THE INTERNATIONAL LAW OF THE HUMAN PERSON. PERIOD OF WAR. PERSONALITY RIGHTS. SUCCESSORS OF THE VICTIM. INDEMNITY. *1. The scope of the immunity of foreign State jurisdiction in relation to an act of empire offensive to the international law of the human person is a constitutional subject worthy of submission to the system of general repercussion. 2. The controversy consists of defining the viability of the processing and trial of a litigation, which involves a foreign sovereign state by the Brazilian Judiciary. 3. Preliminary general acknowledged repercussion.* **(ARE 954858 RG, Rel. Min. Edson Fachin, j. em 11.05.2017, ELECTRONIC PROCESS DJe-108 DIVULG 23.05.2017, PUBLIC 24.05.2017.)**

CONSTITUTIONAL. EXTRAORDINARY REMEDY. CONSTITUTIONAL PRINCIPLE OF PRESUMPTION OF INNOCENCE (CF, ART. 5, LVII). CONDEMNATION OF CRIMINAL JUDGMENT. PROVISIONAL IMPLEMENTATION. POSSIBILITY. RECOGNIZED GENERAL REPERCUSSION. REAFFIRMED JURISPRUDENCE.

1. *Under a general repercussion, it is reaffirmed the jurisprudence of the Federal Supreme Court that the provisional execution of a condemnatory criminal judgment rendered in a recourse degree, even if subject to a special or extraordinary appeal, does not compromise the constitutional principle of the presumption of innocence affirmed by article 5, item LVII, of the Federal Constitution. 2. Extraordinary appeal dismissed, with recognition of the general repercussion of the topic and reaffirmation of jurisprudence on the matter.*

2. **(ARE 964246 RG, Rel. Min. Teori Zavascki, j. em 10.11.2016, ELECTRONIC PROCESS GENERAL REPERCUSSION—MERIT DJe-251 DIVULG 24.11.2016, PUBLIC 25.11.2016.)**

EXTRAORDINARY REMEDY. PENAL AND PENAL PROCEDURE. ACCIDENT SITE LEAKAGE CRIME. ARTICLE 305 OF THE BRAZILIAN TRANSIT CODE. ANALYSIS OF THE CONSTITUTIONALITY OF THE PENAL TYPE IN THE LIGHT OF ART. 5, LXIII, OF THE FEDERAL CONSTITUTION. RECOGNIZED GENERAL REPERCUSSION. RE No. 971,959. UNIT NO. 907.
(RE 971959 RG, Rel. Min. Luiz Fux, j. em 05.08.2016, PROCESSO ELETRÔNICO DJe-239 DIVULG 09.11.2016, PUBLIC 10.11.2016.)

GENERAL REPERCUSSION. EXTRAORDINARY REMEDY. FUNDAMENTAL RIGHTS. PENAL. CRIMINAL PROCEEDINGS *2. Law 12,654/12 introduced the collection of biological material to obtain the genetic profile in criminal execution for violent crimes or heinous crimes (Law 7,210/84, article 9-A). The limits of the State's powers to collect biological material from suspects or convicted criminals, to trace their genetic profile, to store profiles in databases, and to make use of such information are subject to discussion in the various legal systems. Possible violation of the rights of the personality and the prerogative not to incriminate—art. 1, III, art. 5, X, LIV and LXIII, of CF. 3. There is a general repercussion for the claim of unconstitutionality of art. 9 of Law 7,210/84, introduced by Law 12,654/12, which provides for the identification and storage of genetic profiles of convicted persons for violent or heinous crimes. 4. General repercussions on extraordinary recourse recognized.* **(RE 973837 RG, Rel. Min. Gilmar Mendes, j. em 23.06.2016, ELECTRONIC PROCESS. DJe-217 DIVULG 10.10.2016, PUBLIC 11.10.2016.)**

It is important to emphasize the role of our Constitutional Court, in the sense of guaranteeing the supremacy of Human Rights Treaties, whether through concentrated control or through the diffuse control of constitutionality (what many call conventionality control) (FEILKE, Jan./June 2014: 147-186).

Thus, based on the assumption of the need to apply the Human Rights Treaties, within the jurisdictions of the States it is the Supreme Court, as the constitutional Court, which carries out the so-called horizontal conventionality control of the Human Rights Treaties, the instrument of the General Repercussion and it is extremely important for the judges and the lower courts to guarantee the primacy of the human rights treaties in relation to the domestic legal system.

In order to do so, it is necessary to change the position of the Federal Supreme Court itself, in order to apply the Human Rights Treaties in its decisions, and bring the treaties, and especially those of human rights, to a discussion of the General Repercussion. This is so that their decisions can be followed by judges and the lower courts.

V. Final Considerations

Although the Brazilian Judiciary, through the Federal Supreme Court, has advanced to seek the interpretation and correct application of the Human Rights Treaties ratified by the Federative Republic of Brazil, it becomes increasingly necessary for judges to have awareness in this regard.

One of the major problems within our legal system is the judges' lack of knowledge regarding the actual application of the Human Rights Treaties that, in other words, leads to their implementation. The large number of lawsuits which exist within our Judiciary and which deal with human rights issues evidences this.

Naturally, if the treaty, duly ratified by the State is an integral part of our legal system, it must be interpreted and applied by the Judiciary, under penalty of being held accountable internationally. Specifically, there is mention of the Pact of San José of Costa Rica, 1969, which has a degree of supra legal hierarchy.

Naturally, the Federal Supreme Court plays a preponderant role in the correct interpretation and application of the Human Rights Treaties duly ratified by the Federative Republic of Brazil, either through constitutional actions, through binding precedents or through cases of general repercussion.

Due to the relevance of the topic, this article sought to demonstrate that the Federal Supreme Court is still timid regarding the use and application of Human Rights Treaties, within the actions judged by the Ministers and involving general repercussions.

It is therefore increasingly necessary to promote the debate, through academic circles, congresses and within the Judiciary (mainly involving lawyers), in order to raise awareness of the need for the Human Rights Treaties in their judgments, in order to enforce judicial protection.

Bibliography

BARROSO, Luiz Roberto; OSÓRIO, Aline. *As dez principais decisões da pauta "qualitativa" do Supremo Tribunal Federal.* Disponível em: <http://www.conjur.com.br/2015-dez-28/retrospectiva-2015-10-principais-decisoes-pauta-supremo>. Acesso em: 30 jun. 2016.

BOBBIO, Norberto. *A Era dos Direitos.* 10. ed. Rio de Janeiro: Campus, 1992.

DANTAS, Alexandre Fernandes. Repercussão Geral dos Direitos Humanos. *Revista Eletrônica de Direito Processual—REDP*, v. VII. Disponível em: <http://www.e-publicacoes.uerj.br/index.php/redp/article/view/21124>. Acesso em: 27 ago. 2017.

FEILKE, Pedro Ribeiro Agustoni. O Controle de Convencionalidade e a Jurisprudência do Supremo Tribunal Federal. *Direito em Debate*, n. 41, pp. 147-186, jan./jun. 2014. Disponível em: <https://www.revistas.unijui.edu.br/index.php/revistadireitoemdebate/article/viewFile/2561/2679>. Acesso em: 27 ago. 2017.

RAMOS, André de Carvalho. *Curso de Direitos Humanos.* 3. ed. São Paulo: Saraiva, 2016.

ROCHA, Valéria Maria Lacerda. A Repercussão Geral no Controle de Constitucionalidade e os Efeitos Produzidos no Controle Difuso de Constitucionalidade. *Revista Direito e Liberdade—ESMARN*, v. 12, n. 1, pp. 211-232, jan./jun. 2010. Disponível em: <http://www.esmarn.tjrn.jus.br/revistas/index.php/revista_direito_e_liberdade/article/view/346>. Acesso em: 28 jun. 2017.

VIEIRA, Oscar Vilhena. Que reforma? **Estud. av.** [*on-line*]. 2004, v. 18, n. 51, pp. 195-207. Disponível em: <http://www.scielo.br/scielo.php?script=sci_arttext&pid=S0103-40142004000200012&lng=en&nrm=iso>. Acesso em: 27 ago. 2017.

Sites

<http://www.corteidh.or.cr/cf/jurisprudencia2/casos_en_etapa_de_supervision.cfm>.

<http://www.corteidh.or.cr/index.php/es/casos-en-tramite-pendientes-de-emitirse-sentencia>.

<http://www.corteidh.or.cr/cf/jurisprudencia2/casos_en_etapa_de_supervision.cfm>.

<www.stf.jus.br>.

THEMATIC TABLE 3: CHALLENGES OF FREEDOM OF INFORMATION IN THE XXI CENTURY: INFORMATIVE PLURALISM AND MEDIA CONCENTRATION

CHALLENGES OF FREEDOM OF INFORMATION IN THE 21ST CENTURY: RIGHT TO INFORMATION, CONCENTRATION OF COMMUNICATION MEANS AND THE "STATE'S PROTECTION DUTY"[1]

MÔNIA CLARISSA HENNIG LEAL[2]

I. Introduction

This article intends to analyze, based on the protection of the right to freedom of information, whether the State should intervene to avoid a

---

[1] This article is a result of the activities of the research project "Duty to protect (*Schutzpflicht*) and prohibition of insufficient means of protection (*Untermassverbot*) as criteria for a (qualitative) judicial review of public policies: Theoretical possibilities and critical analysis of their use by the Federal Supreme Court and the Inter-American Court of Human Rights," funded by CNPq (Edital Universal—Edital 14/2014—Process 454740/2014-0) and FAPERGS (Programa Pesquisador Gaúcho–
–Edital 02/2014—Process 2351-2551/14-5), in which the author acts as coordinator. The research project is connected with the Research Group "Open Constitutional Jurisdiction" (CNPq) and is developed at the Integrated Center for Study and Research on Public Policies (funded by FINEP) and at the Observatory of Latin-American Constitutional Jurisdiction (funded by FINEP), which are linked to the Graduate Studies Program in Law of the Universidade de Santa Cruz do Sul (UNISC). It is also part of the international cooperation project "Observatory of Latin-American Constitutional Jurisdiction: Reception of the case law of the Inter-American Court of Human Rights and its use as a parameter for the judicial review of public policies by Constitutional Courts," funded by CAPES (Edital PGCI 02/2015–
–Process 88881.1375114/2017-1 and Process 88887.137513/2017-00).
[2] Post-Doctorate at the Ruprecht-Karls Universität Heidelberg (Germany) and Doctorate in Law at the Universidade do Vale do Rio dos Sinos—Unisinos (with research done at the Ruprecht-Karls Universität Heidelberg, in Germany). Professor of the Graduate Studies Program in Law at the Universidade de Santa Cruz do Sul—UNISC, where she teaches Constitutional Jurisdiction and Judicial Review of Public Policies. Coordinator of the Research Group "Open Constitutional Jurisdiction," linked to CNPq. Scholarship holder of productivity in research from CNPq.

concentration of means of information. For this purpose, it adopts as a frame of reference the notion of an objective dimension of fundamental rights, from which a "State's duty to protect" is derived. Thus, it initially develops an approach to its central categories, focusing especially on their emergence and shaping in the realm of German constitutional theory, and then analyzes their repercussion regarding the main problem of this article, which involves the possibility of a State intervention designed to avoid a concentration of means of communication. In this way it seeks to contribute to a consolidation of democracy in its close connection with fundamental rights, recognizing that the State has the duty to create the necessary conditions for their exercise by acting on the basis of the principle of proportionality. Therefore, it should neither intervene excessively in the sphere of the rights of freedom of means and information (*Übermassverbot*) nor insufficiently protect the citizens' freedom of access to plural information (*Untermassverbot*).

II. The Objective Dimension of Fundamental Rights and the "State's Protection Duty" (Schutzpflicht): Theoretical Approaches

The notion of the objective dimension of the fundamental rights proves to be—along with the principle of proportionality[3]—according to some authors,[4] one of the most important innovations in the post-World War II dogmatics of fundamental rights, making it possible to apply them in new realms.

The development of that notion by the German Federal Constitutional Court[5] in connection with the notion of human dignity[6] is partly due to the

---

[3] The principle of proportionality constitutes, along with the limitation of fundamental rights and the reserve of the possible, what Denninger calls "key concepts of constitutional law," which is directly linked to this turning point in the view of the fundamental rights as objective rules. See Erhard Denninger, "Verfassungsrechtliche Schlüsselbegriffe," in: *Festschrift für Rudolf Wassermann zum 60. Geburstag*, ed. by Christian Broda (Darmstadt: Luchterhand, 1985), p. 176.

[4] "In der Grundrechtsdogmatik der Nachkriegszeit haben sich die Entdeckung des Verhältnismässigkeitsprinzips und die Entfaltung des objektivrechtlichen Gehalts der Grundrechte als die folgenreichsten Neuerungen erwiesen." Dieter Grimm, "Rückkehr zum liberalen Grundrechtsverständnis?", in: *Die Zukunft der Verfassung* (Frankfurt a.M.: Suhrkamp, 1991), p. 221.

[5] But the embryonic development of that theory could already be found in authors such as Günter Dürig (*Festschrift für Nawiasky*, 1956) and Henrich Lehmann

insight—based on the experiences of dictatorship—that the merely formal Rule of Law is not sufficient to guarantee rights. In this context, in order to avoid "emptying" the Constitution, it is necessary to refer to a theory of values, which presupposes also a material binding of laws, so that the constitutional rules are seen as value references and as guidelines.[7]

On that basis, the *Bundesverfassungsgericht*, in the exercise of its role as guardian of the Constitution, began to develop the idea that the fundamental rights contained in it have a double dimension, i.e. they denote both a subjective and an objective character.[8]

The embryonic development of this view appeared for the first time in the so-called *Lüth-Urteil,*[9] a historical decision made by that Court on January 23, 1958, in which the controversy involved the possibility or impossibility of a boycott—as a free expression of the freedom of speech—of a movie

---

(*Laufke in der Festschrift*, 1956). The *Bundesverfassungsgericht*, in turn, expressed this view for the first time in a decision by the First Panel on October 23, 1952 (BVerfGE, 1952, 2, p. 1) involving the topic of political parties and terms. Thus, the objective dimension of the fundamental rights comes from the German literature and a construction by the German Constitutional Court, which prompts Böckenförde (1991, p. 160) to conclude that the objective dimension of the fundamental rights is a theory constructed "under" the precepts of the Constitution's text, rather than "on the basis" of it.

[6] Human dignity is considered by some authors as a veritable metavalue of the constitutional and legal order. According to Sarlet, however, one must be aware that, although this value has a certain supremacy, it ends up being submitted to a necessary relativization when contrasted with the equal dignity of third parties. Ingo Sarlet, *Dignidade da pessoa humana e direitos fundamentais na Constituição de 1988*, 2nd ed. (Porto Alegre: Livraria do Advogado, 2002), pp. 131-132.

[7] Wiltraut Rupp von Brünneck, *Verfassungsgerichtsbarkeit und gesetzgebende Gewalt: wechselseitiges Verhältnis zwischen Verfassungsgericht und Parlament* (Tübingen: J. C. B. Mohr, 1977), p. 3 (Archiv des öffentlichen Rechts [AöR], Band 102).

[8] These issues are developed specifically by Robert Alexy, "Grundrechte als subjektive Rechte und als objektive Normen," in: *Der Staat: Zeitschrift für Staatslehre, öffentliches Recht und Verfassungsgeschichte* (Berlin: Duncker & Humblot, 1990), 29, pp. 49ff.

[9] BVerfGE 7, 198, in: Deutschland/Bundesverfassungsgericht, *Entscheidungen des Bundesverfassungsgerichts: Studienauswahl.* 2nd ed., ed. by Dieter Grimm and Paul Kirchhof, rev. by Michael Eichenberger (Tübingen: Mohr, 1997), p. 41.
This idea surfaces, however, in a less elaborate manner, already in previous decisions of that Court, such as in the *Elfes-Urteil* of 1957. BVerfGE 6, 32, in: ibid., p. 25. Since then the theory of the order of values has been constantly developed by the German Constitutional Court.

that was considered anti-Semitic and had been produced by a filmmaker who had collaborated with Hitler's regime. The then president of the Press Club of Hamburg City, Erich Lüth, who tried to exclude the movie from the film schedule of the local movie theaters and incited the mentioned boycott, was sued for damages by the movie producers. The controversy—and it could not be otherwise—raised the issue of the extent to which civil laws must take the fundamental rights into account.[10]

The trial court had decided in favor of the film producers under the allegation that the incitement to the boycott violated the morals and good customs established by the German Civil Code. But when the case was taken to the higher instance the *Bundesverfassungsgericht* changed the decision by looking at the case from a constitutional point of view and considering that Lüth's manifestation was part of his freedom of expression, a condition that is essential for human dignity, as the fundamental rights are rights of defense (*Abwehrrechte*), but also a historical and principled order of values.[11]

---

[10] On the binding of private persons to the fundamental rights, i.e. on their binding force in the private sphere, both in their objective and subjective dimension, see Ingo Wolfgang Sarlet, "Direitos Fundamentais e Direito Privado: algumas considerações em torno da vinculação dos particulares aos direitos fundamentais", in: *A Constituição concretizada: construindo pontes com o público e o privado*, ed. by Ingo W. Sarlet (Porto Alegre: Livraria do Advogado, 2000), pp. 107ff. In his view, it is necessary to overcome the classical contrast between the conceptions of direct (immediate) and indirect (mediated) effectiveness through weighing.
The opposite view that the fundamental rights are not binding, do not have immediate effectiveness for private persons and only apply to the State is held by Dieter Grimm, "Die Grundrechte als objektive Gestaltungsprinzipien," in: *Einführung in das öffentliche Recht—Verfassung und Verwaltung*, ed. by Dieter Grimm (Heidelberg: C. F. Müller, 1985), p. 69: "Besässen die Grundrechte auch unter Privatleuten unmittelbare Geltung, käme es zu ständigen Grundrechtskollisionen, deren Auflösung die Grundrechte selbst nicht mehr bewirken könnten. Deswegen bleibt es dabei, dass die Grundrechte ihre unmittelbare Wirkung nur gegenüber dem Staat entfalten."

[11] We can see her, in a way, a communitarian notion, based on the issue of the sharing of values. In Brugger's opinion, the communitarian view of the *Bundesverfassungsgericht* undoubtedly surfaces in some of its decisions: "das Menschenbild des Grundgesetzes ist nicht das eines isolierten souveränen Individuums; das Grundgesetz hat vielmehr die Spannung Individuum—Gemeinschaft im Sinne der Gemeinschaftsbezogenheit und Gemeinschaftsgebundenheit der Person entschieden, ohne deren Eigenwert anzutasten." In other words, in the Court's view, the concept of person incorporated by the Constitution is not the concept of an isolated individual, but of an individual in their relationship/tension with

Such a conception might initially appear paradoxical, since the integration of these two—in principle opposed—realms is supposed to be irreconcilable.[12] In Alexy's view,[13] however, the seeming conflict can be settled through an abstraction, a practical example of which can be found in the right to freedom of expression, which is a typical subjective and individual right; at the same time, however, it can also be considered a basic principle of the legal system as a whole, which is an aspect that reveals its objective and consequently binding dimension.

In the Court's argument one can find the view that the *Grundgesetz* is not a neutral order, but provides objective principles that guide life in the community, which is an aspect that leads to an increase of the binding force of fundamental rights (*Verstärkung der Geltungskraft der Grundrechte*).[14]

Thus, the judge must test the force of the constitutional provision to determine whether and to what extent the applicable law has to be influenced and limited by that value-based sphere. Therefore, the double character of those rights is an aspect that emanates from and applies to all realms and branches of Law.

Thus, the fundamental rights have the function of being, at the same time, "rights of defense" (*Abwehrrechte*) of the citizen vis-à-vis the State and a support of an objective order of values (*Wertesystem*) that is projected onto the whole of Law,[15] so that all laws must be interpreted and limited by the fundamental rights.

---

society, although it also considers their value in themselves. BVerfGE 4, 7, 15. See Winfried Brugger, *Liberalismus, Pluralismus, Kommunitarismus: Studien zur Legitimation des Grundgesetzes* (Baden-Baden: Nomos, 1999), p. 258.

[12] On the different theoretical currents that try to explain the relationship and/or connection established between the subjective and objective dimension of the fundamental rights, see Ernst-Wolfgang Böckenförde, "Grundrechte als Grundsatznormen: Zur gegenwärtigen Lage der Grundrechtsdogmatik," in: *Staat, Verfassung, Demokratie: Studien zur Verfassungstheorie und zum Verfassungsrecht* (Frankfurt a.M.: Suhrkamp, 1991), p. 180.

[13] Robert Alexy, "Grundrechte als subjektive Rechte und als objektive Normen," p. 57.

[14] BVerfGE 7, 198, in: Deutschland/Bundesverfassungsgericht, *Entscheidungen des Bundesverfassungsgerichts*, p. 41.

[15] "Danach hat der Grundrechtsabschnitt des Grundgesetzes eine doppelte Bedeutung. Er gewährt in erste Linie 'Abwehrrechte' des Bürgers gegen den Saat. Darüber hinaus aber soll er eine 'objektive Wertordnung' oder ein 'Wertesystem'

Such a position causes a reciprocal effect (*Wechselwirkung*)[16] in the relationship between fundamental rights and legislation. This phenomenon is called *Ausstrahlungswirkung* (irradiation effect) by German legal scholarship, as the fundamental rights, in their status of objective rights, provide guidelines for the application and interpretation of the whole infraconstitutional Law.[17]

This *Ausstrahlungswirkung*, however, does not imply an annulment of the various branches of Law (civil, criminal, administrative), which subsist as "autonomous"[18] branches; it only means that they are now intertwined and directly influenced by the Constitution[19] and by the objective dimension of the fundamental rights, binding not only the Judiciary, but all functions of the State.[20]

---

enthalten, das als 'verfassungsrechtliche Grundentscheidung für alle Bereiche des Rechts gilt." Robert Alexy, "Grundrechte als subjektive Rechte und als objektive Normen," p. 49.

16 The phrase was coined by Ralf Dreier, "Konstitutionalismus und Legalismus: zwei Arten juristischen Denkens im demokratischen Verfassungsstaat," in: *Rechtsstaat und Menschenwürde: Festschrift für Werner Maihofer zum 70. Geburtstag* (Frankfurt a.M.: Klostermann, 1988), p. 91, and refers to the previous characteristic of the connection of rights to the law that is typical of European constitutionalism.

17 In the same way, it is possible to speak of an effectiveness of the fundamental rights in the private sphere (*Drittwirkung*) in relation to third parties. See Bernhard Schlink, "Die Entthronung der Staatsrechtswissenschaft durch die Verfassungsgerichtsbarkeit," in: *Der Staat: Zeitschrift für Staatslehre, öffentliches Recht und Verfassungsgeschichte* (Berlin: Duncker & Humblot, 1989), 28, p. 169. Also Ingo W. Sarlet, *A eficácia dos Direitos Fundamentais* (Porto Alegre: Livraria do Advogado, 1998), p. 145.

18 Autonomy is understood here—and it could not be otherwise—in a relative sense. On this aspect, which involves the effects of the objective dimension of the fundamental rights, see Böckenförde, "Grundrechte als Grundsatznormen: zur gegenwärtigen Lage der Grundrechtsdogmatik," p. 168.

19 According to Hesse's analysis, in this new phenomenon being produced in the logic of law a *Gemengelage* (mixture, interaction) between ordinary law and constitutional law is established. See Konrad Hesse, *Verfassungsrecht und Privatrecht* (Heidelberg: C. F. Müller, 1988), p. 24.

20 Hence one can claim, agreeing with Ebsen, that through the guarantee of the fundamental rights an improvement of legislation and of the legal system itself is operated to a certain extent. See Ingwer Ebsen, *Das Bundesverfassungsgericht als Element gesellschaftlicher Selbstregulierung: Eine pluralistische Theorie der Verfassungsgerichtsbarkeit im demokratischen Verfassungsstaat* (Berlin: Duncker & Humblot, 1985), p. 73.

Therefore, the expansion of the content of the fundamental rights corresponds to and implies a process of *material constitutionalization*[21] of Law that directly affects all State powers[22] by binding them with its principled character.[23]

This objective dimension results, in turn, in the notion of a "State's duty to protect" (*Schutzpflicht*), i.e. the idea that the State has a duty to protect the fundamental rights, not only "in face of" but also "by" the State (*Grundrechtsschutz vor und durch den Staat*).[24]

In this way, there is an application of fundamental rights to the State agencies in their different functions,[25] which prompts Böckenförde to even speak of a "hypertrophy of the fundamental rights" (*Hypertrophie der Grundrechte*) and makes them operate as a veritable principle that has to be respected by the whole legal system.[26]

Thus, fundamental rights concern a subjective position of the citizen towards the State (*Abwehrrechte des Bürgers gegen den Staat*); but, based on the recognition that they are part of an objective order of values, there is a larger, multidimensional[27] projection, according to which there must be a protection and application of the fundamental rights not only in the

---

[21] The phrase was coined by Robert Alexy, *Verfassungsrecht und einfaches Recht: Verfassungsgerichtsbarkeit und Fachgerichtsbarkeit* (Berlin: Walter Gruyter, 2002), p. 10 (Veröffentlichungen der Vereinigung der Deutschen Staatsrechtslehrer [VVDStRL], Band 61).

22 Ralf Dreier, "Konstitutionalismus und Legalismus: zwei Arten juristischen Denkens im demokratischen Verfassungsstaat," p. 99.

[23] According to Alexy, the objective dimension of the fundamental rights can only subsist if its rules are considered legally binding (*bindend*). See Robert Alexy, "Grundrechte als subjektive Rechte und als objektive Normen," p. 56.

[24] Josef Isensee and Paul Kirchhof (eds.), *Handbuch des Staatsrechts des Bundesrepublick Deutschland*, 3rd ed. (Heidelberg: C. F. Müller, 2011), Band IX, p. 413.

[25] Johannes Dietlein, *Die Lehre von den grundrechtlichen Schutzpflichten*, 2nd ed. (Berlin: Duncker & Humblot, 2005), p. 51.

[26] According to Kischel, that dimension constitutes the central point of the Rule of Law and of democracy itself. See Uwe Kischel, *Die Begründung* (Tübingen: Mohr Siebeck, 2003), pp. 151-152.

[27] Robert Alexy, "Grundrechte als subjektive Rechte und als objektive Normen," p. 49.

relationship between the State and the individual, but also in the relationships of the individuals among themselves.[28]

From this perspective, according to Canaris,[29] the fundamental rights operate in two dimensions, both in relation to the State and to private persons: a) a prohibition of intervention (*Eingriffsverbote*), which is related to the idea of an "essential core" and of limits to its restriction (*Schranken-Schranke Theorie*); and b) a postulate of protection (*Schutzgebote*).

These "protection duties" unfold in three different aspects: a) prohibition of behaviors that violate fundamental rights (*Verbotspflicht*); b) legal security and a duty to adopt various measures designed to guarantee the fundamental rights (*Sicherheitspflicht*); and c) a duty to avoid risks to the fundamental rights, especially considering the development of science and technology (*Risikopflicht*).

In other words, the objective dimension ascribed to the fundamental rights, resulting from the idea that they embody and express certain fundamental objective values of the community, implies the insight that even the classical rights of defense must have their efficacy valued not only from an individualistic angle, i.e. not based only on their position vis-à-vis the State, but also from a social perspective.[30]

---

[28] Based on the objective dimension of the fundamental rights, which has repercussions on the State, citizens and community, one can even perceive a need for a rereading of the very notion of the relationship between the State branches. See Jorge Reis Novais, *As restrições aos direitos fundamentais não expressamente autorizadas pela Constituição* (Coimbra: Coimbra, 2003), p. 66.
[29] Claus-Wilhelm Canaris, *Grundrechte und Privatrecht* (Tübingen: J. C. B. Mohr [Paul Siebeck], 1984), pp. 201-247 (Archiv für die civilistische Praxis, Band 184).
[30] On these consequences of the objective dimension ascribed to the fundamental rights, see Ingo W. Sarlet, *A eficácia dos direitos* fundamentais, pp. 138ff., where interesting contributions from German legal scholarship on the topic can be found. According to Sarlet, the objective character of the fundamental rights has many implications, both of a theoretical and practical nature, such as the recognition of autonomous legal effects beyond the subjective perspective; a binding and guiding function for the State powers (including the constitutionally recognized power) and also for individuals in the private sphere.

Therefore, the notion of a concrete order of values has not that much to do with a new function of these rights, but rather with the foundation for other, broader functions.[31]

Thus, the principled character of the rules on fundamental rights establishes not only that these rights can be restricted by other rights or in the presence of opposing principles, but also that their limitation is itself limited.[32] The need for weighing these rights and principles is inevitable and leads to a series of new questions, especially concerning the rationality of that weighing.

It should be noted, however, that the rights that impose positive obligations are fundamentally different from the negative obligations, which correspond to the rights of defense or abstention (*Abwehrrechte*). This is so because when something is prohibited—which is characteristically the case of the latter—then each and every action that means or implies a violation or destruction of that protected right is prohibited. On the other hand, when something is imposed in a positive dimension, in the sense of protecting or promoting a right, then not each and every action that protects or promotes that right is seen as mandatory, which once again leads to a weighing.

One example can be found in the analysis of the following situation: when what is at stake is the prohibition to kill, this prohibition has to do, prima facie, with each and every form of death (regardless of the means employed). In the case that there is a duty in the opposite sense, a duty to save—whose dimension is objective—not all available means for that are automatically imposed.[33] If, for example, a drunken person is drowning and it is possible to save her by using a life boat or a life buoy, then not all of these actions are mandatory; rather, one has to choose one *or* the other, i.e. to adopt an alternative logic. This means, then, that the addressee of the command has an open space (*Spielraum*)[34] within which it is possible

[31] Ingo W. Sarlet, *A eficácia dos direitos* fundamentais, p. 148.

[32] One can distinguish two views on the protection of the essential core (*Wesensgehalt*) of these rights: an absolute view and another one that interprets them in a relative manner. On this, see Ludwig Schneider, *Der Schutz des Wesensgehalts von Grundrechten nach Art. 19 Abs. 2 GG* (Berlin: Duncker & Humblot, 1983), pp. 93ff.

[33] Robert Alexy, "Grundrechte als subjektive Rechte und als objektive Normen," p. 62.

[34] In his book on constitutional law and constitutional review, Alexy classifies different kinds of *Spielräume*, subdividing them into structural (*strukturelle*

to choose how this duty will be fulfilled in the best manner, based on an analysis that takes into account the adequacy between the means and the proposed ends,[35] constituting what is usually called the "legislator's freedom of conformation."

This "freedom of conformation," however, is not absolute; from the notion of the "State's duty to protect" are derived the concepts of "prohibition of excess"—in terms of a restriction or intervention in the fundamental rights (*Übermassverbot*)—and of "prohibition of insufficient protection" (*Untermassverbot*), which are closely connected with the notion of proportionality[36] (although in opposite directions, since one operates with the logic of "beyond" and the other with the logic of "below").[37]

Considering this recognition, the State is no longer seen as a mere violator or addressee of the prohibitions imposed by those rights but is also responsible for protecting them and ensuring the conditions for their actual guarantee.[38] The problem is that the parameters of this protection are not

---

Spielräume, those that appear when the Constitution leaves open conformation spaces, requiring elements such as attribution of meaning, choice of means and weighing) and epistemic ones (*epistemische Spielräume*, related to situations in which the Constitution is not clear about what is due, prohibited or allowed; thus, this is an openness of a hermeneutical nature, unlike the previous situation, where the openness resides in the very structuring of the Constitution). See Robert Alexy, *Verfassungsrecht und einfaches Recht*, pp. 15ff.

[35] A reference to this space of deliberation appears in many decisions of the German Constitutional Court, including the so-called *Cannabis-Urteil*, which involved forms of limitation of the use of drugs and their effects on the use of alcohol and cigarettes. The decision mentions the need for an adequacy between means and ends and recognizes that the legislator has the possibility of choosing: "Bei der vom Verhältnismässigkeitsgrundsatz geforderten Beurteilung der Eignung des gewählten Mittels zur Erreichung des erstrebten Zwecks sowie bei der in diesem Zusammenhang vorzunehmenden Einschätzung und Prognose der dem einzelnen oder der Allgemeinheit drohenden Gefahren steht dem Gesetzgeber ein Beurteilungsspielraum zu, welcher vom Bundesverfassungsgericht nur in begrenztem Umfang überprüft werden kann." BVerfGE 90, 145, in: Deutschland/ Bundesverfassungsgericht, *Entscheidungen des Bundesverfassungsgerichts*, p. 519.

[36] Miguel Carbonel, *El principio de proporcionalidad y la interpretación constitucional* (Quito: V&M Gráficas, 2008), p. 11.

[37] Paulo Gilberto Cogo Leivas, *Teoria dos direitos fundamentais sociais* (Porto Alegre: Livraria do Advogado, 2006), p. 76.

[38] Maria Luiza Schäfer Streck, *O direito penal e o princípio da proibição de proteção deficiente: A face oculta da proteção dos direitos fundamentais*, Master's Thesis, Universidade do Vale do Rio Sinos, Programa de Pós-Graduação em Direito, São Leopoldo, 2008, p. 81.

explicitly established, so that German case law determined, in the second decision on abortion (*BverfGE* 88, 203), that in this case the principle of proportionality should be observed, for

> the Constitution establishes protection as the goal but does not go into detail about its shaping. However, the legislator must observe the prohibition of insufficiency … they are subject to the constitutional judicial review (by the Federal Constitutional Court) … What is decisive is that the protection be efficient as such. The measures taken by the legislator must be sufficient for and adequate and efficient protection and also be based on a careful inquiry into the facts and on rationally sustainable assessments. … The state must adopt sufficient normative and factual measures to fulfill its duty to protect, which will make it possible—considering the conflicting goods—to reach an adequate and, as such, efficient protection (prohibition of insufficiency). For that purpose, it is necessary to have a protection project that will combine elements of preventive and repressive protection.[39]

The concept of "duty to protect" (*Schutzpflicht*) also serves, from this perspective, as a foundation and parameter for the recognition of the State's "duty" to act and, consequently, for the pointing out of potential "omissions" or "distortions" by the State, and for this purpose the criteria to be used are the notions of "prohibition of insufficient protection" (*Untermassverbot*) and "prohibition of excess" (*Übermassverbot*), for

> it is the legislator's task to determine, in a detailed manner, the kind and extension of the protection. The Constitution establishes protection as a goal but does not go into detail about its shaping. However, the legislator must observe the prohibition of insufficiency … Considering that there are opposing legal goods, an adequate protection is necessary. What is decisive is that the protection be efficient as such.[40]

Thus, the provision of an adequate protection of the fundamental rights is not the faculty of those who act on behalf of the government, and their acts should be guided by proportionality, so that it will not be provided in an insufficient or excessive manner,[41] which is an aspect that suggests the

---

[39] Leonardo Martins (ed.), *Cinqüenta anos de jurisprudência do Tribunal Constitucional Federal Alemão* (Montevideo: Konrad-Adenauer-Stiftung, 2005), pp. 276-280.
[40] Brasil, Supremo Tribunal Federal. *HC 104.410/RS*, Segunda Turma, julgado em 06/03/2012. Judge-rapporteur: Justice Gilmar Mendes. Available at: <http://www.stj.jus.br>. Retrieved on: 10 May 2013, p. 18.
[41] I. W. Sarlet, L. G. Marinoni and D. Mitidiero, *Curso de Direito Constitucional* (Porto Alegre: Revista dos Tribunais, 2012), p. 338.

existence of a scale of intensities and possibilities of intervention by the State that should not be surpassed either in one direction (excess) or in the other (insufficiency),[42] under penalty of frontally violating the Constitution.

The case of the concentration of the means of information, which is closely connected with the fundamental right to the freedom of information, characterizes a situation in which this complexity becomes evident, leading to the question of whether the State should intervene or not. In this case, the State's role would consist of preventing the concentration of means, based on the protection of the fundamental right to freedom of information; in this regulation, the State should act in a proportional manner, not intervening excessively (*Übermassverbot*) in the autonomy of the means of communication, but providing sufficient protection for the fundamental right of each individual.

Here we would have what Callies calls "multipolar constitutional relations,"[43] characterized by relations that exhibit conflicts between fundamental rights that are much more complex than those that are posed in terms of bilaterality and require an even more accurate action by the State in the fulfillment of its duty to protect the fundamental rights.

III. Conclusion

The notion of an objective dimension of the fundamental rights proves to be, along with the principle of proportionality, one of the most important innovations of the dogmatics of the fundamental rights in the post-World War II period, making it possible to apply them in new domains.

From this perspective, the *Bundesverfassungsgericht*, in the exercise of its role as guardian of the Constitution, developed the idea that the fundamental rights contained in it have a double dimension, i.e. they denote both a subjective and an objective character.

The embryonic development of this view appeared for the first time in the so-called *Lüth-Urteil* in 1958. In the Court's argument one can find that the *Grundgesetz* is not a neutral order, but provides objective principles that guide life in the community, which leads to an increase of the binding

[42] Juan Carlos Gavara de Cara, *La dimensión objetiva de los derechos sociales* (Barcelona: JMB Bosch, 2010), p. 54.

[43] Christian Caliess, *Rechsstaat und Umweltstaat: Zugleich ein Beitrag zur Grundrechtsdogmatik im Rahmen mehrpoliger Verfassungsrechtsverhältnisse* (Tübingen: Mohr-Siebeck, 2001).

force of the fundamental rights (*Verstärkung der Geltungskraft der Grundrechte*).

This objective dimension results, in turn, in the notion of the "State's duty to protect" (*Schutzpflicht*), i.e. the idea that the State has a duty to protect fundamental rights. This is a view of the protection of fundamental rights "before" and "by" the State.

From this perspective, the fundamental rights operate in two dimensions, both in relation to the State and to private persons: a) a prohibition of intervention (*Eingriffsverbote*), which is related to the idea of an "essential core" and of limits to its restriction (*Schranken-Schranke Theorie*); and b) a postulate of protection (*Schutzgebote*).

This means that the addressee of the command has an open space (*Spielraum*) within which it is possible to choose how this duty will be fulfilled in the best manner, based on an analysis that takes into account the adequacy between the means and the proposed ends, constituting what is usually called the "legislator's freedom of conformation."

This "freedom of conformation", however, is not absolute, and from the notion of the "State's duty to protect" are derived the concepts of "prohibition of excess"—in terms of a restriction or intervention in the fundamental rights (*Übermassverbot*)—and of "prohibition of insufficient protection" (*Untermassverbot*), which are closely connected with the notion of proportionality (although in opposite directions, since one operates with the logic of "beyond" and the other with the logic of "below").

Thus, the State is no longer seen as a mere violator or addressee of the prohibitions imposed by those rights but is also responsible for protecting them and ensuring the conditions for their actual guarantee.

The case of the concentration of the means of information, which is closely connected with the fundamental right to the freedom of information, characterizes a situation in which this complexity becomes evident, leading to the question of whether the State should intervene or not. The State should act in a proportional manner, not intervening excessively (*Übermassverbot*) in the autonomy of the means of communication, but providing sufficient protection for the fundamental right of each individual.

Here we would have what Callies calls "multipolar constitutional relations," characterized by relations that exhibit conflicts between fundamental rights that are much more complex than those that are posed in terms of bilaterality and require an even more accurate action by the State in the fulfillment of its duty to protect fundamental rights.

INFORMATIVE FREEDOM, INFORMATIVE PLURALISM AND MEDIA CONCENTRATION

LUIS ALBERTO HUERTA GUERRERO*

I. Introduction

The Thematic Table No. 3 at the IV Inter-American Journey on Fundamental Rights is dedicated to the Challenges of Freedom of Information in the XXI Century, in particular to analyze from a constitutional perspective, and in accordance with international human rights law, the actions that must be adopted by the States to guarantee informative pluralism and avoid the concentration of communication media.

On this matter, based on the interpretation of the 13° Article of the American Convention on Human Rights (ACHR), there are pronouncements of the inter-American system for the protection of human rights organizations, such as the Inter-American Commission (IACHR) and the Inter-American Court (I/A Court or Supranational Court or the Court), which must be taken into consideration by the national authorities when interpreting the 2° Article, clause 4, and the 62° Article of the Political Constitution of 1993, as provided for in the Fourth Final and Transitory Provision of the constitutional text. This paper seeks to explain the relationship between these sources in order to define the obligations of the State aimed at guaranteeing citizen access to a plurality of information sources.

---

* Lawyer, Master in Constitutional Law and Doctor in Law at the Pontifical Catholic University of Peru [*Pontificia Universidad Católica del Perú*]. Professor in Constitutional Law and in Procedural Constitutional Law at the same university.

II. Informative Plurality and the State Obligation Regarding the Concentration of Media

The study of every fundamental right must begin by identifying its foundations, i.e., the reasons that justify its importance, and the special recognition it receives in a Constitutional State. In the case of freedom of expression and information, study and analysis cannot be considered as simply one of the several fundamental rights recognized in the constitutional texts. It is necessary to pay special attention to the theories that have been elaborated regarding their foundations, in such a way that the obligations that exist around their respect and guarantee can be understood.

The modern foundations of freedom of expression and information are framed in a legal-constitutional perspective, because they are theories developed from the recognition of these rights in constitutional texts. Among them we can mention the libertarian theory, which finds its guiding principle in the personal self-realization of the individual, intrinsically related to the autonomy and dignity of the person; or the democratic theory, which emphasizes the importance of this right for the strengthening of the democratic system, so it is a political foundation, where the protected discourse is one that helps citizens to adopt the necessary decisions for the development of the government.

The variety of foundations on these rights does not imply choosing the one that seems best prepared, but all of them must be integrated, given that they reinforce the measures to strengthen their exercise and face contrary acts to it. In practice, an *integrator* position offers a wide margin of action to guarantee its validity. Only with this approach will it be possible to materialize the real dimension of freedom of expression and information, which represents not only an individual interest, but also one of collective scope. This perspective acquires special importance when analyzing the actions that the State should adopt in the matter of informative plurality.

The recognition of freedom of expression and information as fundamental rights implies that states have two obligations: those of respect and guarantee. For the first one, they are prevented from performing acts against both rights, while for the second, they must take all measures to allow everyone enjoyment and performance, as well as to prevent, investigate, punish and repair any act that affects the free dissemination of ideas and information. These obligations derive from international human rights standards, as well as from the constitutional texts themselves.

Regarding the freedom of expression and information, there are several situations that can be considered as opposed to their exercise, such as prior censorship or the establishment of arbitrary sanctions for the issuance of a certain idea or information. Like all fundamental rights, acts contrary to their exercise are varied, being necessary to identify those that occur more frequently, in order to adopt measures that are aimed to reversing them and preventing them from happening.

In practice, the problems that originated in various countries due to the concentration of communication media have led to the consideration of this situation as a measure that limits or restricts freedom of expression. Concentration can occur with regard to various means of communication, be carried out by the State or individuals and be oriented to various objectives. About this problem Delgado Taboada (2016: 36) pointed out:

> The concentration of the media is a universal phenomenon and is one of the most important legal problems of the XXI Century. The problem described is not alien to the Latin American countries, where it is vitally important to develop institutional mechanisms that prevent the private investors or the State from concentrating the mediatic power. The dangers to the democratic system are not only measured with respect to the detriment of informative pluralism, but also by how much capacity the communication media have to define a country's public agenda and thus determine what is being discussed and what the society is taking in importance [original in Spanish].

In attention to the former, it is the responsibility of the State to adopt measures aimed at guaranteeing the existence of an informative plurality, as well as those actions that avoid the concentration of the communication media.

These are two approaches that, while complementary, should not be confused. The first involves a constant effort to ensure that citizens have access to various sources of information. The second is aimed at preventing or, in any case, at reversing specific situations in which a concentration of media is present, given that it is contrary to informative plurality. In general, this second approach has been the most used for the analysis of a subject that also requires the active work of the State in order to promote the access of citizens to different sources of information.

Regarding the measures to avoid media concentration, it is up to the States to have a regulatory framework on the matter. The absence of a debate on media concentration in the corresponding regulatory bodies only encourages the solution to arising problems to be derived from the jurisdictional scope, whose legitimacy to intervene is fully justified insofar as it seeks to protect the informative freedom.

Although the debate and the implementation of measures in favor of informative plurality must be permanent, this should not ignore the fact that only a serious analysis on the subject will be possible if there are minimum guarantees for a democratic debate on a matter that is quite sensitive according to the diverse interests that exist around it.

III. Political Constitution of Peru of 1993

3.1 Regulatory framework

The Political Constitution of Peru of 1993 states in the 2° Article, clause 4, that "Every person has the right: (…) to freedom of information, opinion, expression and dissemination of thought either orally, or in writing or by images, by any means of social communication whatsoever, and without previous authorization, censorship or impediment in accordance with the law." Through its jurisprudence, the Constitutional Court [*Tribunal Constitucional*] has pointed out some aspects related to these rights, as well as analyzed several cases related to restrictions on its exercise.

For this paper it is appropriate to mention the second paragraph of the 61° Article of the Constitution, which states the following:

> The press, radio, television and other means of expression and social communication and, in general, enterprises, goods, and services related to freedom of speech and communication, cannot be objects of exclusivity, monopoly or hoarding, directly or indirectly, by the State or private parties.

The location of this provision is understood if it is taken into account that the 61° Article is part of the general principles that guide the Economic System of the Constitution of 1993. In turn, its context must be taken into account, given that it is part of an article that emphasizes, in its first paragraph, that "the State facilitates and oversees free competition. In this sense, it fights any practice that would limit it and the abuse of dominant or monopolistic positions. No law or arrangement may authorize or establish monopolies."

In a systematic interpretation of the Constitution of 1993, the second paragraph of the 61° Article must not only be considered as a rule related to the economic regime of the constitutional text, but as part of the established guarantees in the supreme law of the legal order in favor of the freedom of expression and information which implies that the State is obliged to adopt measures to avoid the exclusivity, monopoly or hoarding of "the press, radio, television and other means of expression and social communication", either by the State itself or by individuals.

Consequently, this constitutional norm must not only be interpreted from an economic perspective, aimed at avoiding the concentration of a certain activity, but also from a perspective aimed at guaranteeing informative plurality and avoiding the concentration of the media in order to guarantee the informative freedom recognized in the 2° Article, clause 4, of the Constitution. In this way, the actions or omissions of the State regarding the media concentration could lead to a judicial process against it. For this purpose, the judicial path will depend on the measure in favor of the information freedoms that one wishes to achieve. A similar situation arises in the case of individuals, for the actions they carry out imply a concentration of media.

Regarding the measures that the State must adopt to avoid media concentration it is interesting to mention the following (Institute of Democracy and Human Rights of the San Martín de Porres University, 2015: 22-23):

> In particular, legal regulations should be adopted and institutional reforms and public policies should be outlined that include, among others:
>
> a. Limits to the multiplicity of licenses for the use of radio spectrum frequencies under the control of the same single natural or legal person or the same economic conglomerate.
> b. Limits to cross-ownership of media (inside and outside of a given sector, vertical or horizontal property).
> c. Wider scope antitrust laws for the communication media, including printed media.
>
> (….)
>
> In this line, as a projection of the democratic principle of transparency and publicity in media management, it should guarantee;
>
> a. Legislation and concrete practices, to guarantee transparency and access to information on the ownership and control of communication media.
> b. Rules that oblige the media to publish and make known the owners, shareholders and/or those who control the companies behind the media.
> c. Permanent updating of the information handled by the State about ownership, control, assignment and transfers of media [original in Spanish].

Regarding this issue, it should be noted that there are positions contrary to these types of measures, alleging respect for the right to property. In this sense Farfán Sousa (2014: 355) has pointed out that:

> [...] those who are opposed to the limitation of property in the concentration of media have constructed a series of arguments that would make it evident that, even though it is necessary to favor free expression and democracy, restrictions in this market are not necessary. In this way, the advances in technology, the sufficiency of antitrust measures, the communicative weakness of the printed press, the dangers posed by State intervention and the warning of the difficulty of the concept of diversity (required by pluralism) as the affirmation of the impossibility of achieving it through this measure, are perhaps the main arguments used against the limitation in media concentration [original in Spanish].

3.2 Specific problems

Especially in authoritarian periods, several situations have presented in Peru, in which the media concentration was quite evident. For example, during the 1970s, the military dictatorship confiscated the communication media for its own benefit. During the 1990s, and under the validity of the Constitution of 1993, the government carried out acts of corruption to buy the editorial lines of the media in order to attack the opposition and misinform public opinion about the political juncture. In both cases, there were no normative mechanisms or effective judicial channels that would allow opposing situations like those. With regard to what happened in the 1990s, the IACHR pointed out in its Second report on the situation of human rights in Peru (IACHR, 2000):

> 30. The Commission notes that, in effect, some press outlets disseminate information and opinions unfavorable to the government. Nonetheless, claiming to gauge the freedom of expression based on the number of publications critical of the authorities is a fallacious exercise. Respect for freedom of expression should be considered in light of the direct and indirect restrictions on its exercise. The amount of information disseminated is insufficient to appreciate the enjoyment of this right. The value of the information is mainly in its content, not only its amount.
>
> 31. It should be noted that the media that appear to speak out with more freedom are the press and the radio, while television appears to have become completely stripped of its critical tone.

More recently, the debate around the informative pluralism and the media concentration was retaken as a result of acts between individuals regarding the ownership of printed media. This is a matter that for several years has been pending resolution in the courts, regarding an application for protection filed at the end of 2013 by a group of journalists. The IACHR also convened a public hearing on this matter,[1] which was reviewed, by the Office of the Special Rapporteur for Freedom of Expression in its annual report for 2014 (IACHR, 2014), as follows:

> 921. At the hearing on the "Situation of the Right to Freedom of Expression and Concentration of Communications Media Ownership in Peru" [*"Situación del derecho a la libertad de expresión y concentración de propiedad de medios de comunicación en Perú"*], held on March 24, 2014, during the 150th ordinary period of sessions of the IACHR, the Office of the Special Rapporteur received information on what could be a concentration of communications media ownership. According to the petitioners, there is a concentration of printed communications media ownership in the country, stemming from the acquisition of four daily newspapers by the Grupo El Comercio from the Grupo Epensa. As a result of this transaction, the acquiring group has a total of 9 daily newspapers, which translates into a concentration of 78% of the media outlets. Secondly, the petitioners referred to the topic of cross-ownership of media outlets, explaining that the Grupo El Comercio owns the country's main television channel *(América Televisión)*. They emphasized that these situations of concentration also affect radio, because certain groups have various radio stations with national coverage, which affects the access and survival of certain local media outlets. The petitioners expressed their concern over the abusive use of the right of private property that could affect freedom of expression in the country, stating that the judicial channel would be suitable for achieving acceptable levels of concentration that guarantee plurality and diversity of information. (…)
>
> 922. The Government of Peru stated that it fully intended to respect the judicial ruling issued regarding the concentration of the Grupo El Comercio, expressing that there are conditions in the country that ensure the issuance of an independent judicial ruling. The State clarified that it does not have any specialized body charged with evaluating the conduct of printed media outlets. It also said that in local legislation (Law 28278), there is a provision that establishes that radio and television cannot be the

---

[1] The hearing was requested by two non-governmental organizations, the Legal Defense Institute [*Instituto de Defensa Legal—IDL*] and the National Coordinator of Human Rights [*Coordinadora Nacional de Derechos Humanos—CNDDHH*]. The Peruvian State was represented by me, because at that time I was the Specialized Supranational Public Prosecutor, and by Juan Jiménez Mayor, as the representative of the Peruvian State before the Organization of American States. The Rapporteur for Freedom of Expression of the IACHR, Catalina Botero, was present at the hearing.

> object of exclusivity or monopoly or of direct or indirect hoarding by the State or by private parties and that this provision sets criteria and percentages to identify when there is a situation of hoarding. It explained that the Constitutional Court [*Tribunal Constitucional*] has provided interpretive guidelines for article 61 of the Constitution, but that there is no constitutionally-developed norm regarding antimonopoly laws because until now they have not faced this problem.

It is appropriate to indicate that if the application for protection filed at the end of 2013 receives a rejecting judgment at the Judicial Power, it may come to the attention of the Constitutional Court. To have an idea about the delay that this process has had, it can be mentioned that until now (September 2017) the controversy still has not received a response at the first instance level.

IV. Human Rights Treaties

International human rights law is a source for the study of the freedom of expression and information by the principles of these rights and the obligations of the State, in terms of the components, as well as in the declaratory instruments as conventional or about important decisions (recommendations or sentences) of supranational bodies.

In the Peruvian legal system this importance is evidenced in the 55° Article of the Constitution of 1993, which recognizes that treaties ratified by the Peruvian State, and in force, are part of domestic law. But more important is the Fourth Final and Transitory Provision of the Constitution, which requires the interpretation of the fundamental rights recognized in it in accordance with international norms and international jurisprudence, the latter by the mandate of the Constitutional Court [*Tribunal Constitucional*] and the Constitutional Procedural Code. The importance of the jurisprudence of the I/A Court lies in the established criteria for the analysis of the obligations of the State over freedom of expression and information and the reasoning used to resolve controversies over restrictions on its exercise.

For this paper it is particularly interesting to make reference to the development of Article 13.3 of the American Convention in Human Rights (ACHR) made by the I/A Court. This article says that

> [t]he right of expression may not be restricted by indirect methods or means, such as the abuse of government or private controls over newsprint, radio broadcasting frequencies, or equipment used in the dissemination of

information, or by any other means tending to impede the communication and circulation of ideas and opinions.

As Lovatón indicated (2014: 152), an element that could contribute to an advance towards an authentic plurality and diversity of information in democracy is "the standards that the Inter-American human rights system has already developed. Its implementation should lead us towards a balance between plurality and diversity and certain levels of concentration, otherwise inevitable in today's globalized markets" [original in Spanish].

4.1 Position of the Inter-American Court of Human Rights on informative plurality and media concentration

The Inter-American Court had the opportunity to rule on a specific controversy related to the informative plurality in the Granier vs. Venezuela case, dated June 22, 2015. The facts as they were raised by the IACHR before the supranational tribunal (Inter-American Court, 2015, para. 1), were:

> The present case refers to the alleged violation of "the freedom of expression of [the] shareholders, directors and journalists" of the "Radio Caracas Televisión" channel [RCTV] [...], due to the "decision of the State [...] not to renew [the] concession." Therefore, the Commission concluded that "the State [...] failed to comply [with] its substantive and procedural obligations regarding the assignment and renewal of concessions [; and] that the controversy regarding the non-renewal of the concession [...] occurred in a context of legal uncertainty [as there would be] no clarity about the legal framework applicable to [the] concession." In addition, it stated that the State's decision would have been "based on the channel's editorial line [, constituting] a clear act of misuse of power and an indirect restriction incompatible with Articles 13.1 and 13.3 of the Convention [original in Spanish].

In this controversy, the Inter-American Court focused its analysis on assessing whether there was an indirect restriction on freedom of expression, as a result of the abuse of official or private controls over the radio frequencies referred to in Article 13.3 of the ACHR. Regarding this, it was stated:

> 170. In this sense and in relation to media pluralism, the Court recalls that the citizens of a country have the *right to access to information and ideas from a variety of positions, which must be guaranteed at various levels, such as types of media, sources and content* [emphasis added]. This Court considers that, since the radioelectric space is a scarce resource, with a

> certain number of frequencies, this limits the number of media that can access them, so it is necessary to ensure that in that number of media a diversity of views or informative positions or opinions is represented. *The Court emphasizes that the pluralism of ideas in the media cannot be measured from the number of communications media, but rather that the ideas and information transmitted are effectively diverse and are addressed from divergent positions without there being a unique vision or position* [emphasis added]. The foregoing must be taken into account in the granting processes, the renewal of concessions or broadcasting licenses. In this sense, the Court considers that the limits or restrictions that derive from the regulations related to broadcasting must take into account the guarantee of media pluralism given its importance for the functioning of a democratic society [original in Spanish].

In accordance with the foregoing, the Inter-American Court stated that in order to guarantee informative plurality, States must establish regulations on the subject with certain procedural guarantees. In this regard, it pointed out:

> 171. [...] the Court emphasizes the need for States to regulate in a clear and precise manner the processes that deal with the granting or renewal of concessions or licenses related to the broadcasting activity, by means of objective criteria that avoid arbitrariness. Specifically, it is necessary to establish the safeguards or general guarantees of due process, which each State determines as necessary in these processes in the light of the American Convention, with the purpose of avoiding the abuse of official controls and the generation of possible indirect restrictions [original in Spanish].

In its analysis of the specific facts of this case, the I/A Court determined that the Respondent State (Venezuela) violated the 13° Article of the ACHR, for the following reasons:

> 197. The Court then concludes, as it has done in other cases, that the facts of the present case implied a misuse of power, since it made use of a permitted faculty of the State with the objective of editorially aligning the communication media with the government. The aforementioned statement is derived from the two main conclusions to which this Court may come as described above, namely, that the decision was made earlier and was based on the inconvenience generated by the editorial line of RCTV, added to the context on the "deterioration of the protection of freedom of expression" that was proven in the present case (supra paragraph 61).
>
> 198. The Court also considers it necessary to stress that the misuse of power declared here had an impact on the exercise of freedom of expression, not only on the workers and directors of RCTV, but also on the

> social dimension of that right (supra para., 136), that is, the citizenship that was deprived of having access to the editorial line that RCTV represented. In effect, the real purpose was to silence voices critical of the government, which are constituted along with pluralism, tolerance and the spirit of openness, in the demands of a democratic debate that, precisely, the right to freedom of expression seeks to protect.
>
> 199. Therefore it was proven that, in this case, an indirect restriction was placed on the exercise of the right to freedom of expression resulting from the use of media, designed to prevent the communication and circulation of ideas and opinions when deciding that the State would reserve the portion of the spectrum for itself and, therefore, prevent participation in administrative procedures for the awarding of titles or the renewal of the concession to a medium that expressed critical voices against the government, which is why the Court declares the violation of 13.1° and 13.3° Articles, in relation to 1.1° Article of the American Convention [...] [original in Spanish].

When determining the measures of reparation related to the affected right, the supranational court ruled on measures aimed at preventing similar situations to those that gave rise to the concrete case from recurring. In this regard, it ordered the respondent State to:

> […] take the necessary measures to ensure that all future processes of allocation and renewal of radio and television frequencies that are carried out are conducted in an open, independent and transparent way. All these processes must be conducted without discriminatory criteria that seek to limit the granting of concessions and should be aimed at strengthening informative pluralism and respect for judicial guarantees (I/A Court, 2015, para. 394) [original in Spanish].

It is important to highlight the emphasis placed by the Inter-American Court on the necessity for measures of non-repetition to strengthen democratic pluralism.

Consequently, as indicated by the supranational court, the 13° Article of the ACHR includes the "right to access to information and ideas from a variety of positions, which must be guaranteed at different levels, such as the types of communications media, sources and content." As a consequence, it is up to the States to adopt the necessary measures to respect and guarantee this right, in accordance with general human rights obligations set forth in the 1.1° and 2° Articles of the ACHR. Although the specific case was related to the arbitrary cancellation of an operational license to a communication medium, the interpretation of the 13° article of the ACHR is of general scope and of obligatory observance for the States.

4.2 Position of the Inter-American Commission on Human Rights on informative plurality and media concentration

The IACHR has made different decisions and reports related to informative plurality and media concentration, since unlike the Court, it does not limit its work only to petitions that come to its attention for certain violations of Article 13° of the ACHR. The work of the IACHR is broader, based on its competences, and it even has a Special Rapporteurship on Freedom of Expression.

One of the most important IACHR references on the subject of this paper is in its Declaration of Principles on Freedom of Expression (2000), whose 12th Principle states:

> 12. Monopolies or oligopolies in the ownership and control of the communications media must be subject to anti-trust laws, as they conspire against democracy by limiting the plurality and diversity, which ensure the full exercise of people's right to information. In no case should such laws apply exclusively to the media. The concession of radio and television broadcast frequencies should take into account democratic criteria that provide equal opportunity of access for all individuals.

For its part, the Rapporteurship of the IACHR for Freedom of Expression has made important analyses in relation to media concentration and has reached the following conclusions:

> 1. The Office of the Special Rapporteur reiterates that monopolistic and oligopolistic practices in mass media ownership have a serious detrimental impact on the freedom of expression and on the right to information of the citizens of the Member States, and are not compatible with the exercise of the right to freedom of expression in a democratic society.
>
> 2. The continuous complaints received by the Office of the Special Rapporteur in relation to monopolistic and oligopolistic practices in mass media ownership in the region indicate that there is grave concern in several sectors of civil society with respect to the impact that concentration of media ownership may represent where it comes to ensuring pluralism as an essential element of the freedom of expression.
>
> 3. The Office of the Special Rapporteur for Freedom of Expression recommends to the OAS Member States that they take measures to impede monopolies and oligopolies in media ownership, and adopt effective mechanisms for implementing them. Such measures and mechanisms must be compatible with the framework of Article 13 of the Convention and Principle 12 of the Declaration of Principles of Freedom of Expression.

> 4. The Office of the Special Rapporteur for Freedom of Expression considers it important to develop a legal framework that establishes clear guidelines for defining criteria for a balancing test that accords weight to both efficiency in the broadcasting market and pluralism in information. The establishment of mechanisms for supervising these guidelines will be fundamental for ensuring pluralism in the information that is made available to society.

Consequently, the IACHR has as one of its axes of work and analysis the monitoring and evaluation of the situation regarding the concentration of communications media that is presented in various countries, with respect to which it has made recommendations to the States to guarantee informative plurality.

V. Conclusions

The identification of specific actions that States must take to guarantee informative pluralism has as its starting point the Constitution and its interpretation in accordance with human rights treaties. In this sense, according to what is established in the Fourth Final and Transitory Provision of the constitutional text, the 2º Article, clause 4, and the 62º Article of the Political Constitution of 1993, related to the freedom of expression and the prohibition of communications media concentration, must be interpreted in accordance with the 13° Article of the American Convention on Human Rights.

Supranational bodies for the protection of human rights, based on the content and interpretation of Article 13 of the Convention, have identified that the concentration of communications media is contrary to the freedoms of expression and information, before which States are obliged to establish effective measures aimed at guaranteeing the existence of a plurality of information, such as having a regulatory framework that guarantees people's access to various sources of information.

The absence of legislation on the subject, leads to the solution of the problems that arise being derived from the jurisdictional scope, whose legitimacy to intervene is fully justified insofar as it seeks to protect, through the courts, the informative freedoms recognized at a constitutional and international level, with the necessity of pronouncements being issued within a reasonable time.

Bibliography

DELGADO TABOADA, B. A. (2016). "La concentración de los medios de comunicación y el derecho humano a la libertad de expresión" [The media concentration and the human right to freedom of expression]. *Inter-American Institute of Human Rights Journal* Vol. 63, pp. 35-63. Retrieved on: September 25, 2017. Retrieved from http://www.corteidh.or.cr/tablas/r35510.pdf.

FARFÁN SOUSA, R. (2014). "La prohibición constitucional de concentración de la propiedad de los medios de comunicación" [The constitutional prohibition of concentration of media ownership]. *Journal of Administrative Law* N° 14, pp. 341-362. Retrieved on September 25, 2017, from http://revistas.pucp.edu.pe/index.php/derechoadministrativo/article/view/13456/14083.

INSTITUTO DE DERECHOS HUMANOS Y DESARROLLO DE LA UNIVERSIDAD SAN MARTÍN DE PORRES (2015). "Concentración de medios. Un análisis desde la jurisprudencia nacional e internacional" [Concentration of Media. An analysis from the national and international jurisprudence]. *Communicative Freedom Series. Research Notebook* Year 2 N° 3, pp. 22-23. Retrieved on September 25, 2017, from http://www.usmp.edu.pe/IDHDES/pdf/Concentraci%C3%B3n_de_Medios.pdf.

INTER-AMERICAN COMMISSION ON HUMAN RIGHTS (2000a). *Declaration of principles on freedom of expression.* Retrieved on August 18, 2008, from http://www.oas.org/en/iachr/expression/showarticle.asp?artID=26&lID=1.

INTER-AMERICAN COMMISSION ON HUMAN RIGHTS (2000b). *Background on the interpretation of the declaration of principles on freedom of expression.* Rapporteurship for Freedom of Expression of the Inter-American Commission on Human Rights. Retrieved on August 18, 2008, from http://www.oas.org/en/iachr/expression/showarticle.asp?artID=132&lID=1.

INTER-AMERICAN COMMISSION ON HUMAN RIGHTS (2000c) *Second report on the situation of human rights in Perú.* Chapter V—The freedom of expression in Peru. Retrieved on August 18, 2008, from http://www.cidh.org/countryrep/peru2000en/chapter5.htm.

INTER-AMERICAN COMMISSION ON HUMAN RIGHTS (2005). *2004 Annual Report of the Inter-American Commission on Human Rights*. Retrieved on September 25, 2017, from http://www.oas.org/en/iachr/expression/showarticle.asp?artID=459&lID=1.

INTER-AMERICAN COMMISSION ON HUMAN RIGHTS (2015). *Annual report of the office of the Special Rapporteur for Freedom of Expression*. Annual report of the Inter-American Commission on Human Rights, 2014. Vol. 2. Edison Lanza, Special Rapporteur for Freedom of Expression. Retrieved on September 25, 2017, from http://www.oas.org/en/iachr/docs/annual/2014/docs-en/Annual2014-freedom-of-expression.pdf.

INTER-AMERICAN COURT OF HUMAN RIGHTS (2015). *Granier and other (Caracas Radio and Television) v. Venezuela. Preliminary objection, merits, reparations and costs.* Judgment of June 22, 2015. Retrieved on September 25, 2017, from <http://www.corteidh.or.cr/docs/casos/articulos/seriec_293_esp.pdf>.

LOVATÓN PALACIOS, D. (2014). "El equilibrio interamericano entre pluralidad de información y concentración de medios" [The Inter-American balance between plurality of information and media concentration]. *Revista Derecho PUCP* N° 73, pp. 131-153. Retrieved on September 25, 2017, from http://revistas.pucp.edu.pe/index.php/derechopucp/article/view/11305/11814.

SALAS VÁSQUEZ, P. P. (2016). "Acaparamiento en los medios de prensa escrita: Análisis del caso Epensa" [Hoarding in the written media: Analysis of the Epensa case] (Master's thesis in Business Law from the Pontificia Universidad Católica del Perú). Retrieved on September 25, 2017, from http://tesis.pucp.edu.pe/repositorio/bitstream/handle/123456789/7936/SALAS_VASQUEZ_PEDRO_ACAPARAMIENTO.pdf?sequence=1&isAllowed=y.

THEMATIC TABLE 4: JUDICIAL GUARANTEES: JURISDICTIONAL PROTECTION AND DUE PROCESS

THE MULTIDIMENSIONALITY OF FUNDAMENTAL RIGHTS, WITH A SPECIAL FOCUS ON THE THEORY OF THE STATUS ACTIVUS PROCESSUALIS

JORGE LEÓN VÁSQUEZ*

I. Introduction

The main purpose of this article is to analyze the procedural dimension of fundamental rights based on the doctrine of the *status activus processualis*. The idea here is not to develop procedural fundamental rights (*Verfahrensgrundrechte*), but to study the procedural dimension of fundamental rights (*Grundrechte*). The initial thesis is as follows: the assertion and procedural protection of all fundamental rights are themselves part of the very essence of such rights (Häberle, 1997: 292). In other words, according to the doctrine of the *status activus processualis*, all fundamental rights have a procedural dimension that not only strengthens their effectiveness, but also gives rise to objective, concrete duties to guarantee them. This, in turn, has significant consequences, such as the necessary restructuring of the functions of fundamental rights, moving beyond the classical conception of their twofold nature, and above all, demanding the implementation of a *dynamic protection of fundamental rights*, matters that will be developed based on an understanding of the Peruvian Constitution as essentially a plural and open public process.

II. The Constitution as a Public Process

The Constitution, as well as its interpretation, is a public process in which both the State and society take part. This process thus transcends the old

---

* Doctor of Law, graduated from the University of Hamburg in Germany. Professor of Constitutional Law at the Pontificia Universidad Católica del Perú and the Universidad Nacional Mayor de San Marcos.

dichotomy of absolute separation between the State and society, which can no longer be sustained today. Social life is impossible without the State's organization, planning, and responsibility, while the democratic State is founded on society's interactions and cooperation, giving rise to a plurality of reciprocal dependences and influences (Hesse, 1995: 8). The State does not exist prior to the Constitution. Society—and even the structural elements thereof—is *constituted* by the Constitution itself. Political and social forces are channeled by the Constitution, to the point that neither the State nor society can exist "on the margins of" or "outside of" the Constitution. Jellinek's theory of the "normative force of the factual" (*die normative Kraft des Faktischen*) is alien to this understanding. The assertion that both the State and society only exist as permitted by the Constitution is rooted in the fact that the Constitution "comprises the fundamental structures of a pluralist society" (Häberle, 1980: 46 *ff.*).

As a public process, the Constitution tends to waver between stability and change, between permanence and transformation. Without this flexibility, the Constitution would be hard pressed to keep up with social and scientific developments. Openness is an essential feature of the Constitution as a public process. The Constitution requires instruments and procedures that enable it to grasp new realities and offer a framework of rationalization and stabilization. Given its nature as a fundamental juridical-normative body of law, the Constitution only establishes partial substantive presuppositions for the State and society. The rest must be developed, over time, through the structuring of a wide range of processes that are open and plural as possible. It is in this regard that the Constitution presents itself as a task (Scheuner, 1978: 172 *ff.*), that is, an unfinished process under constant construction. This reading is reinforced by those who interpret the constitution *in sensu stricto*, but also by those diverse and plural social forces (individual and collective) that form part of the open society hailed by constitutional interpreters.

Fundamental rights and their interpretation are not relegated to the side lines of this public process. Fundamental rights must be understood "as public interests" in the sense that—without stripping them of all references or ties to their holders—their protection and effectiveness transcend the individual plane and become a public matter. On many occasions, even their scope of protection is defined in relation to the public. Observed from this standpoint, fundamental rights exhibit a *private dimension* and a *public dimension*. This assertion is complemented by an understanding of the interpretation of fundamental rights as a public process, too. The insertion of the public dimension into the interpretative process expands and enriches not only the possibilities of interpretation, but also the procedures and the subjects that interpret the constitution. The interpretative process thus involves all public forces (Häberle, 1980: 45). The Constitution does not lose its normative nature, nor is it left to merely restate social changes. The opening and expansion of the Constitution do not mean that it is dissolved into an all-encompassing dynamic; indeed, its function of the direction and limitation of public and private power remains intact (León, 2016: 42).

III. The Functions of Fundamental Rights: A Reconsideration

The conception of the Constitution as a public process also leads us to a revision of the (classical) functions of fundamental rights. Georg Jellinek is attributed with the theorization of the functions of fundamental rights (Jellinek, 1892). His theory of statuses (*Die Status-Lehre*) is an attempt to explain the relationship between the individual and the State. In other words, the idea of *status* describes the individual's different positions in relation to the State. *Status negativus* (*status libertatis*) comprises, for example, individuals' liberty *against* the State; *status positivus* (*status civitatis*) refers to the individual's liberty *through* the State; *status activus* (*Status der aktiven Civität*) describes individuals' liberty *in* the State; and finally, *status passivus* refers to individuals' obligations *to* the State.

While the theory of statuses is still considered an essential part of fundamental rights theory (Pieroth and Schlink, 2008: 16-19), its continued relevance has only been made possible thanks to the introduction of new approximations and clarifications. For example, *status negativus* corresponds to the understanding of fundamental rights as defensive rights or negative liberties. It is now understood, however, that fundamental rights as defensive rights also apply to the State's regulation of social conflicts, and reflexively penetrate into legal relations within society. This also explains why fundamental rights, in their understanding as defensive rights, continue to be relevant in the praxis of domestic and international courts (Poscher, 2003: 153 *ff.*).

Indeed, with his proposal of the *status activus processualis*, Häberle is not trying to dispense with Jellinek's contributions. With that said, however, he is aware that the theory of statuses must be erected on a clearly democratic foundation, stripping it of any late-period Absolutist trappings (Häberle, 1972: 80 *ff.*). On the other hand, while Jellinek focuses first and foremost on the negative and passive statuses (*status passivus subiectionis*), Häberle finds these to be the least of the statuses. Instead, he focuses on the *status activus*, which is considered to be the fundamental *status* of all rights.

It is here that the *status activus processualis* is inserted as an essential element, by virtue of which the duties of the welfare State and social fundamental rights take on new dimensions, in the form of the protection of claims, rights of participation, rights to benefits, and procedural rights. This protection, in turn, may be "derived" (when the protection is rooted in previously existing institutions, benefits, or processes), or "original," in which case the State must create and organize new processes to protect fundamental rights (Pieroth/Schlink, 2008: 17).

In short, thanks to the developments essentially made by Häberle, the *status activus processualis* has become the first juridical-substantive *status activus*. Fundamental rights thus embody the status of participation "together with" and "in the" State (Häberle, 1972: 81).

IV. The Multidimensionality of Fundamental Rights

Nowadays, everyone knows that fundamental rights have a twofold nature. They are personal rights that correspond, depending on the nature of the right, to the individual person or to groups of persons (*subjective dimension*). This, in turn, is complemented by their conception as an order of objective values (*objective* or *institutional dimension*). This understanding of fundamental rights has been deemed adequate, up to this point, in explaining their nature. But further advances have now been made. It has been some time now since Häberle, their main proponent, proposed that we move beyond this conception, which has yet to be abandoned. The assertion of the multidimensionality of fundamental rights must translate to the enrichment of each right's content, but not the exclusion of some dimensions in favor of others (Schillaci, 2010: 216).

The proposal of the Constitution as a public process calls for a much broader understanding of fundamental rights. The basis for this understanding can be found, on the one hand, in the constant transformation of the normative sphere, the forms of intervention (increasingly more subtle and complex), and the limits on fundamental rights; and on the other, in the realization that relations between the State and the citizen (no longer the mere individual) are diverse and require the most varied of duties by the State to the citizen, but also by the citizen to the State. The twofold dimension of fundamental rights only partially explains this transformation. Together with the subjective and objective dimensions, it thus becomes necessary to take into account the *corporate and cooperative, generational, and procedural* dimensions of fundamental rights.

1. Corporate and Cooperative Dimension

Fundamental rights, such as the *status activus corporativus* are based on the social nature of the human being. The exercise of these rights—even those of a decidedly individual sort (such as freedom of opinion, for example)—only makes complete sense when they are exercised with regard to others. One's opinion has no relevance when speaking to the wall or the mountains, only when it is addressed to others. The "social function" of fundamental rights is applied to all of them and must not be restricted solely to the right to property. Other fundamental rights may only be exercised to the extent that one forms part of a group of citizens (associations, unions, movements, citizens' collectives, political parties, etc.). Some clear examples of this include the right to assemble and the right to protest, rights of political participation that one can only imagine being exercised "in groups," "through groups," but also "against groups." Fundamental rights, in their corporate and cooperative dimension, are inconceivable without being oriented toward the dimension of groups (Häberle, 1997: 293 *ff.*).

It is not only in the group or through groups that the possibility of realizing or protecting fundamental rights is increased, however. This is true of freedom of assembly and the freedom to protest, with labor and union rights, with freedom of association, with consumers' and users' rights, with the right to a healthy environment, and with the rights of peasant and native communities. The list could go on and on. Thus, the *status activus corporativus* is not an external element or one that comes from outside; it is an element that is already inserted into the very essence of fundamental rights. This requires (and here we may now begin to note the influence of their procedural dimension) broad and plural participation in the organization of groups, but also in the implementation of the processes and procedures for participation in groups.

2. Generational Dimension

Häberle was quite right, in the 1980s, when he asserted that "in the future, there is a 'new' dimension of fundamental rights that must take on greater immediacy: the generational" (1997: 298). The problems we now face with regard to the environment, the unchecked pillaging of natural resources, the risks always latent in the non-pacific use of atomic energy, and the anti-ethical use of genetic engineering prove that we are at a stage in humanity's development where we can no longer think only about those of us who are here right now; we must also think about future generations. Fundamental rights, through their generational dimension, provide an abstract protection for the coming generations. They set forth an early effect of protection in favor of the said generations.

Fundamentally, the exercise of economic freedoms does not grant those of us who live in the present the right to make our planet uninhabitable. Fundamental rights must now ensure not only specific guarantees for those who suffer from current, concrete effects in this area; they must also protect the abstract interest "of those yet to come." This now supposes an essential transformation in the very conception of these rights, as well as the possibilities for their protection. Protection of fundamental rights such as the right to a healthy environment, natural resources, and peace may now be invoked on behalf of future generations. The prerequisite of a current and concrete violation must also be interpreted in the sense of an abstract protection that even applies to "future" holders of fundamental rights. It is thus necessary for judges to take up the role of guarantors of the new generations' rights, since these generations cannot presently seek protection on their own behalf.

The fact that future generations must not be burdened by our acts or omissions entails the duty not to condemn those generations. Just as the present generations must not find their aspirations dashed by the decisions of past generations, so the present generations must not live at the expense of future generations. The fundamental liberty of today determines, for better or for worse, the liberty of the coming generations, although a fight must be waged to ensure that the protection of these coming generations can be satisfied by fundamental rights (Häberle, 1997: 299). This, in short, is the generational dimension of fundamental rights.

3. Procedural Dimension

The procedural dimension of fundamental rights is recognized as a complement to the material or substantive aspect of fundamental rights. Under the doctrine of the *status activus processualis*, organization and procedure become appropriate instruments for the protection of fundamental rights. All fundamental rights contain, in their essence, a procedural element that gives them effect. This dimension, like those studied hereinabove, does not come "from outside." It is not a mere accessory to the substantive component of fundamental rights, given that an exclusively substantive guarantee would be partly useless (Häberle, 1997: 292). This is an understanding of fundamental rights as "procedural guarantees," as a strengthening of the material dimension through organization and procedure.

This can be illustrated with a concrete example from Peruvian constitutional law. A recent constitutional amendment recognized the fundamental right to clean drinking water (Section 7-A of the Peruvian Constitution). According to this constitutional provision, this fundamental right is not subject to any non-delegable Act of Congress, nor does it have any direct constitutional limitations. The question that immediately arises, then, is whether this material recognition is sufficient for the effective realization of this fundamental right. According to the traditional, still dominant conception, we must wait until the legislative branch implements the process or indicates a pre-existing process for the protection of this right. From this standpoint, the effectiveness of the fundamental right is left hanging until the legislative branch, which is almost always "late to the party," establishes and organizes the respective procedure, especially considering that the constitutional amendment has erroneously established a progressive implementation of the right to clean drinking water, as if basic necessities were not, in fact, needs.

The doctrine of the *status activus processualis* reaches its full potential in cases such as this, where the mere recognition of a new fundamental right already simultaneously includes its procedural guarantee. It is no longer sufficient to establish legal restrictions to guarantee a fundamental right. Such rights must now be accompanied by a "procedural restriction," given that the assertion and procedural protection of these rights form part of their very essence (Häberle, 1997: 292). Ideally, there should be a pre-existing instrument of guarantee, or a simultaneous recognition of such an instrument that meets the minimum procedural standards. Now then, the doctrine of the *status activus processualis* gives rise to a dimension of fundamental rights that strengthens participation in public decision-making processes (*Teilhaberechte*); while on the other hand also strengthening participation in ordinary and constitutional judicial proceedings.

In terms of public participation in decision-making processes, it becomes clear that the most pressing need is to strengthen the material aspect of social fundamental rights in the welfare State through specific processes. Citizens must have processes available to them that allow them a wide-ranging participation in the planning, promotion, and implementation of the public policies inherent to the welfare State. Unilateral action or action "from above" on the part of the State is no longer sufficient.

Through their procedural dimension, fundamental rights take on a constituent relevance. The most important thing now is that specific processes for their satisfaction have in fact been initiated (Häberle). The procedural dimension gives rise to the need to create and organize processes that guarantee adequate communication between civil society and the welfare State. Conflicts over social rights, which primarily occur *ex post facto*, must be foreseen and accounted for precisely through such processes. Many conflicts within the framework of the welfare State arise not because of the absence of material rights, but because of the lack of suitable processes, or the existence of processes that only offer deficient, or—in the best of cases—partial satisfaction.

Another area for the specific development of the *status activus processualis* can be found in regard to participation in judicial processes. The protection of fundamental rights is implemented through their strict guarantee, i.e., through procedural fundamental rights (the right to be heard and to effective judicial protection). The judgment by the German Federal Constitutional Court (BVerfGE 49, 220 (235), dissenting opinion by Judge Böhmer) emphasizes, in this regard, that

> State organs do not only have the duty to observe material fundamental rights; they must also seek to give them effect through the corresponding procedural configuration. Wherever procedural law is not aimed at giving effect to fundamental rights, harm may be done to their substantive content. Ultimately, a process compatible with the legal system is the only possibility for effectively realising or guaranteeing fundamental rights. This binds the State organs to an interpretation in accordance with fundamental rights and the implementation of procedural law.

In its judgment on the Joined Cases C-402/05 P and C-415/05 P, of 3 September 2008, the Grand Chamber of the European Court of Justice ruled on the appeals to the higher court filed by Mr. Yassin Abdullah Kadi and the Al Barakaat International Foundation, who had been subjected to certain specific restrictive measures aimed at persons and entities associated with Usama bin Laden, the Al-Qaeda network, and the Taliban. The specific point in which we are interested here is the Grand Chamber's finding that the restriction of Mr. Kadi's right to property was adopted without allowing him to set forth his case before the competent authorities (Grounds 367 *et seq*.), or more specifically, without allowing him to "participate" in the determination of the restrictive measures. This decision captures the meeting point between security and the protection of fundamental rights through an effective articulation of procedural guarantees (Schillaci, 2010: 237). Note that the participation of the person who must bear the encumbrances of such restrictions is decisive even in the determination of the measures restricting freedoms, and not only in the determination of the normative sphere of fundamental rights.

Separate mention should be made of the treatment of constitutional procedural law from the standpoint of the *status activus processualis*. Elsewhere, we have specifically argued that, more than a procedural right, it is a right to participation and pluralism (León, 2016: 185 *ff*.). It is closer to constitutional theory than to the general theory of procedure. This position is bolstered by the constitutionalization of its tasks, its material and procedural principles, its interpretation, the subjects that participate therein, and its juridical and jurisprudential sources. The constitutional proceeding provides courts with an open and plural public forum for decision-making in which all citizens take part. Thus, courts' decisions are legitimized not only by the fact that they are an institution enshrined in the Constitution, nor by the mere rational explanation of their decisions.

Essentially, a court is democratically legitimized by the possibility of participation granted to all plural public forces. Unlike any other procedural order, constitutional proceedings place special importance on public hearings, the institution of the amicus curiae, third-party participation, and dissenting opinions. This understanding also offers constitutional courts the ability to settle constitutional conflicts by taking on "new" roles in addition to that of mere fact finder. It is with good reason that the German Federal Constitutional Court has been dubbed the "*Friedensjudikatur*," or "jurisdiction for peace" (Häberle, 2017: 11). In the constant search for peace, it is legitimate and necessary for constitutional courts to take on other roles in response to certain types of conflict. Acting as a mediator, an arbitrator, and, on an exceptional basis—when dealing with the public sphere and the mass media—as an agenda-setter, must not be dismissed outright.

In a broad sense, on the other hand, fundamental rights are guaranteed through other instruments for protection, such as the Ombudsman's Office, for example, or the non-judicial institutions that are also tasked with protecting fundamental rights. No evidence is needed in saying that judicial protection often arrives too late. We therefore need prior processes that protect fundamental rights, such as those of an administrative nature, for example. With this goal in mind, the standards of protection in administrative procedures must be raised with regard to fundamental rights, and administrative entities must evaluate, time and again, whether their procedures are organized and oriented toward a better protection of rights. The interpretative principle of the maximum effectiveness of fundamental rights has concrete implications in this process. The fact that these are not jurisdictional procedures does not mean that they must offer lesser guarantees than judicial proceedings. Only if we accept this premise can we acknowledge that fundamental rights can also be protected specifically by non-judicial processes (Häberle, 1993: 157).

V. The "Dynamic Protection" of Fundamental Rights

The doctrine of the *status activus processualis* offers still more possibilities. One of these is the "dynamic protection of fundamental rights" (BVerfGE 53, 30 (76)). The dynamic protection of fundamental rights is a principle that prohibits the legislative branch from establishing the state of the science and the state of the art. As a result of the rapid changes in science and technology, the legislative branch is often only able to offer a relative—and in many cases, insufficient—protection of fundamental rights. The knowledge available to the legislature at a given moment is limited, even though it is bound to provide suitable processes for the effectiveness of these rights. Its prognosis of events is thus incomplete, and not infrequently mistaken.

The procedural guarantees that the legislative branch is able to offer are, in this sense, partial. The processes organized and shaped by the legislative branch for the protection of fundamental rights run the risk of remaining static. Especially problematic are those matters tied to the risks posed by atomic energy, genetic manipulation, and health, as well as information technology. It is the task of the judge and the administration to provide those processes established by the legislative branch with an interpretation and application capable of meeting the demands of the dynamic protection of fundamental rights. This dynamism also entails an intense flexibilization of procedural forms, which shall remain in place only if following them does not leave fundamental liberties unprotected, either wholly or in part.

Dynamic protection can also take the form of processes not initially established for a given purpose, but which—due to the particularities of the case—may be more adequate than others to protect the right in question. The "repurposing" of constitutional proceedings is a clear example of this in Peruvian constitutional law. From this standpoint, dynamic protection must always opt for that process or procedure with an organization and openness that allow for the best possible protection of fundamental rights.

Finally, it is worth saying a few words about so-called "multilevel constitutionalism." This notion is based on the use of "level," which, in turn, is related to the concept of hierarchy, that is, to a hierarchical subordination or superposition. The "multilevel" concept is rightly criticized by Häberle, given that the relationship between the domestic order and the international order is based on complementarity, expansion, and concurrence. As far as the dynamic protection of rights is concerned, such protection has a better chance of realization under a relation of coordination between the internal and international orders, as opposed to rigid hierarchical relations.

VI. Conclusion

The *status activus processualis* has become a decisive element of the democratic constitutional State for ensuring the protection and effectiveness of fundamental rights. The mere positivization of a long list of fundamental rights might turn them into solely symbolic instruments, if they lack standards of organization and suitable processes aimed at their protection (Mendes, 2009: 400). The essence of these rights encompasses not only substantive or material elements, but also a procedural dimension that comprises the contents of all fundamental rights. The organization and the processes—which do not come "from outside" fundamental rights—must meet certain minimum standards of suitability and effectiveness. The processes must be arranged in such a way that they do not lead to a devaluation of the material position of the fundamental right. Violations of procedural norms are a sign that the material right is being affected, which thus calls for a much more intense judicial control (Jarass, 2006: 646) and a dynamic protection of fundamental rights.

Bibliography

PIEROTH, Bodo, and SCHLINK, Bernhard (2008). *Grundrechte. Staatsrecht II.* 2. Aufl. Heidelberg: C. F. Müller.

HÄBERLE, Peter (2017). *Die "Kultur des Friedens"—Thema der universalen Vefassungslehre. Oder: Das Prinzip Frieden.* Berlin: Duncker & Humblot.

HÄBERLE, Peter (1980). *Die Verfassung des Pluralismus. Studien zur Verfassungstheorie der offenen Gesellschaft* . Königstein/Ts.: Athenäum.

HÄBERLE, Peter (1972). "Grundrechte im Leistungsstaat." In *VVDStRL* 30. Berlin: Walter de Gruyter, 43-140.

HÄBERLE, Peter (1997). *La libertad fundamental en el Estado Constitucional.* Lima: Fondo Editorial de la PUCP.

HÄBERLE, Peter (1993). "Recientes desarrollos sobre derechos fundamentales en Alemania." *Derechos y libertades* I (1), 149-168.

HESSE, Konrad (1995). *Grundzüge des Verfassungsrechts der Bundesrepublik Deutschland* (20. Aufl. ed.). Heidelberg: C. F. Müller Verlag.

JARASS, Hans D. (2006). "§ 38 Funktionen und Dimensionen der Grundrechte." In Josef Isensee/Paul Kirchhof (Hrsg.), *Handbuch des Staatsrechts,* Bd. IX, 3. Aufl. Heidelberg: C. F. Müller, 626-654.

JELLINEK, Georg (1892). *System der subjektiven öffentlichen Rechte.* Freiburg im Br.: Mohr Siebeck.

LEÓN, Jorge (2016). *Verfassungsgerichtsbarkeit, Verfassungsprozeßrecht und Pluralismus. Zugleich ein Beitrag zu Peter Häberles Theorie der Verfassungsgerichtsbarkeit als gesellschaftliche Funktion und des Verfassungsprozessrechts als Pluralismus- und Partizipationsrecht.* Berlin: Duncker & Humblot.

MENDES, Gilmar (2009). "Proteção judicial efetiva dos direitos fundamentais." In George Salomão Leite and Ingo Wolfgang Sarlet (Coordinação), *Direitos Fundamentais e Estado Constitucional. Estudos em homenagem a J. J. Gomes Canotilho.* São Paulo: Editora Revista dos Tribunais, 372-400.

POSCHER, Ralf (2003). *Grundrechte als Abwehrrechte. Reflexive Regelung rechtlich geordneter Freiheit.* Tübingen: Mohr Siebeck.

SCHEUNER, Ulrich (1978). *Staatstheorie und Staatsrecht. Gesammelte Schriften.* Berlin: Duncker & Humblot.

SCHILLACI, Angelo (2010). "Derechos fundamentales y procedimiento entre libertad y seguridad." *Revista de Derecho Constitucional Europeo* (13), 209-242.

The Tension between the Judiciary and Legislature in Concretization of the Fundamental Right to Health in Brazil: Judicial Actions for the Obtainment of Medicines

Eduardo Rocha Dias[1]
and Gina Vidal Marcílio Pompeu[2]

I. Introduction

The examination of the so-called judicialization of health in Brazil, from the study of the evolution of jurisprudence concerning the supply of medicines, allows interesting considerations regarding the relationship between the Judiciary and Legislature, as well as the limits to the creative activity of the judge.

The right to health, in spite of its terminological imprecision, as to the object and extent, was enshrined verbatim in arts. 6 and 196 of the Brazilian Constitution of 1988, which, over time, gives rise to different positions on the part of the subjects of subjective right, and on the functions of the State: executive, legislative and judicial.

---

[1] Doctor in Law by the University of Lisbon (2007). Master in Law by the Federal University of Ceará (1997). Professor of the Law Post-graduation Program at the University of Fortaleza. Federal Prosecutor. Part of the Center of Studies on Labor Law and Social Security Research Group—NEDTS, at the University of Fortaleza, as well as the International Group of Research on Human Development and Social Security in Latin America. E-mail: eduardordias@hotmail.com.

[2] Doctor in Law by the Federal University of Pernambuco (2004). Master in Law by the Federal University of Ceará (1994). Lawyer registered in OAB/CE under nº 6101. Coordinator and Professor of the Constitutional Law Post-graduation Program at the University of Fortaleza, Master's and Doctor's Degrees. Legal Consultant at the Legislative Assembly of Ceará. E-mail: ginapompeu@unifor.br.

At the outset, a more reticent position is identified regarding the granting of requests for the supply of medicines; in a second moment, due to the constitutional order of immediate applicability of the constitutional precepts, the Judiciary, even through the action of the Federal Supreme Court, will intervene more vehemently, and in this bias determines the systematic granting of drugs, which generates greater impacts on the health budget in Brazil; the confrontation between the judiciary and the executive reveals itself and the resulting judicialization of politics. In the second decade of the 21st century, we identify the phase of rationality seeking in judicial intervention, a situation in which jurisprudence seems to be at present.

This quest for greater rationality seems to be a result of factors of two orders, internal to the Judicial Branch itself, and to the Federal Supreme Court's actions, as well as external ones, materialized in the work of the Legislature. Among the first ones, reference should be made to the holding of a public hearing in 2009, in which the need to establish parameters for the Supreme Court's action in judicial actions involving the right to health was discussed, as well as the work of the National Council of Justice, a Judiciary agency, chaired by the President of the Federal Supreme Court, issuing recommendations and resolutions on the subject.

On the other hand, the Legislative Branch has worked to establish criteria for the incorporation of new technologies, among which are inserted medicines (Law 12401/04/2011), which undoubtedly becomes a matter that judges should consider in their decisions, and also in the search for dialogued and consensual solutions, which materialized mainly in the 2015 edition of the Code of Civil Proceedings and Law 13.140/06/2015. As will be seen, such diplomas favor the search for mediation and conciliation, among other fields, regarding the right to health. The Judiciary, on the other hand, in the search for alternative solutions to conflict resolution, also favored this second group of measures.

To this end, it initially deals with the right to health, content and extent, and the evolution of jurisprudence regarding the granting of medicines, based on the way the Judiciary has positioned itself. It then examines the way in which the Legislature has reacted and how excesses identified in the work of the Judiciary have been subject to containment by legal measures. Finally, it seeks to assess the prospects for change in case law and what measures may contribute to more appropriate decisions. The constitutional parameters are analyzed in the field of the right to health, and whether this discussion reveals the existence of fields where the

Judiciary should be more deferential toward legislative and administrative choices, above all because it does not detain technical expertise and because its exaggerated intervention has the power to systemically affect public health by prioritizing individual interests to the detriment of collective interest.

II. Right to Health and Evolution of Jurisprudence on Judicialization

Defining health, and specifically the right to health, its object and extent, is not an easy task. If it is decided to depart from the concept contained in the 1946 Constitution of the World Health Organization,[3] the difficulty is further amplified. In fact, such a "state of complete well-being" seems unreal. At most, there is an ideal to be achieved, but in practice it demands multiple stages and modalities of action by public authorities and society. Such imprecision undoubtedly contributed to greater intervention by the Judiciary in the fulfillment of its content, through the determination of the supply of medicines.

The interpretation of art. 196 of the Constitution, therefore, should consider two aspects which are more objective (Santos, 2014: 130): one that considers health as the effect of social and economic policies that avoid risks of aggravation (protection in a broad sense) and another that imposes the universal and equal access to actions and services that promote, protect and recover health. The first part requires the adoption by the State of public policies (Nunes and Scaff, 2011: 79) that guarantee the conditions for quality of life (education, sanitation, transportation, among other dimensions); the second part covers access to services and actions that recover the health already affected by some disease and protect it in a strict sense, since in a broad sense protection is obtained through the conditions that ensure quality of life. One dimension is more preventive; the other, more curative.

Health protection and promotion translate, synthetically, the evolution of the legal protection of this legal asset from a phase in which one had health as an individual asset, involved in a doctor-patient relationship, to a phase in which one identifies in health a collective good. The public relevance of health as an asset was soon affirmed by the adoption of measures to combat epidemics, which had already arisen in the Roman

---

[3] "Health is a state of complete physical, mental and social well-being, and it does not consist only in the absence of disease or infirmity".

Empire (Estorninho and Macieirinha, 2014: 10), and which constitute the embryo of the future sanitary administrative police, nowadays characterized as sanitary surveillance. Industrialization and the urbanization of societies have created other risks and turned a new role for the State into a necessity, this time as a provider of health services, initially for workers who contributed to insurance or social security systems, or later, for the population as a whole, with the idea of universality.

Health as an integral care, inheriting such evolution, presupposes a set of services, goods and supplies (Santos, 2014: 132) that "have direct costs for the Unified Health System, with a network structure based in health regions, organized in levels of services of greater or lesser technological density built from primary health care". Such a network imposes a division of competences and resources among the entities of the Federation, according to the needs and the economic and demographic conditions of each entity. The second part of the provision of art. 196 of the Constitution is the actions and services of promotion, protection (in the strict sense) and the recovery of health. From the art. 6º of 8.080/09/1990, it can be affirmed that the scope of the Brazilian Unified Health System includes the so-called health surveillance (sanitary and epidemiological) and comprehensive therapeutic care, including pharmaceuticals. This does not neglect science and technology and the training of personnel (Santos, 2014: 137). Assistance is organized in a network, with different levels of complexity (primary, secondary and tertiary care).

This Unified Health System action is not exclusive, since art. 199 of the Constitution allows the participation of private initiative in the field of public health, by means of a contract or agreement (§1 of article 199), configuring complementary health, and also allowing the exploitation of health services for profit purposes (caption of article 199), it being, in this case, supplementary health. Even private (supplementary) health, however, has public relevance, in the form of art. 197 of the Constitution, and the State shall regulate, supervise and control it.

With respect to public health, which is the responsibility of the State, its organization is drawn in principle by art. 200 of the Constitution and implemented by legal instruments, such as Law 8.080/09/1990 and Complementary Law 141/01/2012. This last one, which deals with the minimum values to be applied annually, by the Federation, State, Federal District and Municipalities, with actions and health services, conceptuates, for financing purposes, such actions and services in its art. 3º. On the other hand, Decree 7.508/06/2011 defines health care as a set of services divided into increasing levels of attention and complexity, and also indicates the "entrance doors" in the Unified Health Systems, in the form of art. 9: primary care, emergency and urgency care, psychosocial care, and special forms of open access.

In the form of art. 6, item I, paragraph "d", of Law 8.080/09/1990, the Unified Health System's field of action includes the execution of actions of "comprehensive therapeutic care, including pharmaceuticals". This topic is where judicialization is allowed with reference to the supply of medicines.

Health judicialization means the determination by judicial decisions of the provision of a particular benefit, of a particular treatment or medicine, by the public authorities and, in the case of supplementary health, by private health plans and health insurance.

Specifically, with regard to the Ministry of Health's spending on the acquisition of medicines by virtue of judicial decisions, that is, without considering the impact for States and Municipalities and for the Federal District, it has gone from R$139.6 million in 2010 to R$838.4 million in 2014.[4] In 2015 the amount went to R$1.2 billion. By 2016, up to June, R$ 686.4 million had already been spent.[5]

In the Brazilian case, the degree of intervention of the Judiciary leads to decisions that: a) do not, as a rule, consider the scientific efficacy of treatments and drugs sought in court (Dias, Silva Júnior, 2016); b) do not analyze the cost-effectiveness of the measures sought; c) result in purchases made without bidding, due to the urgency generated by the judicial determination, and entail excessive expenses for the treasury; d) subtract high volumes from the public budget; e) benefit people without considering the criteria of distributive justice, but only the success in having access to justice and obtaining favorable decisions, and f) disregard priorities and public policies drawn up by the bodies that are legitimized for this purpose (Wang, 2013: 3).

---

[4] According to the Ministry of Health as in a piece of news available at http://portalsaude.saude.gov.br/index.php/cidadao/principal/agencia-saude/20195-em-cinco-anos-mais-de-r-2-1-bilhoes-foram-gastos-com-acoes-judiciais, accessed on 12/04/2016.

[5] Rare diseases affect 13 million Brazilians http://noticias.uol.com.br/saude/ultimas-noticias/estado/2016/06/13/doencas-raras-afetam-13-milhoes-de-brasileiros.htm, accessed on 11/11/2016.

The peculiarities of the Brazilian public health system, which is based on a division of competencies among the different federated entities, can also bring significant impacts to entities with smaller budgets, as is the case of Municipalities, given the recognition, through jurisprudence, that authors can propose actions against any federated entity or against all of them, for being sympathetic.[6]

It is true that there has been a change in jurisprudence, especially if considering the position of the Superior Court of Justice and the Federal Supreme Court (Balestra Neto, 2015: 90-91). If, in the first instance, decisions tended to deny the granting of medicines, there was an increase in favorable decisions initially linked to access to medicines for the treatment of HIV infection. The reference to the constitutional character of the right to health and to the dignity of the human person has become the basis for concessive decisions and for the attainment of indices of claims exceeding 80% (Wang, 2013: 20-21). The work of the Judiciary, under the pretext of effecting social rights, ends up transforming them into individual rights, disregarding the budget and the care of the community (Scaff, 2010: 29-30).

It is worth remembering the hypothesis, referred to by José Augusto Dias de Castro (2008: 155), of a decision based solely on journalistic news, determining the supply of medicine which was still in the testing phase.[7]

---

[6] In accordance with the consolidated jurisprudence of the STF (SL 47 AgR, Tribunal Pleno, judged on 17-3-2010), of the STJ (AgRg no REsp 1136549/RS, judged on 8-6-2010) and the TNU (REQUEST 200481100052205, *DOU* 11-3-2011), the operation of the Unified Health System (SUS) is joint liability of the Union, the Member States and the Municipalities, so that any of these entities have legitimacy ad causam to appear in the passive demand pole that guarantees access to the medication for people deprived of financial resources. This is because there is no constitutional provision that determines that a federated entity only has the duty to provide medicines, to the exclusion of others. Of all sorts of things, it cannot be disregarded that the Constitution itself provides that it is for the law to dispose of the regulation and execution of health services (article 197) and that the respective actions and services are part of a regionalized, hierarchical and decentralized network (article 198 and its item I), which allows for the distribution of tasks among federated entities, including the supply of medicines.

[7] In this case, it was ENBREL, which cost four thousand reais a box. Ordinance of the Ministry of Health recommended the use of another drug, Infliximab, whose effectiveness was best demonstrated. The case reached the Federal Supreme Court in Extraordinary Appeal 271.286, which, however, did not take into account the technical aspects, but only recognized the duty of the State to provide medicines to a person deprived of remedies when linking the right to health with the right to life.

The Federal Supreme Court itself came to recognize the right to treatment abroad for retinitis pigmentosa despite the lack of scientific evidence of the efficacy of the therapy sought.[8]

From 2009, the beginning of a trend alteration starts, motivated by factors of two orders.

Through the initiative of the Judiciary itself, the criteria for judicial intervention were discussed. The public hearing held in the Federal Supreme Court between April and May 2009 should be highlighted, in which specialists from a wide range of areas were heard to obtain subsidies for the Court's actions in actions involving access to benefits in the health area.

As a result of the aforementioned public hearing, the National Council of Justice (CNJ) issued Recommendation 31 of March 30, 2010, urging State Courts of Justice and Federal Regional Courts to conclude agreements aimed at providing technical support from doctors and pharmacists to assist magistrates in the formation of a value judgment regarding the assessment of the clinical issues presented by the health action parties, observing the regional peculiarities. The courts were also requested, through their respective inspecting agencies, to direct the magistrates, among other measures, to seek to instruct the actions in which they act, as far as possible, with medical reports, with a description of the disease, including the ICD, containing a prescription of medicines, with the generic name or active principle, products, orthoses, prostheses and supplies in general, with the exact dosage, avoid authorizing the supply of medicines not yet registered by ANVISA, or in an experimental phase, excepting the ones expressly provided by law, listening, when possible, preferably by electronic means, to the managers, before the assessment of emergency measures.

It is curious to notice that many of such recommendations go as far as to urge judges to comply with the law, using prudence, dialogue between the parties involved, and rationality, when determining the supply of a drug for example.

It is worth mentioning among the measures adopted by the CNJ that the National Forum of the Judiciary was set up to monitor and resolve demands for health care—the Health Forum, through Resolution 107 of

---

[8] RE 368564/DF, Rapporteur Ministro Marco Aurélio, 1ª Class, judged on 04/13/2011.

April 6, 2010. The said Forum subsequently extended its area of operation to include supplementary health and legal actions involving consumer relations. Then, Recommendation 36, dated July 12, 2011, was issued specifically for the lawsuits involving supplementary health.

In the latter, it is also recommended that the Courts of Justice and the Federal Regional Courts conclude agreements aimed at providing technical support without burden to the Courts, composed of doctors and pharmacists, to assist magistrates "in forming a judgment on the value of assessment of the clinical issues presented by the parties".

Secondly, in addition to the work of the Judiciary, it is worth recording the edition of Law 12.401/04/2011, which established criteria for the action and incorporation of new health technologies by the Unified Health System and clearer competences in this regard. It is to be hoped that such a diploma will serve to instill greater deference from the Judiciary to administrative decisions, to help overcome the prevailing conception that the Judiciary may ignore the public policies drawn up by the legitimized bodies (Wang, 2013: 40-50).

III. The Actions of the Legislature and the Perspectives of Jurisprudence Evolution

Law 12.401/04/2011 inserted Chapter VIII in Title II of Law 8.080/1990, which refers to the conditions for the promotion, protection and recovery of health and the organization and functioning of the corresponding services. According to article 19-Q of the law, the attributions to incorporate, exclude or change new drugs by the Unified Health System were disciplined as follows:

> Art. 19-Q. The incorporation, exclusion or modification by the Unified Health System of new medicines, products and procedures, as well as the constitution or modification of a clinical protocol or therapeutic guideline, are attributed by the Ministry of Health, assisted by the National Commission for the Incorporation of Technologies in the Unified Health System.

The National Commission for the Incorporation of Technologies to the Unified Health System (CONITEC) is responsible for preparing a report and deciding on the basis of "scientific evidence on the efficacy, accuracy, effectiveness and safety of the drug, product or procedure subject to the process, accepted by the body responsible for registration or authorization of use" (item I of § 2 of article 19-Q of Law 8.080/1990). The Commission will also take into account the "comparative economic evaluation of benefits and costs in relation to technologies already incorporated, including in regard to home, outpatient or hospital care, when appropriate" (item II of § 2 of article 19-Q of Law 8.080/09/1990).

The arts. 19-M, 19-N and 19-O, added by Law 12.401/04/2011, deal with the dispensation of drugs and products of health interest, which must observe the therapeutic guidelines defined in the clinical protocol for the disease or injury to be treated. As foreseen in item II of art. 19-N of Law 8.080/1990, clinical protocol and therapeutic guidelines are understood as the:

> document which establishes criteria for the diagnosis of the disease or health problem; the recommended treatment, with medicines and other appropriate products, when appropriate; the recommended dosages; the mechanisms of clinical control; and the monitoring and verification of therapeutic results, to be followed by SUS managers.

As provided in art. 19-O of Law 8.080/1990, clinical protocols and therapeutic guidelines should:

> establish the medicines or products necessary in the different evolutionary stages of the disease or of the health problem they treat, as well as those indicated in cases of loss of efficacy and the appearance of intolerance or relevant adverse reaction caused by the first product, product or procedure choice.

The sole paragraph of art. 19-O of Law 8.080/1990 establishes that "if needed, the medicines or products will be evaluated for their efficacy, safety, effectiveness and cost-effectiveness for the different evolutionary stages of the disease or the health protocol".

In the absence of a clinical protocol or therapeutic guidelines, dispensation will be performed, as provided in art. 19-P of Law 8.080/2011:

> I—based on the relations of medicines instituted by the federal manager of the Unified Health System, observing the competencies established in Law 8.080/1990, and the responsibility for the supply will be agreed in the Tripartite Interagency Committee;
>
> II—within the scope of each State and the Federal District, in a supplementary manner, based on the relations of medicines instituted by the state managers of the Unified Health System, and the responsibility for the supply will be agreed in the Bipartite Interagency Committee;

> III—in the scope of each Municipality, on an additional basis, based on the relations of medicines instituted by the municipal managers of the Unified Health System, and the responsibility for the supply will be agreed in the Municipal Health Council.

The provisions of the Code of Civil Proceedings of 2015 (Law 13.105/2015) and of Law 13.140/2015 seem to be of no minor importance, regarding the search for a consensual solution of conflicts, including in the scope of the public administration. It opens up a vast field to try to arrive at dialogued and consensual solutions, in which the administration can show the Judiciary its role and the alternatives available in the field of public health. It also allows the improvement of the state performance, informing the services and actions made available and allowing the citizen's service.

As Lenir Santos (2014: 138) reminds us, the responsibilities of each member of the Brazilian Federation in terms of the provision of health services are due to the complexity of such services and the compatibility with socioeconomic, demographic and geographical levels. They must, together with society, set guidelines that guide the choices of therapies, since "there isn't money for everything". The Unified Health System cannot be "a concession desk for procedures that are detached from guidelines essential to its systemic organization and sanitary security" (Santos, 2014: 139). Hence the roles of the National Agency of Sanitary Surveillance—ANVISA, acting in the field of efficacy and safety of medicines, products and procedures, and the National Commission for the Incorporation of Technologies in Health—CONITEC, which should evaluate which drugs will be incorporated, as seen above, based on evidence-based criteria on efficacy, accuracy and safety, as well as the costs and benefits of the available alternatives.

It should be emphasized that the Unified Health System guarantees to the population, in what concerns health care, procedures and services contained in RENASES—the List of Health Actions and Services and RENAME—the National List of Essential Medicines, disciplined by arts. 21 to 29 of Decree 7.508/06/2011.

The decision of the Supreme Federal Court, in which the role of ANVISA was recognized, is the one pronounced in the case of synthetic phosphoethanolamine, known as the "cancer pill". This is ADI 5501, whereby the Brazilian Medical Association (AMB) questioned Law 13.269/04/2016, which authorized the dispensing of the said substance without its efficacy and safety being certified by the entity authorized to do so, in this case ANVISA. By a majority, the Supreme Federal Court understood that the legislative action violated the separation of powers, besides opening a dangerous precedent to the health protection of the population. The Rapporteur, Luís Roberto Barroso, alluded to the existence in the species of an "administrative reserve" and that the technical judgment of ANVISA was improperly replaced by a political judgment of the parliament.

In 2017, the Supreme Court of Justice, in deciding Special Appeal 1,663,141/SP, filed by a health plan operator in response to the decision that ordered the supply of imported medicine without registration with ANVISA, approved the appeal, deciding that there was a violation of both the Law 9,656/06/1998, whose art. 10, item V, makes it possible for health plans to exclude from their coverage the supply of imported non-nationalized drugs, as well as art. 12 of Law 6,360/1976, which establishes the need to register with the competent body of imported medicines. The decision is important because it may also reflect a change of understanding regarding the supply of medicines not registered in public health (Schulze, 2017), imposing law enforcement and greater deference to ANVISA's actions.

Another important decision, issued in the judgment of Extraordinary Appeals 566471 and 657718, is related to the supply of high-cost medicines that are neither registered in ANVISA nor made available by the Unified Health System for the treatment or control of rare diseases. According to the World Health Organization (WHO), rare diseases are those that affect up to sixty-five per 100,000 people.[9] In Europe and the United States, studies indicate that between 6% and 8% of the population is affected by some rare disease, but there are no comprehensive studies in Brazil.[10] In a population like the Brazilian one, this implies considering a universe of between thirteen and fifteen million people.

The trial was suspended on September 28, 2016 after three votes were cast. Initially, Minister Marco Aurélio proposed the following thesis at the trial:

---

[9] Ministry of Health launches clinical protocols for 12 rare diseases, in http://portalsaude.saude.gov.br/index.php/cidadao/principal/agencia-saude/18086-ministerio-da-saude-lanca-protocolos-clinicos-para-12-doencas-raras, accessed on 11/11/2016.

[10] Information available at http://rederaras.org, accessed on 11/11/2016.

> recognition of the individual right to the provision by the State of a high-cost drug not included in a National Drug Policy or an Exceptional Dispensing Drug Program, in exceptional character, a constant list of the approved ones, depends on the demonstration of the indispensability—adequacy and necessity—, the impossibility of replacing the drug and the financial incapacity of the patient, and the lack of spontaneity to help from the members of the family in solidarity, respected the dispositions about food of articles 1,694 to 1,710 of the Civil Code, and the right of return is guaranteed.[11]

Subsequently, Minister Luís Roberto Barroso, after stating that the discussion of the subject should be subtracted from the Judiciary, which is not responsible for defining public health policies, but only intervening in extreme situations, affirmed that, as a rule, in the case of unincorporated drugs, including high cost, the State cannot be obliged to provide them. "There is no health system that can withstand a model in which all medicines, regardless of their cost and financial impact, must be offered by the State to all people," he added.[12] Afterwards, he proposed five cumulative criteria that must be observed by the Judiciary so that certain health benefits can be inferred:

> A financial inability to bear the corresponding cost; a demonstration that the non-incorporation of the drug did not result from an express decision of the competent organs; the inexistence of a therapeutic substitute incorporated by the Unified Health System; evidence of the efficacy of the medicinal product sought in the light of evidence-based medicine; since the responsibility for the final decision on the incorporation or non-incorporation of medicines is exclusive of this federative entity.[13]

Minister Luís Roberto Barroso also defended a dialogue between the Judiciary and the people and organs endowed with knowledge in the area of health, either to verify, initially, the presence of the requirements for

[11] "Request for examination of case dockets postponed trial on access to high cost drugs by judicial process" in http://www.stf.jus.br/portal/cms/verNoticiaDetalhe.asp?idConteudo=326275, accessed on 11/11/2016.

[12] "Request for examination of case dockets postponed trial on access to high cost drugs by judicial process" in http://www.stf.jus.br/portal/cms/verNoticiaDetalhe.asp?idConteudo=326275, accessed on 11/11/2016.

[13] "Request for examination of case dockets postponed trial on access to high cost drugs by judicial process" in http://www.stf.jus.br/portal/cms/verNoticiaDetalhe.asp?idConteudo=326275, accessed on 11/11/2016.

dispensing the drug, or, once its supply is determined in the judicial process, in order to evaluate the possibility of its incorporation. Regarding medicines not registered with ANVISA, he proposed the following thesis with general repercussions:

> The State cannot be required to supply experimental medicines without proven efficacy and safety under any circumstances. Regarding medicines not registered with Anvisa, but with proof of efficacy and safety, the State can only be obliged to provide them in the event of unreasonable delay of the agency in assessing the application for registration (a term longer than 365 days), when three requirements are met: 1) the existence of an application for the registration of the drug in Brazil; 2) the existence of the registration of the drug in renowned regulatory agencies abroad; and 3) the inexistence of a therapeutic substitute with registration in Brazil. The actions that demand the supply of medicines without registration in Anvisa must necessarily be proposed to the Union.[14]

Finally, Minister Edson Fachin considered that there is a subjective right to public health care policies, and there is a violation of individual rights due to a failure, omission or delay in the provision, then suggested that it is preferable to take collective actions, not individual ones, in the fulfillment of the right to health, and that the management of individual actions should be exceptional, in addition to requiring a large probative output regarding the inefficacy of the existing public policy, also proposing criteria for the Judiciary to impose the provision or costing of medicines or health treatments:

> 1) necessary to demonstrate prior administrative application to the public network; 2) preferential prescription by a physician connected to the public network; 3) preferred designation of the drug by the Common Brazilian Denomination (DCB) and, in the absence of the DCB, the IND (International Common Denomination); 4) justification of the inadequacy or lack of medication/treatment dispensed in the public network; 5), and in the case of the refusal of dispensing in the public network, it is necessary to carry out a medical report indicating the necessity of the treatment, its effects, studies of evidence-based medicine and advantages for the patient, and compare with eventual drugs provided by the Unified Health System.[15]

---

[14] "Request for examination of case dockets postponed trial on access to high cost drugs by judicial process" in http://www.stf.jus.br/portal/cms/verNoticiaDetalhe.asp?idConteudo=326275, accessed on 11/11/2016.

[15] "Request for examination of case dockets postponed trial on access to high cost drugs by judicial process" in

The Minister also stressed that the Judiciary should take a more deferential stance regarding the technical and democratic choices of the competent bodies, which must also be accountable for their actions and be transparent regarding the criteria adopted.

A concern with the respect for public policies and the criteria established by law and the Administration for the registration and incorporation of new technologies has been expressed in the votes of the Ministers who have pronounced themselves until now, especially in the vote of Minister Luís Roberto Barroso. There is still a possibility of judicial intervention and the proposed criteria may actually lead to a replication, in the judicial sphere, of procedures that should be adopted in the administrative sphere, which is not reasonable, except in exceptional cases. The Judiciary does not have the structure and the expertise, does not involve the participation of all those interested in the public policy in question and does not appreciate problems of equity regarding access to budget funds (Wang, 2013: 50).

It is interesting to observe that the discussion undertaken here approaches the identification of limits to the institutional capacities of the Judiciary. Cass Sunstein and Adrian Vermeule (2002: 48) argue that the issue of interpretation in law, in particular the greater or lesser deference to the textual meanings of legal norms, must take into account institutional aspects. Among these aspects, they point out the reliability of the judges, especially if they have specific knowledge regarding the legislation they intend to apply, and the systemic effects that their decisions may entail. That is, can generalist judges adopt broader interpretations of texts on unknown specific subjects, such as those related to health, for example? Or is it better to adopt narrower, more formal interpretations? Can judges assess the consequences of their decisions on the health system and the budget? The paths indicated by the votes given above point to a possible reversal in the tendency to grant everything in the field of health judicialization from institutional elements as well.

On the other hand, concern about the transparency of administrative procedures for registering and incorporating new drugs is commendable. This may lead to a type of judicial intervention, of a collective nature and no longer individual, that questions the public policy itself and includes the possibility of demanding the presentation of the criteria for the

---

http://www.stf.jus.br/portal/cms/verNoticiaDetalhe.asp?idConteudo=326275, accessed on 11/11/2016.

decision, which eventually determines that the matter is reviewed in the administrative level and which is concerned with equity in the distribution of public resources and with the scientific effectiveness of medicines and treatments.

Brazilian legislation, as in Law 12.401/04/2011, may fulfill in this field a pedagogical role, of reminding judges that they cannot do everything and that there are technical aspects to be considered that their decisions inevitably hide. A reserve of administration or greater deference to legislative and administrative decisions is thus affirmed, which can only be dismissed by the Judiciary in exceptional situations. The so-called Chevron doctrine, elaborated by the US Supreme Court, can still be invoked in this sense.

The concrete case which led to the affirmation of the Chevron doctrine involved the questioning of the legality of norms issued by the environmental protection agency of that country (Schwartz, 1991: 701-702). According to this doctrine, the Judiciary must maintain the interpretation of a law made by the agencies, by means of regulations, for example, unless such interpretation is inconsistent with clearly expressed parliamentary intent. For this reason, the Chevron doctrine implies respect or judicial deference to administrative interpretations (judicial deference), about which it is important to define not whether they are correct, but whether they are admissible. That is, the Judiciary should not replace the interpretation adopted by the agency, unless it clearly violates the law. If it does not violate it, the administrative interpretation must prevail.

Above all, it seems necessary to establish an institutional dialogue and affirmation of the powers of public officials, since sometimes not even the health professionals themselves seem to know the clinical protocols and the procedures they envisage, not demonstrating sensitivity to the aspect of cost and the effectiveness of treatments and impacts for the budget and society.

Such dialogue could take place in a consensual solution of litigation, such as mediation, transaction and other forms of amicable dispute settlement, encouraged by the 2015 Code of Civil Proceedings and Law 13.140/06/2015; also, through technical conciliation nuclei, which allow the intermediation between health plans or the Unified Health System and the Judiciary, already adopted in some Brazilian courts.

This bias reveals a mechanism whose study and application may prove interesting, for this purpose: the so-called meaningful engagement, developed by the Constitutional Court of South Africa (Vieira Junior, 2015: 29). It is a case law construction that seems to serve to respect the separation of powers and at the same time ensure the realization of fundamental rights that require the allocation of resources from the budget. In the Olivia Road case of 2008, which resulted from a building eviction order issued by the city of Johannesburg to the detriment of more than 400 people for health and safety reasons, the Court determined that the city and the occupants should make a significant commitment to resolve the conflict in the light of the values of the Constitution, to guarantee living conditions for those living in the buildings, ensure health and safety, and report back to the Court later on the results of the compromise.

The main advantage in adopting such a commitment is the overcoming of a unilateral imposition by the Judiciary, which affects the budget, through a consensual and participatory solution, under the supervision of the Judiciary, with greater respect for the separation of powers (Vieira Junior, 2015: 50). There is already a Brazilian Senate bill (PLS 736, 2015) that seeks to include a significant commitment to the country's constitutional control system (Vieira Junior, 2015: 34).

IV. Conclusion

The analysis of the evolution of jurisprudence related to the topic of health judicialization shows an interesting dynamic. From a phase of self-restraint, a maximization of the Judiciary's action followed, in the context of the Brazilian Constitution of 1988 and the affirmation of new rights and promises that it had set up.

However, the excesses of this phase were noticed, due to the lack of consideration, among other aspects, of legal forecasts, limits of budgets and the consequences for the public health system of judicial intervention. Not to mention problems of equity in the care and distribution of public resources.

The fundamental right to health, based on the general prediction of art. 196 of the Constitution and the consideration of human dignity, cannot lead to granting extremely expensive or untested drugs and unproven results to all applicants, without considering the competence established by the Legislature for technical instances, the cost of incorporation of new drugs and the scientific evidence regarding its effectiveness.

The problems caused by the excesses of the judicial intervention were faced by the Judiciary itself, and also by the Legislature, as highlighted in this work. It can even be said that the edition of Law 12.401/04/2011 has fulfilled the scope of reaffirming the technical competencies of the Executive, for example, regarding the incorporation of new technologies in health and the definition of clinical protocols. The legislator, therefore, may play an important role in reaffirming the Executive's technical competencies, and in a pedagogical way, set limits for judicial intervention.

The pendulum must return to the position of greater balance between individual interests and rights and collective needs, and it is necessary to consider the greater institutional expertise of the entities to whom the legislation gives competence, for example, to decide on the effectiveness and safety of new drugs, as is the case in Brazil, of ANVISA, as well as from the bodies that design and implement public health policies and the incorporation of new technologies.

It is reaffirmed that the judicialization may take a new course, no longer purely individual, but to consider the way in which these policies are exercised and the actions of the institutions which have to decide. In this sense, it is essential to have a permanent dialogue between the Judiciary and these bodies, in order to clarify the limits of their institutional capacities and to find consensual solutions, to remove obstacles, incomprehension and mutual distrust. Dialogue, mediation, partnership and advice from scientists and technicians seem to be a timely way forward, with a view to realizing the right to health without affecting budgets and the implementation of public policies in this area.

Bibliography

BALESTRA NETO, Otávio. (2015). "A jurisprudência dos tribunais superiores e o direito à saúde—evolução rumo à racionalidade." *Direito Sanitário magazine* (São Paulo). V. 16, n. 1, March/June de 2015, pp. 87-111.

DIAS, Eduardo Rocha. SILVA JÚNIOR, Geraldo Bezerra da. (2016). "Evidence-based medicine in judicial decisions concerning right to healthcare." Einstein (São Paulo). Vol. 14, n. 1, Jan./Mar. 2016, pp. 1-5.

DIAS DE CASTRO, José Augusto. (2008). "A questão do direito fundamental à saúde sob a ótica da análise econômica do direito." *Direito Público da Economia magazine*, year 6, n. 21, pp. 149-158, Jan./Mar. 2008.

ESTORNINHO, Maria João e MACIEIRINHA, Tiago. (2014). *Direito da saúde*. Lisbon: Universidade Católica Editora.

NUNES, António José Avelãs and SCAFF, Fernando Facury. (2011). *Os tribunais e o direito à saúde*. Porto Alegre: Livraria do Advogado.

PORTAL DA SAÚDE. "Doenças Raras: Ministério da Saúde lança protocolos clínicos para 12 doenças raras." Available at: < http://portalsaude.saude.gov.br/index.php/cidadao/principal/agencia-saude/18086-ministerio-da-saude-lanca-protocolos-clinicos-para-12-doencas-raras>. Last accessed on Nov 11th, 2016.

—. "Judicialização: Em cinco anos, mais de R$ 2,1 bilhões foram gastos com ações judiciais." Available at: <http://portalsaude.saude.gov.br/index.php/cidadao/principal/agencia-saude/20195-em-cinco-anos-mais-de-r-2-1-bilhoes-foram-gastos-com-acoes-judiciais> Last accessed on Dec 4th, 2016.

REDE RARAS. "Observatório de Doenças Raras da Universidade de Brasília." Available at: <http://rederaras.org/> Last accessed on: Nov 11th, 2016.

SANTOS, Lenir. "Judicialização da saúde e a incompreensão do SUS. Judicialização da saúde no Brasil." Campinas: Saberes Editora, 2014, pp. 125-160.

SCAFF, Fernando Facury. "A efetivação dos direitos sociais no Brasil. Garantias constitucionais de financiamento e judicialização." A Eficácia dos Direitos Sociais – I Jornada Internacional de Direito Constitucional Brasil/Espanha/Itália. São Paulo: Quartier Latin, 2010, pp. 21-42.

SCHULZE, Clenio Jair. "STJ inaugura nova posição na judicialização da saúde." Available at: <http://emporiododireito.com.br/stj-inaugura-nova-posicao-na-judicializacao-da-saude-por-clenio-jair-schulze/> Last accessed on Sept 4th, 2017.

SCHWARTZ, Bernard. (1991). *Administrative law*. Boston: Little, Brown and Company.

SUNSTEIN, Cass e VERMEULE, Adrian. "Interpretation and institutions." University of Chicago Law School. Coase-Sandor Working Paper Series in Law and Economics, 2002, pp. 1-48. Available at <http://chicagounbound.uchicago.edu/cgi/viewcontent.cgi?article=1279&context=law_and_economics> Last accessed on Sept 4th, 2017.

SUPREMO TRIBUNAL FEDERAL. "Pedido de vista adia julgamento sobre acesso a medicamentos de alto custo por via judicial." Available at: <http://www.stf.jus.br/portal/cms/verNoticiaDetalhe.asp?idConteudo=326275> Last accessed on: Nov 11th, 2016.

VIEIRA JUNIOR, Ronaldo Jorge Araújo. "Separação de poderes, estado de coisas inconstitucional e compromisso significativo: novas balizas à atuação do Supremo Tribunal Federal." Senado Federal: Brasília, 2015, pp. 1-38. Available at: https://www12.senado.leg.br/publicacoes/estudos-legislativos/tipos-de-estudos/textos-para-discussao/td186, last accessed on: 12/18/2016.

WANG, Daniel. "Courts as healthcare policy-makers: the problem, the responses to the problem and the problem in the responses." São Paulo Law School of Fundação Getúlio Vargas—Direito GV. Research Paper Series—Legal Studies. Paper n. 75. In http://bibliotecadigital.fgv.br/dspace/bitstream/handle/10438/11198/RPS_75_final.pdf?sequence=1, Last accessed on: 04/20/2014.

THEMATIC TABLE 5:
NEW TECHNOLOGIES AND FUNDAMENTAL RIGHTS PROTECTION

NOTES ON THE SO-CALLED RIGHT TO BE FORGOTTEN IN BRAZIL AND ITS ACKNOWLEDGMENT AND IMPLEMENTATION BY THE SUPERIOR COURTS

INGO WOLFGANG SARLET[1]

I. General Considerations

Considering that the acknowledgment and protection of the dignity of the human person and of personality rights in the face of the advances and challenges represented by the new technologies, particularly in the sphere of information technologies, are—also in Brazil—a central problem for the political and legal system, the discussion about the right "to be forgotten" soon caught not only the attention of the Brazilian legal scholarship[2] and case law,[3] but also of the legislative sphere, given the existence of several bills on the topic that are currently being examined in the National Congress.

Furthermore, it is evident that also in this field—hence the use of some references to international and foreign law—there is a (greater or smaller) reception of foreign normative (legislative in the broad sense), theoretical

---

[1] Doctorate in Law at the Ludwig-Maximilians-Universität München, Germany. Professor of Constitutional Law and Head of the Graduation Program in Law (Master and Doctorate) at the Pontifical Catholic University of Rio Grande do Sul (www.pucrs.br). Judge at the State Appeal Court of Rio Grande do Sul (TJRS).

[2] Limiting ourselves here to the sphere of the Brazilian books dedicated specifically to the topic, see especially Pablo Dominguez Martinez, *Direito ao Esquecimento. A proteção da memória individual na sociedade da informação*, 2014; Viviane Nóbrega Maldonado, *Direito ao Esquecimento*, 2016; Clarissa Pereira Carello, *Direito ao Esquecimento. Parâmetros jurisprudenciais*, 2016; Zilda Mara Consalter, *Direito ao Esquecimento. Proteção da intimidade e ambiente virtual*, 2017; Sérgio Branco, *Memória e esquecimento na Internet*, 2017.

[3] The presentation of some of the main cases adjudicated by the superior courts in Brazil and their analysis will be performed in sections 3 and 4 of the present article.

and case law categories, which even come from international law, that has influenced the political debate and fed the discourse of Brazilian legal scholarship and case law.

However, although the broader context that transcends the borders of the national territory and law should be the object of consideration, it is certain that, also as regards the acknowledgment and protection of a fundamental right, it is necessary to prioritize a comprehension that is constitutionally appropriate, i.e. attuned to the peculiarities of the Brazilian legal-constitutional system.

Thus, even if in the coming sections there will be mention of topics that have already been discussed, it is essential to try to ground (justify) a right to be forgotten in the Brazilian legal-constitutional architecture, from the perspective of a systematic understanding, so as to define its boundaries and scope (and also its limits), as well as its consequences and possibilities of implementation.

For this purpose, it is necessary to begin by examining potential constitutional foundations for a right to be forgotten, continuing with the identification and brief analysis of its diverse dimensions (even though not direct and explicit) in the infraconstitutional legislation and its acknowledgment and protection by case law, which—also due to the need to establish priorities—will be limited to the most important decisions of the Superior Court of Justice (SCJ) and of the Federal Supreme Court (FSC).

II. The Legal-Constitutional Framework and the Inference of a Fundamental Right to "Be Forgotten"

2.1 Constitutional foundations

Similar to the development of the institute of the right to be forgotten in Europe (as in the case, among others, of Germany, Spain, France and Italy) and even in other countries, such as the USA (although in the latter country there are strong objections to acknowledging this right), likewise in Brazil this legal concept is not expressly established in the sense of being textually and specifically expressed in the Constitution's text.

As shown by the German experience, the acknowledgment of a right to be forgotten is founded—from the constitutional perspective—in the dignity of the human person, in the general clause of personality protection (or rather, in the right to a free development of personality), besides being related to and inferable from other special personality rights, such as the right to informational self-determination, and the rights to a private life, honor and image.[4] Furthermore, it is broadly recognized that the acknowledgment of a so-called right to be forgotten is justified by the protection of personality in the face of potential abuses resulting from the exercise of freedom of speech and information, not only, but especially in the internet environment.

The legal foundation and shaping of the right to be forgotten, despite the existence of sparse legal provisions (even if they are not direct), should clearly start from a constitutional perspective, also for the purpose of rendering feasible an integrated and coherent understanding of the infraconstitutional legislation, their consistency from the constitutional point of view and even the legislative updating in this domain.

In this context, it is essential to take into account that the right to be forgotten holds the double condition of a fundamental right in the material and formal sense; corresponding to the former its justification both philosophically and from the constitutional perspective of its relevance as a legal good connected to fundamental principles and rights, will be prioritized here.[5]

Its condition as a fundamental right in the formal sense corresponds to the qualified legal regime of fundamental rights that was attributed to them directly and even indirectly by the Constitution, such as the prerogative of immediate applicability and direct binding of State agencies and even of private entities, its condition as a material limit to constitutional reform and its reinforced protection from restrictions imposed by the lawgiver, administrator, judiciary power and even by acts performed by private actors.[6]

---

[4] See, pars por toto, Gabrielle Buchholz, Das "Recht auf Vergessen im Internet—Eine Herausforderung für den demokratischen Rechtstaat", in*: Archiv des öffentlichen Rechts* (AÖR) vol. 140 (Tübingen: Mohr-Siebeck, 2015), pp. 127ff.

[5] See, pars pro toto, Arthur M. Ferreira Neto, "Direito ao Esquecimento na Alemanha e no Brasil" in: *Diálogo entre o Direito Brasileiro e o Direito Alemão. Fundamentos, métodos e desafios de ensino, pesquisa e extensão em tempos de cooperação internacional*, ed. by Claudia Lima Marques, Christoph Benicke and Augusto Jaeger Junior (Porto Alegre: RJR, 2016), vol. II, pp. 278-323.

[6] For the development of this point see, pars pro toto, Ingo Wolfgang Sarlet, *A eficácia dos Direitos Fundamentais. Uma teoria geral dos direitos fundamentais*

In a first approach—turning here to the material dimension of its fundamentality—one must begin with the general and structuring fundamental principle of the dignity of the human person, provided for in Brazil in art. 1, item III of the Federal Constitution (= FC), in the article that lists the foundations of the democratic rule of law. This principle has assumed—in a practically settled manner in legal scholarship and case law—the condition of a general clause of protection of personality and of foundation for the right to free personality development.[7]

Notwithstanding the fact that the right to be forgotten can already be well anchored from the point of view of its justification and acknowledgment, as a fundamental right implicit in human dignity and in the right to free development of personality, this justification is reinforced by the possible and necessary relationship between the right to be forgotten and some special personality rights, be they expressly or even implicitly established, particularly the right to privacy (and intimacy), the rights to honor and image, as well as the rights to the protection of data and to informational self-determination.

These special personality rights—save the right to informational self-determination—were objects of express acknowledgment by the framers of the FC and allow, especially in the case of tension and even conflict with the freedom of speech and information, the reinforcement of the justification for the inference of a right to be forgotten as an implicit and necessary projection to its protection, especially in relation to the personal and public exposure/confrontation with facts from the past—whether one's own or especially of third parties—of an offensive, embarrassing or even inconvenient and untrue nature.

On the other hand, the right to informational self-determination, which, as in other countries, is not expressly provided for in Brazil's constitutional text, has been inferred from the principle of the dignity of the human

---

na perspectiva constitucional, 12th ed. (Porto Alegre: Livraria do Advogado Editora, 2015).

[7] In Brazilian law, see among others, Gustavo Tepedino, *Temas de Direito Civil* (Rio de Janeiro: Renovar, 1999), pp. 44ff.; Fabio Siebeneichler de Andrade, "Considerações sobre a tutela dos direitos da personalidade no Código Civil de 2002", in: *O novo Código Civil e a Constituição*, ed. by Ingo Wolfgang Sarlet, 2nd ed., p. 101; Maria Celina Bodin de Moraes, *Danos à pessoa humana. Uma leitura civil-constitucional dos danos morais*, 2nd ed. (Rio de Janeiro: Editora Processo, 2003), pp. 117ff.; Anderson Schreiber, *Direitos da Personalidade*, 3rd rev. and updated ed. (São Paulo: Atlas, 2014), especially pp. 7ff.

person as a general clause of personality protection, from the right to the inviolability of personal data enshrined in art. 5, item XII of the FC (together with the confidentiality of correspondence and communications by telephone). Furthermore, the right to informational self-determination is related to the right to information and also to the institute of habeas data, a constitutional action instituted by art. 5, item LXXII of the FC, according to which

> *habeas data* shall be granted: a) to ensure the knowledge of information related to the person of the petitioner, contained in records or databases of government agencies or of agencies of a public character; b) for the correction of data, when the petitioner does not prefer to do so through a confidential process, either judicial or administrative.

Moreover, although here we are dealing with a more specific aspect that refers more directly to criminal law, but that, even indirectly, reinforces the constitutional justification of the right to be forgotten as a fundamental, currently implicit right, it is cogent to invoke the right of the convict to resocialization, recognized by the FSC also as an implicit fundamental right, even if this acknowledgment is previous to and originally not associated with a right to be forgotten.

In the particular dimension connected to the right to be forgotten, the right to re-socialization implies ensuring that the convict has a real possibility of becoming reintegrated into family and social life and not being constantly confronted with this fact. Here, in turn, legal scholarship and case law have repeatedly invoked a precedent from the Federal Constitutional Court of Germany, specifically the famous "Lebach I" case, which will be the object of some attention later on, in the critical evaluation of the decisions of the Brazilian courts.

Obviously, acknowledging a right to be forgotten as a statement inferred, in general terms, from the dignity of the human person and from the personality rights, or even, particularly, as a legal position associated with specific constitutional rights and guarantees, as in the case of the criminal sphere, does not subtract the right to be forgotten from the legal regime of fundamental rights. This includes its limits and the limits to the imposition of restrictions. Such limits and the correlated imposition of restrictions (restrictive interventions) have precisely the purpose of ensuring other fundamental rights and goods with constitutional stature, which in turn are also limited by the right to be forgotten, as in the case of the already mentioned freedoms of speech and information, particularly the right of access to information.

In brief, what matters here are precisely the limits to the right to be forgotten, as a particular manifestation and demand of the dignity of the human person and the personality rights, in addition to other fundamental rights, which will be examined further on in the light of the selected court decisions.

2.2. Partial legislative manifestations

At the underconstitutional level, although also not nominally, a few aspects (and problems) that involve a right to be forgotten have already been regulated and protected, but there is still the lack of a broader, systematic and efficacious comprehension of the right to be forgotten, its dimensions and effectiveness. So far, however, there has not been a general and cross-sectional comprehension, which, at least in Brazil, depends on an approach from the perspective of the Constitution, especially as regards the fundamental rights and guarantees.

An initial and traditional dimension of a right to be forgotten—although until recently this term was not even invoked—can be found in the domain of criminal law and criminal procedure law, especially as regards art. 135 of the Criminal Code, art. 748 of the Criminal Procedure Code and art. 202 of the Sentence Execution Act, which is in clear harmony with the Constitution's perspective (the convict's right to resocialization and the prohibition of life sentences), not only supporting and giving additional content to legal protection, but also making it concretely possible in some aspects.

Indeed, according to the provision in art. 135 of the Penal Code, "once rehabilitation has been declared, the criminal record will be cancelled through an entry." Besides, in the single paragraph of the aforementioned article, it is stated that "once rehabilitation has been granted, the official record of criminal convictions can only be communicated to the police or judiciary authority, or to the representative of the Public Prosecutor's Office, for the production of evidence in a criminal procedure that might be instituted against the rehabilitated person." Along the same lines, art. 748 of the Criminal Procedure Code establishes that the "previous conviction or convictions will not be mentioned in the criminal record of the rehabilitated person, nor in a certificate extracted from the court books, save when ordered by a criminal court judge", which, in general terms, was also provided for in article 202 of the Sentence Execution Act.

Another specific statement that has been associated with a right to be forgotten is supported by the Consumer Protection Code (Law n. 8,078, of September 11, 1990), more precisely in its art. 43, which, besides implementing, in this domain, aspects of the right to informational self-determination, is also related to the object of a right to be forgotten.

Thus, at the head of art. 43 it is set forth that "the consumer, without prejudice to the provisions of the art. 86,[8] shall have free access to any of their own data informed in reference files, index cards, records, personal and consumer data, as well as their respective sources", and in par. 2 of the same legal rule the Code assures the consumer that whenever they find "any inaccuracy in their data and records, the consumer shall be entitled to require the prompt correction, and the person in charge of such records shall communicate the alteration, within five weekdays, to any possible addressee of the incorrect information."

Likewise, the cadaster information on the consumers who are in the lists of defaulters (negative cadasters) can only be stored and used for five years (art. 43, par. 1 of the Consumer Protection Code), and they have the right to demand cancellation (exclusion of information, besides holding accountable the entities responsible for maintaining and using the data if the rule is violated). In addition, in par. 4 of art. 43 the Consumer Protection Code establishes that the cadasters and databases concerning the consumers are public, which has been used to justify an extensive reading of the scope of the habeas data action as regards the passive parties to the action.

The Brazilian Civil Code (Law n. 10,406, of January 10, 2002), particularly in arts. 11, 12 and also and especially in arts. 16 to 21, in the chapter concerning personality rights, also offers a foundation for the protection of aspects connected to the right to be forgotten. Whereas arts. 11 and 12 establish general rules for the protection of personality rights, in arts. 16 to 21 norms are enshrined that are, although indirectly, related to important aspects that also concern a right to be forgotten.

In art. 16, the Civil Code acknowledges that "every person has the right to a name, which includes forename and surname." This right, absent from a specific and express constitutional provision, has been, from the constitutional point of view and as a fundamental right, of the dignity of

[8] This provision was vetoed by the President.

the human person, a general clause of protection of personality.[9] On the other hand, in arts. 17 to 19 the Civil Code says that a) "a person's name cannot be used by another in publications or representations which expose them to public contempt, even when there is no defamatory intention" (art. 17); b) "the name of another cannot be used in commercial advertising without authorization" (art. 18); and c) "the pseudonym adopted for lawful activities enjoys the protection that is given to the name" (art. 19).

In more general terms, art. 21 of the Civil Code provides that "the private life of a natural person is inviolable, and the judge, at the request of the party concerned, will adopt the necessary measures to prevent or make cease acts contrary to this rule," a normative precept to be handled in tune with both the constitutional framework and the other legal provisions that concern the topic. Anyhow, the first part only reproduces in the ordinary legislative sphere the right to privacy set forth in the FC. The second part, however, concerns matters connected to the judicial protection of private life (applicable also, to a certain extent, to the right to be forgotten), which is the object of attention, as already mentioned, in the last chapter.

Particularly controversial is the statement of art. 20, according to which, in the original draft,

> Unless authorized, or if necessary to the administration of justice or maintenance of public order, the dissemination of written material, the transmission of words, or the publication, exhibition or use of a person's image may be forbidden, at their behest and without prejudice to the compensation, if appropriate, if their honor, good name or respectability are affected, or if they are used for commercial purposes.

Although one might say that the legal claim to forgetting information that has become public, but that over time became irrelevant or unreasonable can also be derived—and implemented by a specific legal rule—from the protection of the personality right provided for in art. 20 of the Civil Code, insofar as the overexposure of facets of the intimate sphere of an individual—without any social pertinence of the informational content that

[9] See as an illustration representing the orientation in constitutional case law the decision of the FSC in RE 454903/SP, j. 07.12.2009, judge-rapporteur Joaquim Barbosa: "The right to a name is part of the concept of dignity of the human person and expresses their identity, the origin of their ancestry, the acknowledgment of the family, which is the reason why the state of affiliation is an inalienable right, because of the greater common good to be protected, derived from the very binding force of the public order precepts that regulate the matter (Child and Adolescent Statute, art. 27)."

is to be restricted or eliminated—prevents the full autonomous development of this person, violating the maintenance of their "honor, good name and respectability," the fact is that there are well-founded reasons to question the constitutionality of aspects that concern the legal precept mentioned.

Indeed, based on dissent in precedents already established by the lower courts, as well as on major criticism that had already been made by legal scholars, the FSC—in ADI 4815,[10] whose judge-rapporteur was Cármen Lúcia and which was judged in 2015—though it did not declare the unconstitutionality in itself— not even partial—of the text of art. 20 of the Civil Code, gave it an interpretation in accordance with the FC, without any reduction of the text, in the sense of not making requirable a prior authorization by the person whose biography is involved, or their representatives, for third parties to write biographies.

The relatively recent Federal Access to Information Act (n. 12.444/2011), despite its particular scope and although it is basically aimed at public agencies, is also relevant for the protection of personality rights and is, thus, related to aspects of the right to be forgotten. Although here it is not possible to offer a cross-sectional and profound approach, there is no way to not mention the main provisions of the aforementioned law which, within the sphere of an interpretation in tune with the constitutional framework and systematically associated with the other legal precepts in force on the matter, not only help justify and ground, from the legal point of view, the right to be forgotten, but also contribute to the definition of its contours and limits.

Thus, for instance, in art. 31, the Access to Information Act provides that "personal information must be treated transparently and respecting people's intimacy, private life, honor and image, as well as individual freedoms and guarantees." Besides, art. 38 of the Access to Information Act refers to Law n. 9,507, of September 12, 1997, which regulated access to information that was in public registries or databases, as well as the already mentioned procedure of "habeas data". Despite its relatively restricted scope—according to Law 9,507/97, all records or databases containing information that is or could be transmitted to third parties or

[10] For non-Brazilian readers, it should be explained that the procedure in which this matter was decided is called Direct Action for the Declaration of Unconstitutionality ("Ação Direta de Inconstitucionalidade"), which, within the sphere of an abstract and concentrated control of rules, aims to declare the unconstitutionality of a federal or state normative act or then, among other modalities of decision, to promote an interpretation according to the Constitution.

that is not for the exclusive use of the agency or entity that has produced, or is the depositary of the information—its complementary integration into the system created by the Access to Information Act reinforces aspects of the protection of personality rights which bear a relation to the right to be forgotten itself.

On the other hand, the so-called Statute of the Civil Framework of the Internet (Federal Statute n. 12,965, of April 23, 2014) established a set of principles and provided for guarantees, rights and duties for the use of the internet in Brazil. This statute, even if it does not expressly establish the right to be forgotten, contains important guidelines and concrete rules that can be reconstructed for the purpose of recognizing the need to accept this individual legal claim in certain cases, as can be seen from the following provisions that, if systematically interpreted, lead to the conclusion that points to the existence of the right to be forgotten in national law, besides regulating specific aspects pertaining to this fundamental law and thus implementing it at least partially.

From this perspective, art. 2 of the Statute establishes that "internet use in Brazil is founded on the respect for freedom of expression," which is the reason why its use should always guarantee and fulfill "the human rights, the development of personality and the exercise of citizenship in digital media." On the other hand, art. 7 contains a kind of catalogue of rights and guarantees of internet users that also involve the protection of personal data, privacy and informational self-determination, and even reproduce constitutional provisions, besides rendering them concrete by regulating various aspects that are correlated to them, in the internet environment.

Thus, according to art. 7, "Internet access is essential for the exercise of citizenship, and the users have the following rights: I—inviolability of intimacy and privacy, protection and compensation for property or moral damages resulting from its breach;" "VII—no supply of personal data to third parties, including connection logs, and data of access to internet applications, except by free, express and informed consent or in the cases provided by law;" "IX—express consent to the collection, use, storage and processing of personal data, which should be highlighted in the contract terms;" "X—definitive exclusion of personal data that have been provided to the particular internet application, on request of the user, at the end of the relationship between the parties, except in the cases of mandatory log keeping provided for in this law;" "XIII—application of protective standards and consumer protection in consumer relations carried out on the internet."

This shows that the systematic interpretation of the legal provisions mentioned in the light of the constitutional principle of the dignity of the human person, and particularly the personality rights, makes it possible to identify, implicitly and indirectly, the acknowledgment of the right to be forgotten in the Brazilian legal system. On the other hand, also in the case of Brazil, it is clear that the right to be forgotten does not really constitute a new right, but rather a particular expression of certain principles and fundamental rights. This statement does not mean that the right to be forgotten implies new dimensions, new challenges and new legal problems, especially in the context of the so-called information society, particularly the digital environment.

III. The Right to "Be Forgotten" and its Acknowledgment and Protection by the Superior Courts (SCJ and FSC)

Based on the partial—constitutional and legal—recognition of a right to be forgotten in the sphere of positive law, as well as looking at contributions from national and even foreign legal scholarship, the Brazilian superior courts, especially—for now—the SCJ, have already had the opportunity of invoking and enforcing a right to be forgotten in a number of cases submitted to their examination. However, considering a casuistic practice, which is not always consistent and predictable—as shall be seen further on—it is not possible to speak yet of a consolidation of the right to be forgotten as far as case law is concerned, which is even more relevant if the production of ordinary jurisdictional instances on this topic is considered. Given the broad range of the latter, it will not be considered here, except for possible isolated references, when deemed necessary.

Furthermore, for the sake of an easier understanding and especially of a broad and comparative critical analysis, we shall not only follow the chronological order, but also present separately the cases that concern acknowledging the right to be forgotten in general terms and the cases that refer to acknowledging and protecting this right in the domain of the internet. On the other hand, considering the spatial limits of the present text, we will restrict ourselves to presenting those that could be considered the leading cases in this matter.

3.1. Decisions involving a right to be forgotten outside the internet domains

The first two cases, both judged by the SCJ, were appreciated in the Special Appeals n. 1335153/RJ and n. 1334097/RJ (2013). In these two cases judged by the 4th Panel of the Superior Court on the same day a few parameters were established for the acknowledgment and respective legal consequences of a right to be forgotten in Brazil. However, opposite conclusions were reached in them, since one of the cases assured the protection of this right, whereas in the other prevalence was given to the freedom of information and communication. This discrepancy does not necessarily prove to be contradictory, but already points to the fact that, as in other cases in which there is a collision of rights, it is necessary to analyze the peculiarities of each case, the weight of the rights involved, and also the impact resulting from their greater or lesser protection. This must be done through a weighting operation aiming at establishing a balance and an adequate solution from the legal point of view.

In the first case, known as the “Aida Curi” case (Resp. 1.335.153/RJ), the family of Aida Curi, who was murdered in 1958—a case that became very notorious at the time when the murder was committed—wanted to prevent a TV Globo program called Linha Direta from reproducing and reconstituting, even as a documentary, decades later, the same traumatic episode. They claimed that “old already healed wounds” might be reopened in public. The plaintiffs requested the acceptance of their claim that in this case “their right to be forgotten” be declared, “to not have revived, against their will, the pain that they had previously suffered on the occasion of Aida Curi’s death, and also because of the publicity given to the case decades earlier.” They further requested compensation for intangible damages.

Analyzing the particularities of the case, the judge-rapporteur, Luís Felipe Salomão, found that

> (i) the victims of crimes and their families, theoretically, can also hold the right to be forgotten insofar as they cannot be obliged to submit unnecessarily to “memories of past facts that caused them unforgettable wounds,” besides the circumstance that the protection of the possible offender would be unfair, because of their right to resocialization, leaving the victim and their family at the mercy of their public and permanent exposure;

(ii) the appropriate resolution of the case requires balancing the potential historicity of the fact narrated with the protection to the intimacy and privacy of the victims;

(iii) in this case the crime entered the public domain and thus became a historical fact, which cannot be transformed into a fact that is not accessible to the press and society. Besides, due to the broad dissemination given to the fact at the time it happened, including the investigation and trials, as well as the direct connection with the victim's name, it would be unfeasible to "portray the Aida Curi case without Aida Curi;" and

(iv) considering the concrete situation, a restriction of the freedom of the press would be disproportionate compared to the discomfort generated by the remembrance of the facts by the victim's family, particularly considering the long time elapsed since the date of the events, which has the power of reducing, even if not completely removing, the pain and shock caused by the facts and their dissemination.

In the second decision, known as the case of the Candelaria Slaughter (Resp. n. 1.334.097/RJ), likewise, there was an intention to prevent the transmission of a television program (Linha Direta) and a request for indemnification for intangible damages by Rede Globo de Televisão. The plaintiff of the original claim, also made against Globo Comunicações e Participações, alleged the absence of contemporaneity of the facts and that reopening "old wounds" which had already been overcome by him would have reawakened the suspicion of society regarding his character, and fought for the acknowledgment of his right to be forgotten, that is, not be remembered against his will, because of criminal facts for which he had been indicted and judged but acquitted.

In this decision, considering the particularities of the case, the same Justice, Luiz Felipe Salomão, likewise the rapporteur of the case, found for the plaintiff (appellee), after establishing a few assumptions, arguing that

(i) even if the crimes reported were famous and historical and although the journalistic story was faithful to reality, the protection of the intimacy and privacy of the convicted and the acquitted should prevail, as in the case of the appellee, since the "useful life of the criminal information" had already reached its end;
(ii) the acknowledgment of a right to be forgotten expresses "a cultural evolution of society, conferring concreteness to a legal system that, between memory—which is the connection with the past—and hope—which is the tie with the present—made a clear

option for the latter," and the right to be forgotten is a "right to hope, completely attuned with the legal and constitutional presumption of the possibility of rehabilitation of the human person;"

(iii) The uncontested historicity of the facts to which the television program refers must be concretely examined, affirming the public and social interest, as long as, however, the personal identification of those involved is essential. In the case judged, although it is a historical event and a symbol of the precariousness of the State protection of children and adolescents, the documentary could have portrayed the facts correctly without identifying, by name or by image, those involved, particularly the appellee;

(iv) furthermore, allowing the dissemination of the name and image of the appellee, even if acquitted (who even so would have reinforced his image as accused and involved in the crime), would be the same as allowing a second violation of his dignity, since the very fact and its broad dissemination, including the name of the appellee as a suspect, and also the police inquiry, at the time they took place were already a national shaming.

Thus, in the second case, what prevailed was the criterion of exhaustion of the sanctioning function and the need for the rehabilitation and social reinsertion of the people who had been convicted and acquitted, which would surpass the argumentative weight, not only of the—in this case, evident—historicity of the facts that would be the object of a journalistic story, but also the freedom of speech inherent to the activity of the press.

Particularly relevant for the discussion around the content and scope of a right to be forgotten in Brazil is the fact that the FSC (after the Aida Curi case) acknowledged the General Repercussion of the discussion,[11] since it would be possible to examine in an extraordinary appeal the allegation that

> the right to be forgotten is an attribute that cannot be dissociated from the guarantee of human dignity and is identical with it, and that freedom of

[11] ARE 833248 RG/RJ, Justice Dias Toffoli, judged on Feb 19, 2015. It should be mentioned for the better understanding of non-Brazilians that the FSC, by majority decision of its judges, can accept the allegation of general repercussion (relevance and national character of the case because of a relevant divergence in case law), which implies the suspension of all actions that are going through the ordinary instances up to the definitive judgment of the case, when the decision begins to have general effects (erga omnes) and directly binds all of the bodies and agents of the Judiciary.

> speech is not absolute and cannot be greater than the individual guarantees, notably the inviolability of personality, honor, dignity, private life, and intimacy of the human person.

During the proceedings, the judge-rapporteur, Justice Dias Toffoli, called for a public hearing, held on June 12, 2017, and also the acceptance of utterances by various agents as *amici curiae*. The definitive judgment of the case is still being awaited.

3.2. The right to be forgotten in the internet environment from the perspective of the SCJ

The first case that arrived at the SCJ became known as the Xuxa case, and it was judged in the Special Appeal 1,316,921. Its judge-rapporteur was Justice Nancy Andrigui, and it was judged on June 26, 2012. It was a case brought by Maria da Graça Xuxa Meneguel, then still a presenter of television programs for children and adolescents, against Google Brasil Internet Ltda, aiming to suppress from search mechanisms all and any results of searches based on the term "xuxa pedófila" or any other expression that would associate the name of the plaintiff with any kind of criminal practice.

The SCJ, however, appreciating the defendant's (Google Search) refusal to accept it, ended up by looking into the specific problem involving a right to be forgotten, although it fully granted the appeal. As to what matters to our study, here are, in brief, the reasons on which the decision was based which will be evaluated critically further on:

(i) The provision in art. 14 of the Consumer Protection Code does not apply to Google Search, whose activity is limited to operating as a search mechanism and a research provider, since, on the contrary of what happens with the content providers, Google Search limits itself to indexing terms and "indicating links where the terms or expressions for search supplied by the user themselves can be found." That is why in this type of activity it is not possible to speak of defective service.

(ii) Since the activity of the research provider is carried out in a virtual environment, which allows public and unrestricted access, even if there were no search mechanisms such as those offered by Google Search the contents considered unlawful would still continue circulating and being made available on the internet.

(iii) Given the subjective and arbitrary character involved in the decision to remove—or not—links, results and pages vehiculating offensive (illicit) contents on the internet, this margin of discretion cannot be delegated to the research provider.

(iv) The person who considers themselves affected by the dissemination of some information (content) on the internet should turn against those directly responsible for the insertion of such data in the world wide web of computers, and not against the research providers, who then would not even have any way of giving access to the contents considered offensive. Thus, the only way to exclude the content considered illicit (offensive) lies in identifying the respective URL, specifying the address responsible for its storage on the world-wide computer web.

(v) The conflict between the protection of personality rights and the freedom of speech and communication, especially in its collective dimension, should prevail over the individual interests and greater weight should be attributed to the right to information.

A more recent case judged by the SCJ on May 10, 2016 (Special Appeal n. 1.582.981/RJ, judge-rapporteur Justice Marco Aurélio Bellizze) presents a few peculiarities in relation to the Xuxa case. In this appeal, filed both by Google and by the suing party, the object of the lawsuit against Google concerned the responsibility of the Google Brasil company for the fact that, despite the exclusion of the name of the plaintiff who had been the subject of a comment by a third party who connected him inappropriately to his name and profession (lawyer), it continued showing the aforementioned story in its search mechanisms.

It should be noted that in the lower courts Google had been condemned and ordered to revise its search mechanisms, excluding the association of the name of the plaintiff to the link www.tudosuper.com.br and its derivatives, under penalty of a daily fine if it did not comply. The SCJ, in turn, although it repeated arguments from previous trials, decided that exceptionally the search providers may be compelled to exclude from their database results that are incorrect or damaging, "especially when there is no relationship of pertinence between the content of the result and the criterion researched." Furthermore, besides maintaining the imposition of the compensatory fine, the SCJ underlined that the value of the fine must be dynamic in its character and adequate so as to have "real coercive force" to prevent noncompliance with the judicial decisions, like what happened in effect in that case.

The last case to be collated here was judged by the SCJ in November 2016 (Resp. n. 1.593.873-SP). It was a case of obligation to do brought against Google Brasil Internet (recurrent) for the purpose of definitively blocking in the system searches based on the name of the plaintiff, because they might show nude images of her. In her opinion the judge-rapporteur, Justice Nancy Andrigui, collated precedents from the SCJ itself and the case of *Google Spain vs. Agencia Espanhola de Protección de Datos and Mario Costeja González* but refuted its validity as an adequate precedent to guide the decision in the concrete case because in Brazil there is no general law of data protection. In brief, the arguments used in the previous decisions were reiterated, especially in the sense that research providers are not responsible for the content of the results of the searches carried out by the respective users and cannot be obliged to eliminate results derived from searches based on a given term or name. Besides, the SCJ considered (by a majority) that in Brazil there is no specific legal provision imposing this responsibility on research providers, which would also mean to entrust them with the function of a kind of digital censor.

IV. Summary and Evaluation of the Current Stage of Brazil as Regards the Content and Limits of the Right to be Forgotten

As can be seen, concerning the recognition of the right to be forgotten as a fundamental right in Brazil, there are sufficient foundations in the national legal framework—as long as it is systematically interpreted primarily on the basis of a constitutional perspective—as an implicit particular dimension inferred especially from the principle of human dignity and the correlated general clause of protection of personality, as well as from the special rights to personality (emphasizing informational free self-determination, rights to private life, honor, image and name), and even from the prohibition of life sentences, the right to resocialization and the institute of habeas data. Besides, there are several concrete rules at the level of ordinary legislation, such as the Consumer Protection Code, the Access to Information Act, and the Law of the Civil Framework of the Internet, which provide for the possibility, in some cases, of deleting and rectifying data.

Moreover, as announced, the legal literature has already been dedicating itself to the topic, acknowledging in general terms the existence of a right to be forgotten in the Brazilian legal system but recording a number of divergences as regards its content and limits, especially in relation to the criteria used for its application, by balancing it with other colliding fundamental principles and rights, and also to the means of implementation.

Particularly at the level of case law and taking here as reference the decisions of the SCJ—since they mark and guide all decisions of state and federal ordinary courts—one can see that there is at least a partial lack of consistency and congruence, whether it be among the decisions themselves and their respective foundations, or as regards the different treatment among the cases that do not concern the internet and the judgements that deal precisely with this matter.

Indeed, even though in the digital environment there are peculiarities that have to be taken into account, the fact is that there are some common elements that need to be systematically and consistently dealt with, especially regarding the criteria adopted to establish the content and the limits of a right to be forgotten.

In the case of the decisions of the SCJ what is salient is the use of comparative law and even the important precedent of the Google case judged by the Court of Justice of the European Union.

This happens, for instance, by invoking the famous "Lebach Case" in Germany, where, differently from what happened in the Candelária Slaughter case, the plaintiff who sought to stop the dissemination of the documentary had been convicted and was about to get parole, so that his resocialization was directly and concretely at stake, whereas in the case examined by the SCJ the defendant had been acquitted and not even a distortion of facts and the omission of the fact that he had been acquitted were alleged.

On the other hand, as regards the digital environment, especially trials involving the Google Brasil Internet company, what stands out is the fact that even with the dissemination of contents that were embarrassing and not truthful, prevalence was given to the freedom of speech and information, which, although it does not necessarily mean a complete contradiction with the judgments in the "Ainda Curi" and "Chacina da Candelária" cases, it needs a better solution.

Still in this context, it is strange that, even after the widely disseminated decision of the Court of Justice of the European Union in May 2014, acknowledging (as is also the case of the Spanish Agency for the Protection of Data and of the Superior Court of Justice in Germany) that Google is indeed responsible and a passive legitimate party to be held liable for the insertion and hierarchization of references in its search mechanisms, the SCJ reiterated its view that Google cannot be considered directly liable because it is only a provider of research, except if it was judicially notified and did not comply with the judicial order, in which case then it could be fined.

A central point, however, where substantial gaps are found as regards the acknowledgment and application of a right to be forgotten by the SCJ concerns respecting the criteria used to ensure an appropriate balancing between the colliding constitutional rights and principles and thus to meet the demands of proportionality.

Besides the incongruence and incoherence already pointed out—even if partial—between the decisions, likewise there is no secure orientation regarding the various hypotheses in which a right to be forgotten should (or not) be recognized and applied, and as concerns the respective sanctions, if and when appropriate. For instance, the case law examined does not use as reference the levels of intervention in the freedom of speech and information and the need to apply sanctions that are compatible with such levels.

In effect, it is practically clear that there are various forms of acknowledging and protecting a right to be forgotten, modalities that allow a grading according to the intensity of the restriction, on the one hand, and to the weight of the juridical goods to be safeguarded, on the other.

As an illustration, it seems evident that among the ways of implementing a right to be forgotten the determination to delete (erase) some piece of information posted on the internet is less restrictive than ensuring the deindexation of the search mechanisms. Likewise, and as less invasive but still effective alternatives one could mention the granting of the right to a response, the imposition of the suppression of the identity (name) of the person affected in their personality rights, or even a greater or lesser use of indemnification for intangible and even tangible damages, depending on the case.

Anyhow, it can be seen that—and in this respect Brazil is no different from what is found in other countries and even in the domain of international law—also the right to be forgotten is still a right that is being constructed as regards its sphere of application, content and limits, so that what is expected here is that through the present text it is at least possible to capture some interest in the current state of the art concerning the way the superior courts have handled this right up to the present time.

BRIEF CONSIDERATIONS ON ACCESS TO NEW INFORMATION AND COMMUNICATIONS TECHNOLOGIES AND THE INTERNET, AND THE RIGHT TO NON-DISCRIMINATION AGAINST WOMEN

CAROLINA GARCÉS PERALTA*

I. General Considerations

The emergence and ever-faster development of new information technologies have had direct repercussions on not only the defence of fundamental rights, but also their promotion and even their violation. Against the backdrop of globalization in the digital era, it has now become undeniable that access to and use of these technologies guarantee the real effectiveness of rights worldwide. This possibility is closely tied to the obligation of every constitutional, democratic state under the rule of law to guarantee human rights, especially in view of the fact that today—within this context of globalization in the digital era—there can be no real democracy without a guarantee of pluralism and the consequent access to new information technologies (ICTs) by all citizens, whether male or female.

Access to and use of the internet have become a social phenomenon and an indispensable element in guaranteeing the effective enjoyment of freedoms, such as freedom of expression and information; so-called economic, social, and cultural rights—such as the right to work and the right to education; and even new rights, such as the right to development,

* Attorney at Law, Master of Constitutional Law with PhD studies at the Pontificia Universidad Católica del Perú (PUCP). Former Assistant Head of Women's Rights at the Peruvian Ombudsman's Office. Member of the Peruvian Association of Constitutional Law (APDC). Professor in the PUCP Master's Program in Constitutional Law and the PUCP School of Law, and researcher with the Law, Gender, and Sexuality Group (DEGESE) at the same university.

the right to the truth, and the right to market access. This is directly rooted in the universal, indivisible, and interdependent nature of human rights, as established in the Vienna Declaration and Programme of Action of 1993 (United Nations, 1993).

In keeping with the foregoing, international systems for the protection of human rights have gradually recognized universal access to ICTs. Not only that, but—in view of the true importance of ICTs in guaranteeing the right to have and develop a personality (the right to achieve one's life plans, as established in Subsection 2.1 of the Constitution) and the enforcement of other fundamental rights—a growing number of people now argue that access to the internet must be understood as not just part of the new and indispensable content of one or more fundamental rights, but a specific fundamental right all on its own.

Under these circumstances, it seems a cause for concern that despite the growing importance and significance of ICTs, there are still certain groups of people whose particular vulnerability places them, in practice, in a situation of restricted or limited access to ICTs, and specifically to the internet. Namely, it is women who form the most excluded group, a fact that is due above all to the situation of structural discrimination that they continue to face, despite undeniable advances. Indeed, although they make up approximately half the population, at both the international and domestic levels, they continue to find the real effectiveness of their fundamental rights violated. This problem is complicated by the fact that women are not a homogeneous group. This means that those who live in poverty or those who belong to indigenous communities, for example, are affected even further by the confluence of multiple factors of discrimination.

To grasp the fact that we, as women, have historically been discriminated against merely because of our gender is easier to do, without objection, when it comes to matters such as rape, femicide, reproductive rights, or political participation, without neglecting the persistence of deep-rooted stereotypes that still tolerate or justify these expressions of discrimination. But there are other areas with regard to which society finds it genuinely challenging to admit their true significance, whether because of their newness, their technicality, or some other reason. And yet these issues—if they continue to go unaddressed—will prevent us from eradicating the inequalities to which women are still subjected to this day.

It is precisely these matters—matters we might even classify as pioneering or novel—that are addressed in this Chapter; namely, new ICTs from a gender-based approach. When dealing with this subject, we must stress the importance of the emergence of—and in some cases, the increase in—new forms of discrimination tied to access to ICTs and the internet.

At present, access to the internet and ICTs is becoming an increasingly vital part of human existence. This means that restrictions on this access—which may be legal, but are generally de facto limitations rooted in sociocultural factors—lay bare the disadvantages faced by these persons, who thus find their possibilities for progress and development in all areas of life (social, political, economic, cultural, etc.) limited, all of which perpetuates the relations of subordination and control in which they find themselves, and even reinforces their power relations with those who *do* have access to—and are thus able to benefit from—the use of ICTs.

It is for this reason that we hear increasingly louder calls, both in Peru and around the world, for the state to guarantee access to the internet for all, with the objective of ensuring respect for and the true effectiveness of people's fundamental rights.

Despite this, the work being done in the areas of constitutional law and human rights in terms of access to new information and communication technologies—and specifically, the internet—has not resulted in a true awareness of the problem of discrimination faced by women in the digital age, as in ages past, due to gender relations, roles, spaces, and attributes, as highlighted in the gender gaps— both international and domestic—presented here. Even worse, in cases where women have begun struggling to make spaces for themselves in this area, they have been subjected—by those who seek to cling to power—to manifestations of gender violence in the digital realm, including online stalking, cyber-harassment, invasion of privacy, defamation campaigns, threats of rape, trolling, piracy, viral videos of rape, seduction and abuse through email and websites, etc. (UNESCO, 2014: 68).

This wide-ranging set of problems clearly requires analysis and research from a sociological, political, and economic standpoint, with a crosscutting gender-based approach. Given our area of expertise, however, we will be addressing this issue from a constitutional legal perspective, with a focus on gender and human rights. We seek here to make contributions to the analysis of women's real access to ICTs and the internet; the scope and limitations of the laws currently in force (both internally and in international human rights law); and the adequate interpretation of these laws, based on gender, interculturality, and intersectionality, in an effort to ensure the state's compliance with its obligation to adopt effective measures in response to this situation, and to guarantee the effective defence and protection of women's constitutional rights, and particularly their right to non-discrimination.

The ultimate purpose of this paper is to spur an interest in and analysis of this problem based on constitutional law, from a gender perspective, thus helping to foster awareness of its importance so that, in the near future, more in-depth investigations can be done into the matter in Peru, and so that the different interpreters and operators of constitutional law become aware of their role, carrying out their interpretative tasks based on a true respect for women's fundamental rights in the digital age.

II. Women's Access to and use of New Information and Communications Technologies (ICTs) and the Internet: National and International Statistics

At present, access to ICTs has clearly started to play an increasingly important role in achieving the true effectiveness of fundamental rights and the right to development.

The gender divide in digital technology has significant effects on women, their empowerment and development, not to mention society, companies, and economies. It is thus undeniably important for the different stakeholders involved to take effective, tangible, and measurable actions to overcome the digital gender divide in access, in order to ensure that women, too, can benefit from the development of information and communications technologies (ICTs). It is widely recognized by now that ICTs, including the internet and broadband, have the potential to make a positive contribution to the protection of women's fundamental rights, and to their economic, social, and political empowerment, among other aspects, by reducing the cost of information, expanding the repository of information, and increasing women's financial independence and productivity (UNESCO, 2017: 8-13).

In Peru, the importance of access to information and ICTs has gradually been recognized by the state. For example, the Ministry of Transportation and Communications has noted that ICTs offer many ways to help meet the Millennium Development Goals, and may be used as an effective tool for sustainable development (Ministry of Transportation and Communications, 2016: 6)

These circumstances highlight the particular seriousness of persistent, deep-seated social and cultural patterns that continue to result, in different areas of life in society, in a situation in which women are subordinate to men. This is corroborated by the existence of what are known as discrimination gaps, which can be defined as those objective and verifiable inequalities that have no justification, and which directly affect the real effectiveness of women's fundamental rights, simply because they are women (Ombudsman's Office 2012: 43). As noted by the Centro Andino de Altos Estudios (CANDANE), gender divides are the objective differences between men and women in terms of access to, participation in, and control of resources, services, opportunities, and the benefits of development (Ombudsman's Office 2012: 43), a situation that certainly holds true for ICTs and internet access among women. Unfortunately, this discrimination (which, according to a number of international conventions, such as the CEDAW, as well as the Peruvian Constitutional Court (in its ruling dated November 6, 2008: paragraph 7), may occur on purpose or as a side effect—i.e., unintentionally) can be observed not only in Peru, but around the world.

Some manifestations of these divides are discussed below.

The International Sphere

International bodies and entities have been quicker to acknowledge the existence of gender divides in the access to ICTs and the need to take action in order to reverse these gaps, especially given how few states have begun to address the issue.

There is currently a worldwide gender divide of 12 per cent in internet access between males and females. This gap jumps to nearly 31 per cent in the least developed countries. Women continue to lag behind in the growth of mobile phone ownership. Mobile phones are important tools in improving women's lives in low- and medium-income countries, helping them to feel safer and more connected, save time and money, and gain access to services that improve their lives, such as mobile money or potential education and employment opportunities (UNESCO, 2017: 7).

According to UN Women, only 35 per cent of countries keep gender statistics on means of communication, while just over half keep gender statistics on information and communications technologies (2015: 43-45). On the other hand, this same entity states that while the emergence and growth of new technologies may create gaps and lead to the violation of women's rights, they can also become an important element of change if we address the inequalities that currently structure women's ties to the job market. "Nevertheless, *there are few countries that keep track of their progress in this area, doubtlessly because they are still dealing with basic inequalities that render invisible the need to also worry about these issues and understand the benefits*" (UN Women 2017: 59).

For its part, the United Nations General Assembly has recognized that "(…) there is a gap between genders as part of the digital divide, and encourages all those interested to ensure women's full participation in information society and to make sure that women have access to and use of information and communications technologies, in order to contribute to their empowerment and overall benefit" (United Nations, 2011). The UN subsequently reiterated and expanded upon its position, as follows (United Nations, 2016):

> *21. (…) we express concern that* ***many forms of digital divides remain, both between and within countries and between women and men****. We note that divides are often closely linked to education levels and existing inequalities, and we recognise that further divides can emerge in the future, slowing sustainable development.*
>
> *(…)*
>
> *27. We emphasise our concern that* ***only 41 per cent of women have internet access, and draw attention to the gender digital divide, which persists in women's access to and use of information and communications technologies, including in education, employment, and other areas of economic and social development****. We recognise that ending the gender digital divide and the achievement of Sustainable Development Goal 5 on gender are mutually reinforcing efforts, and we commit to mainstreaming gender in the World Summit on the Information Society process, including through a new emphasis on gender in the implementation and monitoring of the action lines, with the support of relevant United Nations entities, including the United Nations Entity for Gender Equality and the Empowerment of Women (UN-Women).* ***We call for immediate measures to achieve gender equality in internet users by 2020****, especially by significantly enhancing women's and girls' education and participation in information and communications technologies, as users, content creators, employees, entrepreneurs, innovators, and leaders. We reaffirm our commitment to ensure women's full participation in decision-making processes related to information and communications technologies* (emphasis ours).

Particular note should be made of the pronouncements issued by the Office of the Special Rapporteur on Freedom of Opinion and Expression to the Inter-American Commission on Human Rights. After acknowledging that the principle of universal access includes the need to guarantee connectivity, as well as universal and equitable access to ICT services, the Office of the Special Rapporteur goes on to state the following:

> *16. (...) Universal access also places a priority on ensuring equitable access when it comes to* ***gender****, as well as inclusive access for disabled individuals and/or individuals belonging to marginalised communities.*
>
> *(...)*
>
> *39. (...) [It is also] important that authorities make efforts to progressively close the digital divide, broadly recognised by States, whether it is the result of wealth,* ***gender****, geography, or social group, between States and within them.*
>
> *(...)*
>
> *41. (...) [T]here is also a* ***gender divide separating women and men in the access to and use of information and communication technology****.* ***States should take measures to promote the participation of women in the information society*** *in order to contribute to their empowerment and gender equality.* (IACHR, 2013) (emphasis ours)

This same Office of the Special Rapporteur—in information from this year (IACHR, 2017), as well as in the section on equality and non-discrimination as a guiding principle contained in its most recent annual report from 2016—has stressed the importance of women's participation in guaranteeing human rights on the internet:

> *61. The States must promote and guarantee, for instance, the full participation of women in the knowledge society in order to be able to ensure integration and respect for human rights on the internet. The* ***States should ensure the participation of women in decision-making processes, and encourage their input in shaping all spheres of the information society*** *at the international, regional, and local levels. Statistics from the Internet Governance Forum show that* ***in 2015 only 38 per cent of the participants in the forum were women, and in 2016 that percentage rose to 39.6 per cent. The States should take proactive measures to close the gender gap on the internet*** *and in all aspects of its governance.*
>
> *(...)*

65. The obligation of equality and non-discrimination also entails the State's obligation to guarantee the exercise of individual human rights on the internet under equal conditions.

(...)

66. (...) [I]nstances of online discrimination against particularly vulnerable groups, including ***women****, children, the LGBTI community, migrants, disabled persons, and others have also been documented. The States must take measures to foster equality and non-discrimination, both "online" and "offline," prohibiting hate speech that incites violence, documenting instances of discrimination, and promoting tolerance through social programs, training, and education.* (emphasis ours)

Another fundamental issue—one that we only have room to touch on briefly here, but which undoubtedly deserves its own analysis—is that of gender and new media platforms in digital technology. In its report on World Trends in Freedom of Expression and Media Development, UNESCO notes that the distribution of communication capacities is typically influenced by socioeconomic inequalities, and particularly by gender inequalities, resulting in differences in the opportunities offered by new media, with the most evident disparity being linked to access. In fact,

> according to estimates by the ITU, 36 per cent of the world's women use the internet, compared to 41 per cent of men. While internet use rates have reached almost absolute parity in the developed world (just a 2 per cent difference between men and women), it is estimated that in the developing world, 16 per cent fewer women use this platform. As web and mobile platforms become increasingly important in the production, consumption, and dissemination of news, the gender divide in access may have a multiplying effect. (UNESCO 2017: 68)

Lastly, as we will examine in more depth in Section 4 of this paper, the reports and resolutions of bodies such as those noted here constitute binding parameters for the interpretation of women's fundamental rights, even when they are not formally considered as such.

The Domestic Sphere

a) *Population aged 6 and older that uses the internet service, by sex and geographic area* (INEI, 2017). One of the first major gender divides laid bare by these statistics is the gap suffered by women in their access to the internet service. This divide reached its peak between 2007 and 2011; during this period, men had from 7.4 per cent to 8.4

per cent more internet access. This figure is even higher, however, when we compare the urban and rural populations. Here, other factors of discrimination come into play, in addition to gender, such as higher levels of poverty, lower education, and fewer job possibilities. As we can see in the following tables, the gaps in the internet service between men and women are 1.7 (2002 and 2003), 3.5 (2004), 3.8 (2005), 5.1 (2006) and 7.7 (2007), 7.8 (2008) and 8.1 (2009), 8.4 (2010) and 7.4 (2011), 7 (2012), 6.4 (2013), 5.7 (2014), and 4.7 (2015), respectively.

Indicator 8.10: population aged 6 and over that uses internet services, by sex and geographic area

INDICADOR 8.10: POBLACIÓN DE 6 Y MÁS AÑOS DE EDAD QUE HACE USO DE SERVICIO DE INTERNET POR SEXO, SEGÚN ÁMBITO GEOGRÁFICO, 2002-2015

(Porcentaje respecto del total de población de 6 y más años de edad por sexo)

Ámbito geográfico	2002		2003		2004		2005		2006		2007		2008	
	H	M	H	M	H	M	H	M	H	M	H	M	H	M
Total	12.0	10.3	13.1	11.4	17.6	14.1	21.2	17.4	24.9	19.8	34.9	27.2	35.5	27.7
Lima Metropolitana 1/	22.0	18.1	21.6	19.7	25.5	20.5	27.2	23.1	32.6	27.0	51.1	40.7	51.5	40.6
Resto país	7.9	6.8	9.7	8.0	14.3	11.3	18.7	14.9	21.5	16.6	28.1	20.9	28.6	21.8
Área de residencia														
Urbana	16.8	14.1	18.3	15.8	24.0	18.9	28.3	22.9	32.4	25.7	45.3	34.9	45.4	35.1
Rural	1.4	1.0	1.5	1.1	2.8	2.0	4.4	3.2	6.2	4.1	8.8	6.0	10.1	6.7
Región natural														
Costa	16.8	14.4	18.1	16.1	23.2	18.8	26.6	22.1	30.8	24.8	44.6	35.0	44.2	35.0
Sierra	7.8	6.1	8.9	6.7	12.9	9.4	16.9	12.8	19.9	15.0	26.0	18.7	27.2	19.8
Selva	3.7	3.4	4.8	5.0	7.8	6.4	11.1	8.9	13.8	10.6	19.4	15.1	21.8	16.4

Ámbito geográfico	2009		2010		2011		2012		2013		2014		2015	
	H	M	H	M	H	M	H	M	H	M	H	M	H	M
Total	37.9	29.8	38.9	30.5	39.7	32.3	41.6	34.6	42.4	36.0	43.1	37.4	43.2	38.5
Lima Metropolitana 1/	55.7	44.9	56.0	44.9	57.4	48.7	61.3	52.8	62.2	54.6	63.6	56.9	61.8	57.1
Resto país	30.1	22.8	31.4	23.8	31.9	24.6	32.9	26.0	33.5	27.1	33.9	27.9	35.0	29.3
Área de residencia														
Urbana	48.0	37.5	48.7	38.2	49.6	40.3	51.9	42.8	52.4	44.2	52.9	45.6	52.7	46.6
Rural	11.1	7.1	12.1	7.4	12.1	7.7	12.2	8.5	12.8	8.9	13.3	9.5	13.9	9.8
Región natural														
Costa	47.6	37.9	48.1	38.5	49.6	41.4	52.8	44.8	53.6	46.6	55.1	48.8	54.8	49.7
Sierra	28.5	20.8	29.9	21.8	30.7	22.3	31.1	23.1	31.6	24.0	31.1	24.0	31.5	25.1
Selva	22.8	17.3	24.3	18.2	22.3	17.8	23.0	19.0	23.5	19.2	23.9	20.1	25.5	21.0

The gap faced by women in Peru is once again corroborated by other information prepared by the Peruvian National Institute of Statistics and Computer Science (INEI, for its acronym in Spanish), which shows that although internet access and use by men and women increased considerably between 2007 and 2015, the percentage of women surfing the web still lags 4.7 percentage points behind men—a gap that once again widens, it should be noted, when we look at the rural population (Peruvian National Institute of Statistics and Computer Science (INEI), 2017 A: 110-111).

Peru: internet use by women and men, 2007-2015 (Percentage)

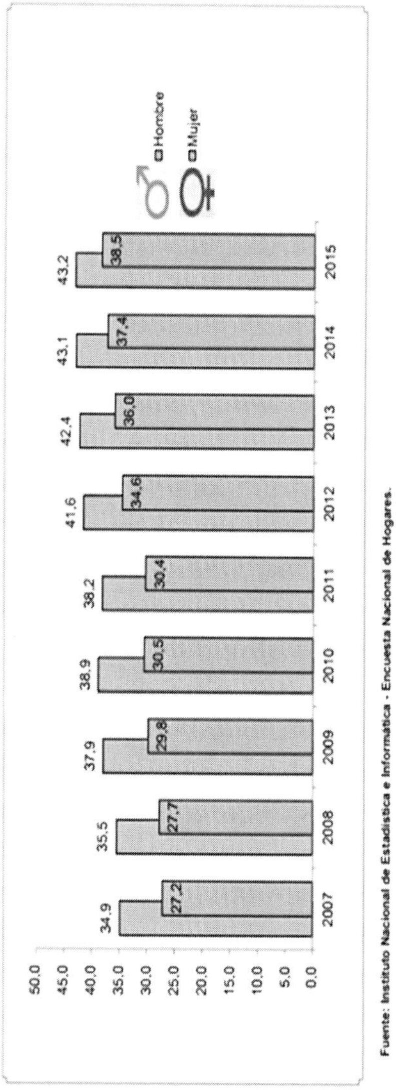

Indeed, as we can see here, between 2007 and 2015 women faced gaps of 7.7, 7.8, 8.1, 8.4, 7.8, 7, 6.4, 5.7, and 4.7, respectively.

c) *Women and men who use the internet, by age groups.* The INEI's analysis of internet access by age group once again shows a greater proportion of internet use by men, with the largest divide found among people between the ages of 19 and 24 (5.9 pp), and the smallest divide among those between the ages of 12 and 18 (2.1 pp) (INEI, 2017 A: 112).

Peru: women and men who use the internet, by age groups, 2015 (Percentage)

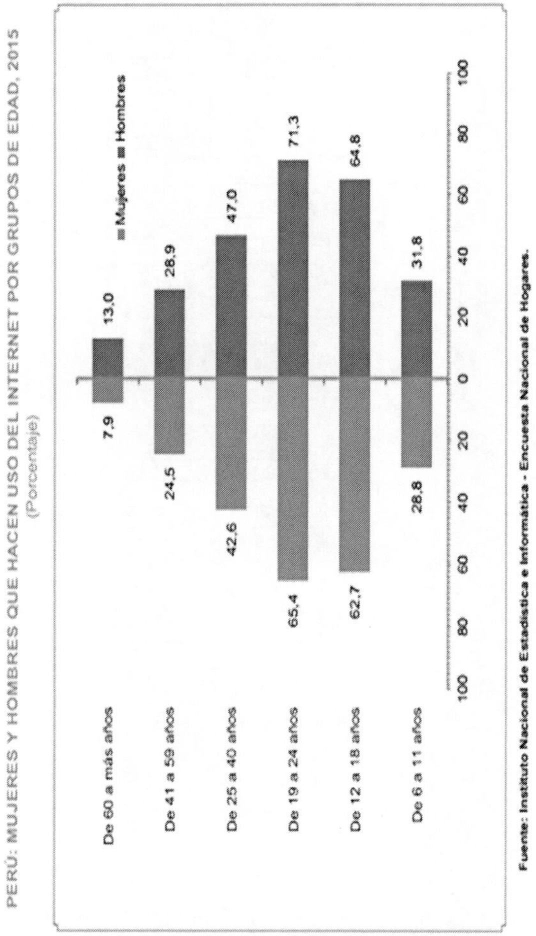

d) *Women and men with internet access by level of education and employment*. One important finding that deserves special note is the fact that the gap between men and women decreases when women have more opportunities; that is, when they have more education or more job opportunities. According to the INEI, the gap in internet use is reversed, with women coming out on top among university students—where women lead men by 1.3 percentage points—as well as among the employed population:

> *[I]t is possible to observe a clear pattern of higher rates of internet use among women than men. Salaried employed women have higher rates of internet use than men. These data show that, as women successfully insert themselves into the job market, as in the case of salaried female employees, they gain an advantage over men in terms of the percentage of technology users. It might be supposed that this is the result of relatively low rates of female participation in the job market, where skills in ICTs use are one variable that is taken into account when hiring many salaried women* (INEI, 2016 A: 112-113).

These data showing higher percentages of internet use among female university students and salaried women may be due to the fact that gender roles, spaces, and attributes force women to make a greater effort than men to achieve their life plans and earn professional recognition in society.

Peru: internet use by women and men, by education level, 2015 (Percentage)

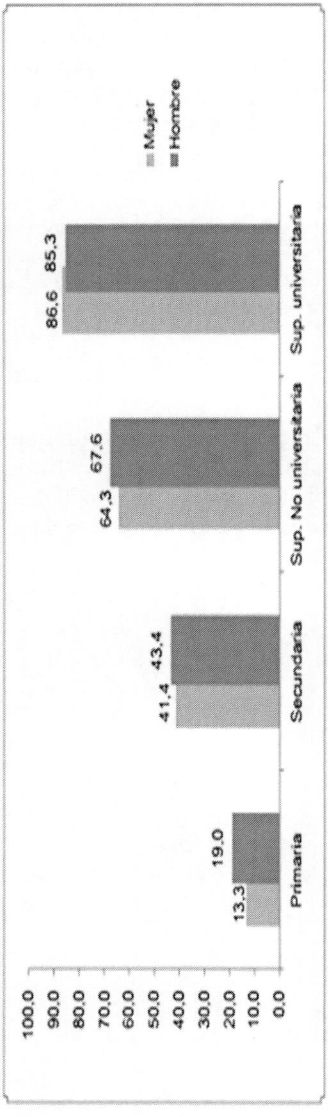

Fuente: Instituto Nacional de Estadística e Informática - Encuesta Nacional de Hogares.

Peru: internet use by women and men, by education level, 2015 (Percentage)

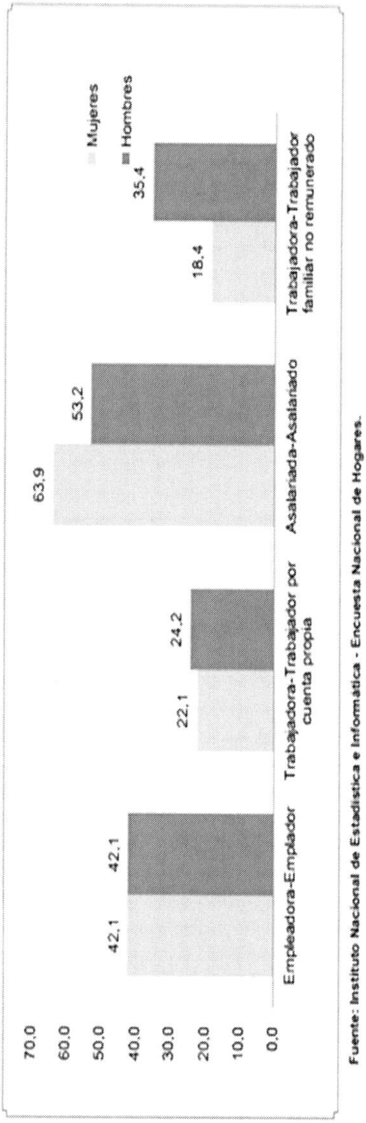

e) *Women and men with internet access by ethnicity*. When looking at data for indigenous women, we once again find them at a disadvantage due to the confluence of discrimination based not only on gender, but also on ethnicity and rurality. In this case, women manifestly face confluent factors of discrimination (multiple or intersectional discrimination), which calls for an analysis based on gender, interculturality, and intersectionality.[1] This, combined with disadvantages such as distance[2] and the lack of accessible means of transport and communications, makes it more difficult for them to access the internet (INEI, 2016 A: 114). All of this is expressed in a digital divide of 6.6 per cent between indigenous men and women, and 4.3 per cent between non-indigenous men and women.

---

[1] In regard to this matter, see Section 3 of this paper: "The need to Incorporate the Gender Approach or Perspective in the Constitutional Analysis of the Prohibition of Discrimination and Women's Access to ICTs, the Internet, and Non-discrimination."

[2] Women often find internet access to be particularly difficult in areas where it is predominantly available outside the home or in unsafe or inaccessible places and/or where social or cultural norms and safety concerns may restrict freedom of movement and the ability to visit, for example, publicly accessible facilities. Publicly accessible facilities in schools, libraries, or other community anchor institutions are particularly important (UNESCO, 2017: 29).

Peru: internet use by women and men, by ethnicity, 2015 (Percentage)

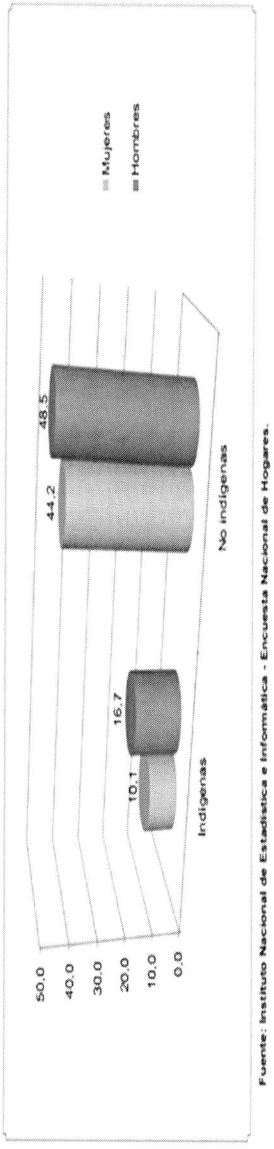

e) *Rural men and women who use mobile telephone services*. Looking beyond the significant increase in women who use mobile telephone services as of 2015, the data also show gender divides, especially with regard to rural women, once again revealing the confluence of at least two factors of discrimination (rural women), combined with the conditions of poverty that, as a general rule, affect the rural population (INEI, 2016 B). Since 2011, the digital divide between women and men has evolved from 6.4 (2011) to 7.3 (2012), 6.4 (2013), 6.3 (2014), and 5.4 (2015).

Rural Peru: population aged 12 and over who use mobile telephone services, by sex, 2011-2015

Cuadro N° 2.23 Perú Rural: Población de 12 y más años de edad que usa el servicio de telefonía móvil, según sexo, 2011 - 2015 (Porcentaje)

Sexo	Año					Variación porcentual (2015 - 2014)
	2011 a/	2012	2013	2014	2015	
Total	52,1	58,2	64,3	66,6	70,3	3,7
Hombre	55,4	61,9	67,6	69,8	73,1	3,3
Mujer	49,0	54,6	61,2	63,5	67,7	4,2

a/ Los datos corresponden al periodo abril - diciembre.
Fuente: Instituto Nacional de Estadística e Informática - Encuesta Nacional de Programas Estratégicos 2011-2015.

f) *Activities performed by women and men who use the internet.* One especially interesting statistic offered by the INEI is that "[o]f the total men and women who use the internet, 88.5 per cent and 89.0 per cent, respectively, use it to communicate via email, chat, etc.; 83.9 per cent of men and 85.2 per cent of women, to obtain information; and 83.4 per cent of men and 80.1 per cent of women for entertainment activities" (INEI, 2017 B: 11). These figures are significant, showing that men are the ones who most use the internet for fun or entertainment. If we consider, furthermore, that according to the latest National Time Use Survey (ENUT, 2010), women in Peru work nine more hours a week than men; and that according to the INEI, female university students and salaried female employees are the ones who access the internet most (see Item c) in this section), we can conclude that access to and use of the internet and ICTs are indispensable for women in their struggle to achieve true equality in society.

Peru: population by sex and age group, according to types of internet activities

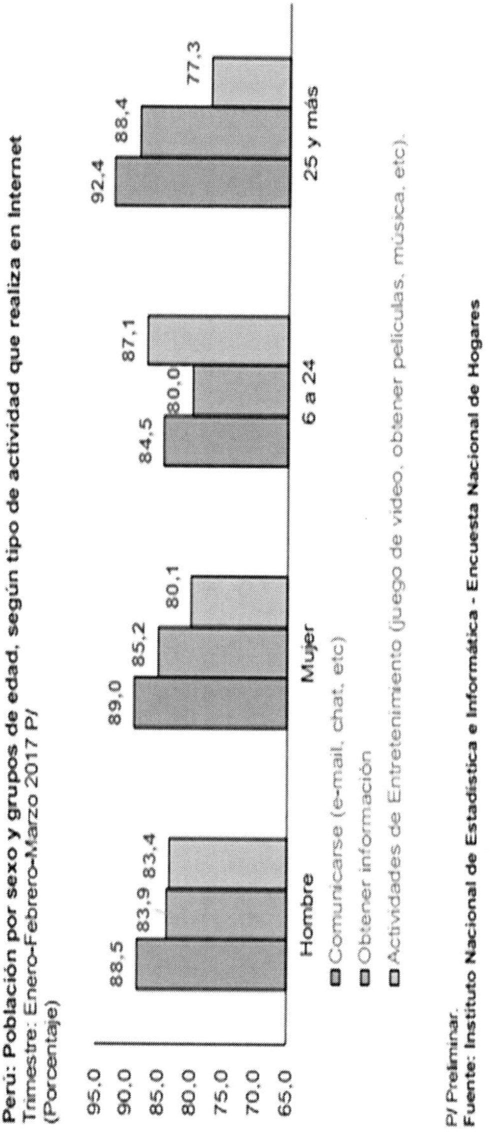

The analysis of this information shows that gender gaps in internet access are not just a numerical or percentage-based difference between men and women. What they represent is nothing more and nothing less than the consequence of "*situations of structural discrimination, which lead to social and economic exclusion, as well as influencing women's condition and position. (...)* ***Given that gender gaps express inequality and levels of wellbeing or difficulty among men and women, as well as degrees of national, regional, and local development, their reduction must be made a policy objective and a priority for public investment***" (emphasis ours) (Ombudsman's Office, 2012: 44).

In view of the foregoing, there is clearly an urgent need to address the problem of gender gaps in access to ICTs and the internet based on an approach prioritising gender, interculturality, and intersectionality. This is especially true given that—at least in Peru—this information was not specially prepared to detect gender gaps. Rather, it is general data on a matter where we can observe clear divides between men and women.

III. Need to Incorporate the Gender Approach or Perspective in the Constitutional Analysis of the Prohibition of Discrimination and Women's Access to ICTs and the Internet

Within the framework of the primacy of the human person and respect for her dignity (Sections 1 and 44 of the Constitution), the principle of equality and non-discrimination (in both its formal and substantive aspects) is not just an enforceable right expressly established in both Section 2, Subsection 2 and Section 191 of the Constitution, along with numerous international conventions on human rights; it is also the source of all other fundamental rights (Landa Arroyo, 2006: 17).

Despite the significant advances made in both normative terms and in the exercise of rights, reality continues to be marked by persistent discrimination committed both by the state and by private individuals. In the case of women, this situation is especially worrisome, since this discrimination is the result of gender relations based on sociocultural patterns of men's and women's conduct that reveal prejudices and customs rooted in the premise of men's superiority. As a result, even the legal system constructed on this premise failed to consider women as true holders of rights and obligations under equal conditions, thus making it necessary to reinterpret these structures from a gender perspective (Garcés Peralta and Portal Farfán, 2016: 107).

In the analysis of these power relations, which explain women's subordination to and oppression by men, it is vital to distinguish between the concepts of sex and gender. While an investigation into this topic is worthy of a more in-depth, interdisciplinary discussion, for the effects of this paper it will suffice to note that—according to the committee responsible for ensuring compliance with the Convention on the Elimination of All Forms of Discrimination against Women (CEDAW)—while the term "sex" refers to biological differences between men and women, the term "gender" refers to socially constructed identities, attributes, and roles for women and men and society's social and cultural meaning for these biological differences (CEDAW Committee, 2010: paragraph 5). This differentiation helps us to understand that biological differences are not the ones that put women at a disadvantage and subject them to oppression, along with the power relations forged on this basis; rather, it is the way in which this difference has been socially and culturally constructed.[3]

For its part, the gender approach or perspective is based on the existence of an asymmetrical power structure between women and men, constructed based on gender differences. This is what is defined nowadays as structural discrimination, i.e., that faced by society as a whole, based on social stereotypes in relation to one's belonging to a group that is oppressed by or subordinated to another. That is why this approach must be used to help design the intervention strategies aimed at achieving equal opportunities between men and women, in order to reverse discrimination in all areas of social relations.

To understand gender relations, it should be recalled that historically, patriarchal organization has led to inequality between women and men, and that in order to maintain this power, a rigid division of labour was created, symbolically linking masculinity to those attributes considered

[3] It is important to note that the evolution of gender perspective analysis has helped create a more complex and refined definition. Today, it has left behind the binary, essentialist conception of the sex/gender system (based on the binomial man/women differentiation) in favour of a constructivist conception that incorporates sexual diversity and protects the right not to be discriminated against based on sexual orientation or gender identity. For the effects of this paper, however, we will limit ourselves to the analysis of gender discrimination against women based on the mere fact of their being such.

positive, and assigning femininity attributes that were deemed less valuable, in both economic and social aspects. These sociocultural constructions of femininity and masculinity are expressed in what we typically refer to as gender roles, spaces, and attributes (Ruíz Bravo López, 1999).

In terms of gender roles, women are typically identified as mothers and men as economic providers and heads of households, resulting in the sexual division of labour whereby women and men are obligated to perform certain tasks for which they are "innately" prepared. This is one of the most powerful core ideas and mechanisms behind the perpetuation of gender discrimination.

It is in those spaces that are attributed based on gender where the aforementioned roles are acted out, identifying the public with masculinity and the private with femininity, thus creating an adverse impact on women. Finally, in terms of personality attributes or characteristics, it is assumed that men and women have a different "nature," associating femininity with emotion, daintiness, sacrifice, and resignation, and masculinity with objectivity, strength, reason, and competition.

Although women now work in the public space, it is because of these roles that they continue to lack the same opportunities as men, given that they are still expected to additionally perform a domestic role as caregiver, where men continue to have little participation. This fact is revealed in the First National Time Use Survey 2010 (ENUT) conducted by the INEI, which shows that Peruvian women work an average of nine hours more than men. This is just one example of how de facto discrimination exists in spite of the formal recognition of the right to equality, as evidenced in all areas of social life. Of course, this discrimination can also be clearly observed in the access to and use of ICTs and the internet.

In light of the foregoing, the need to introduce and mainstream gender perspective in the use of ICTs and the internet is not only an obligation, but an indispensable requirement in all of the state's actions, making it possible to integrate the needs and interests of men and women in the design, implementation, and evaluation of public policies so that they both benefit equally.

This obligation to incorporate gender perspective into women's access to ICTs and the internet is directly connected to the principle of/right to equality (in its substantive, material, or real dimension) and to non-discrimination, which are in turn derived from the Constitution and numerous international instruments ratified by Peru on matters of the protection and promotion of women's human rights. In addition to the provisions set forth in Section 2, Subsection 2 and Section 191 of the Peruvian Constitution, note should be made at the domestic level of Law 28983—the Act on Equal Opportunities for Men and Women (LIO, for its acronym in Spanish); Law 30364—the Act for the Prevention, Punishment, and Eradication of Violence against Women and Family Members; the National Gender Equality Plan 2012-2017; and the National Plan against Gender Violence 2012-2017.

However, for the state to adequately address these gender gaps that lay bare the limitations on women's access to ICTs and the internet, it must necessarily recognize that because women are not a homogeneous group—especially in a multicultural country such as Peru—it is also critical to utilize the approaches of interculturality and intersectionality, as established in norms such as Law 30364.

The *intercultural approach* refers to the need for interaction and dialogue among the different cultures that exist in Peruvian society, in a respectful and equitable manner, allowing for integration and coexistence based on diversity and the enrichment of this diversity.

Finally, *the intersectional approach*, also known as "multiple discrimination,"[4] takes into account the simultaneous confluence, in a person or a group of people, of different types of discrimination and disadvantage (gender, disability, poverty, etc.), resulting in a situation of greater vulnerability due to the negative impact of this convergence in terms of opportunities, as well as the access to and exercise of rights. Without a real awareness of the need to address the simultaneous coexistence or confluence of two or more factors of discrimination that may exacerbate the limitations faced by women when it comes to access to the internet and ICTs (as in the case of women living in poverty, those

[4] The "concept of 'multiple discrimination' is based on the idea of recognising that people may simultaneously belong to several disadvantaged groups, resulting in aggravated and specific forms of discrimination. This type of discrimination is characterized by the interaction of several suspicious factors, such as distinctions based on race or ethnicity, sex, religion, economic status, disability, etc. The way in which these factors of discrimination interact may vary, which has led to the use of different names to refer to this situation. This allows us to assert the existence of different manifestations of what we have up to now dubbed, more generally, 'multiple discrimination'" (Salomé Resurrección, 2015: 112).

without an education, or disabled women)—especially in a multicultural context such as Peru (indigenous and Afro-descendant women)—it will not be possible to adopt policies that guarantee their effective protection.

One aspect of particular importance in the analysis of discrimination, especially in countries such as Peru, is poverty, which is closely tied to women. Indeed, international studies show that 70 per cent of people living in extreme poverty are women (Organización No Gubernamental para la Cooperación Solidaria 2012: 6), who are affected by a complete or partial lack of education and the information necessary to assert their rights, with Africa, Asia, and Latin America ranking among the worst places in this regard (ibid.: 3). This situation is evident in Peru, where women continue to be the "*poorest of the poor*" (UNDP 2012: 16), due to a confluence of factors that result in multiple or intersectional discrimination. It is important to note here that the division of labour, assigned caregiving responsibilities, and time use—all of which are linked to gender stereotypes—help to explain the so-called feminization of poverty (Seara, 2015).

The importance of and need for the use of these approaches when addressing women's access to ICTs and the internet from a constitutional standpoint are tied to the specification process of human rights (which calls for an analysis of citizens' particular situation based on considerations such as gender, disability, cultural identity, and others) (Bobbio 1991: 109). It is crucial to bear in mind that the application of these approaches is not only a legally established obligation, but that they also enable the state to comply with its duty to guarantee the fundamental right to equality and non-discrimination, as expressly provided for in Section 2, Subsection 2 of the Constitution.

Lastly, there are a number of national norms that now incorporate a gender-based, intersectional, and intercultural approach in addressing discrimination against women; for example, the aforementioned Law 30364—the Act for the Prevention, Punishment, and Eradication of Violence against Women and Family Members; the National Plan against Gender Violence 2016-2021; and the recent National Plan against Human Trafficking 2017-2021.

IV. The State's Duty to Guarantee Women's Access to ICTs and the Internet based on a Constitutional Analysis: The Need to Incorporate Feminist Legal Methods in Constitutional Analysis

It is worth underscoring the intrinsic bond that exists between democracy and fundamental rights, given that only a truly consolidated democracy guarantees the effective force of all persons' fundamental rights, without distinction. As such, it can be said that there is no true democracy—understood as government and participation by the majority—without the recognition and protection of women's access to ICTs and the internet.

Under these circumstances, it is important to recall the duty of all constitutional, democratic states under the rule of law to guarantee human rights (Sections 1 and 44 of the Constitution of 1993; and Articles 1 and 2 of the American Convention on Human Rights), which includes their obligation to comply with the national and international commitments assumed with regard to the protection of these rights, since states must be held responsible for any failure to do so. This requires a study of the constitutional regimen for the protection of access to information on the part of persons belonging to groups that have historically faced discrimination, as in the case of women.

As previously noted, the obligation to guarantee women's access to ICTs and the internet is directly rooted in the principle of/right to equality and non-discrimination, as expressly recognised in the Constitution and multiple international instruments ratified by Peru in matters of the protection and promotion of women's human rights; and especially the Convention on the Elimination of All Forms of Discrimination against Women (CEDAW), ratified by the Peruvian state on September 13, 1982, and the Inter-American Convention on the Prevention, Punishment, and Eradication of Violence against Women (also known as the Convention of Belem Do Pará), ratified by Peru on June 4, 1996.[5]

---

[5] It should be remembered that, due to the special situation of vulnerability and discrimination faced by women, there emerged a need—as part of the aforementioned specification process of human rights—for specific international instruments for the protection of women's rights. These instruments do not substitute, but instead supplement, the framework of protection established in treaties of a more general scope.

One important point to be noted here is that, in addition to the treaties ratified by Peru,[6] the decisions of the international courts in charge of their enforcement—such as the Inter-American Court of Human Rights[7]—are also binding.

It must not be forgotten, however, that—by virtue of the provisions established in Articles 26 and 27 of the Vienna Convention on the Law of Treaties, and based on the principle of good faith—the different pronouncements (including notes and recommendations) of the international bodies responsible for supervising compliance with treaties (such as the CEDAW Committee or the Follow-Up Mechanism of the Inter-American Convention on the Prevention, Punishment, and Eradication of Violence against Women (MESECVI)), and even reports by specialised bodies (including reports by entities such as UNESCO, UNICEF, etc.), are also considered parameters for the interpretation of women's fundamental rights, even if they are not formally binding (i.e., "soft law").

In this regard, we must take into account the advances made by different international bodies that have recognised the need to incorporate the gender approach in access to ICTs and the internet as a way of guaranteeing women's fundamental rights, especially their right to equality and non-discrimination.

---

[6] Peru's mandatory compliance with these treaties is established in Sections 55, 3, and the Fourth Final and Temporary Provision of the Constitution of 1993, as well as Section V of the Preliminary Title of Law 28237—the Constitutional Code of Procedure. On the other hand, it is important to recall that according to the Peruvian Constitutional Court, treaties on human rights have a constitutional rank (PCC, April 24, 2006: 32-33; and PCC, October 28, 2015: 26).

[7] An increasing degree of relevance has been taken on by the so-called conventionality control, developed by the Inter-American Court of Human Rights in the cases of Almonacid Arellano v. Chile (2006) and Gelman v. Uruguay (2011). This technique for the normative control of internal law is based on the use of instruments from the Inter-American Human Rights System, in an effort to guarantee that national norms and internal actions are in accordance with the human rights conventions ratified by the state, as well as the interpretation of these conventions by the bodies responsible for their enforcement. In addition to the foregoing—especially given the state's responsibility to engage in conventionality control—there is also the need for an ever-greater use of international human rights law and international standards, which—as we have seen—include gender equality in the legal reasoning and resolution of cases. Some of the judgments under analysis have made indisputable advances, thus leading to high expectations for further development in the near future.

As a social democratic state, Peru is subject to the dialogue between international and internal law—the constitutionalization of international law and the internationalization of constitutional law. This brings with it a series of obligations that Peru must meet with regard to the effectiveness of fundamental rights (Alvites 2011: 122), in an effort to achieve substantive equality and equal opportunities for all persons, especially those in a situation that renders them particularly vulnerable. This circumstance is directly linked to the state's duty—as recognised by the Peruvian Constitutional Court (PCC)—to adopt all measures "*that, to varying degrees, are aimed at removing those obstacles that do not foster conditions of equal opportunities*" (PCC, January 6, 2006: 10), as well as the provisions set forth in Section 4 of Law 28983—the Act on Equal Opportunities for Men and Women, which call for the adoption of temporary measures of positive action to accelerate the de facto equality of men and women, which are not considered discriminatory.

Thus, in its substantive role as the promoter of women's effective fundamental rights, the state is bound to intervene, adopting measures to guarantee women's access to ICTs and helping to gradually transform the economic, social, or cultural order in an effort to contribute to effective equality as a principle and right, while guaranteeing the force of people's constitutional rights within the frame of a pluralist state that seeks to ensure that all people are able to achieve their life plans, with the sole limitation that they not violate the rights of others or disrupt the public order. It must be stressed that a social democratic state under the rule of law does not limit people's life plans. On the contrary, it seeks to intervene (in the social and economic order) in an effort to remove obstacles, thus aiding human beings in achieving—within a framework of true equality—the real effectiveness of their fundamental rights.

It is important to bear in mind that the state's obligation to adopt affirmative or positive actions that remove obstacles restricting women's rights is also expressly established by the international normative framework. Indeed, Article 4.1 of the CEDAW establishes states' adoption of special measures of a temporary nature aimed at accelerating de facto equality between men and women, measures that shall cease once the objectives of equal opportunity and equal treatment have been achieved.

This requirement is set forth in General Recommendation No. 25 of the CEDAW Committee (2004) on temporary special measures. With the goal of eliminating discriminatory dimensions of societal and cultural contexts that impede women's enjoyment of their human rights, this Recommendation provides for the application of temporary special measures as part of a necessary strategy and form of accelerating *the equal participation of women in all areas*. In 2014, this same Committee recommended the application of these measures—in a report issued specifically for Peru—to achieve women's substantive equality in all areas where they are underrepresented or face disadvantages (CEDAW Committee, 2014).

Based on the foregoing, we may conclude that it is constitutionally valid, in response to the gender divides that affect women and their access to ICTs and the internet, to evaluate the adoption of exceptional measures, provided such measures meet the indispensable concurrent requirements for their adoption, i.e., necessity, objectivity, temporariness, legality, and proportionality.

It is cause for concern, then, that in Peru's case—despite the growing consciousness of the importance of access to ICTs in guaranteeing fundamental rights—there is little being done to eradicate the discrimination faced by women in this regard. Indeed, this is so even though the state itself has become aware of such needs. The Ministry of Transportation and Communications, for example, has acknowledged that *"[t]he majority of people are unaware of the potential of ICTs. Beyond the technical barriers, many limitations to the incorporation of ICTs are social, cultural, or economic. Therefore,* ***the government's first objective should be to increase digital literacy, especially among disadvantaged groups, such as women****"* (emphasis ours) (Peruvian Ministry of Transportation and Communications, 2016: 6).

This situation is made worse, as we will see below, by the fact that—according to information from 2016 provided by the UN Economic Commission for Latin America and the Caribbean (ECLAC)—Peru has not even included the issue of "women and ICTs" in its digital policy focus (2016: 43):

Table 1: Issues Included in Digital Policies in the Countries of Latin America and the Caribbean

Cuadro 1
Temas incluidos en las políticas digitales en países de América Latina y el Caribe

Tema	ARG	BOL	BRA	CHL	COL	CRI	ECU	HND	MEX	PAN	PRY	PER	DOM	URY	TOTAL
Infraestructura	×	×	×	×	×	×	×	×	×	×	×	×	×	×	14
Gobierno electrónico		×		×	×	×		×	×	×	×	×	×	×	11
Difusión de TIC		×		×	×	×	×		×	×	×	×	×	×	11
Educación		×	×	×	×		×		×		×	×	×	×	10
Innovación digital		×	×	×		×			×	×		×	×	×	9
Desigualdad y pobreza		×	×		×	×					×	×	×	×	8
Marco normativo		×		×	×			×		×					5
Desarrollo de aplicaciones					×	×					×				3
Reducción de tarifas							×				×				2
Mujer y TIC				×											1

Fuente: ORBA de la CEPAL.

In light of the foregoing, a constitutional assessment of the limitations currently faced by women in their access to the internet, and, in general, to new information technologies—based on the obligation of the state and society to remove obstacles to the achievement of substantive equality—requires an evaluation of general proposals or suggestions such as the following:

a) Preparation of diagnoses and studies on Peruvian women's needs and problems in accessing ICTs, as well as the causes of these problems, along with any violations of fundamental rights that are now occurring due to this situation. Emphasis should be placed on the importance of preparing these diagnoses within a framework that is both unified and decentralised at the same time, i.e., taking into account the particularities of each of the country's geographic areas, as well as other criteria such as urban and rural population, education, poverty, etc. All of this is vital if we are to establish adequate and effective policies and strategies.
b) Identification of gender divides linked to women's limitations in accessing ICTs and the internet. While credit must be given to the work done thus far by the Peruvian National Institute for Statistics and Computer Science (INEI), which has provided us with statistics on women and their access to the internet and ICTs, we still believe this information could be refined in an effort to monitor this problem more extensively and specifically. More developed data regarding women's access to the internet, broken down by factors such as economic or social situation, or surveys among users themselves, could play an especially important role.
c) The proposals set forth in Items a) and b) would enable the formulation of suitable and comprehensive policies (by the public and private sectors involved) for the gradual review of the problems involved in women's access to ICTs and the internet. This includes the adequate planning and implementation of policies, plans, and actions, as well as their assessment and monitoring, with the application of gender-based, intersectional, and intercultural approaches to the establishment and implementation of strategies that help guarantee women's access to ICTs and the internet.

To prepare policies and action plans that adequately address the problem, it is first necessary to establish baselines, indicators, and goals. "The integration of gender equality goals and key performance indicators in all internet-related strategies, policies, plans, projects, and budgets is vital to effectively address the digital gender divide" (UNESCO 2017: 25).

d) The establishment of the aforementioned public policies must include, on the one hand, strategies and actions to train and raise consciousness among officials with regard to this problem, its direct repercussions on the country's improvement and development, and the state's obligation to guarantee real equality in access to the information society. On the other hand, it is critical to carry out social programmes, strategies, and actions for the promotion and training of women regarding the use of ICTs and the internet.
e) The establishment of plans that reverse this situation of discrimination against women in terms of access to new information and communications technologies requires the progressive transformation of deep-seated social and cultural patterns that affect the force of women's rights. To achieve this, it is necessary to establish programmatic policies and actions for digital literacy in education systems, and to design policies for services and applications. All of this requires a budget (funding) that guarantees an adequate design and effective compliance.
f) Although the majority of problems regarding this matter should be solved, as a rule, through general actions and public policies, we must be careful not to rule out the possibility that—in exceptional situations, based on an analysis of each specific case—there may be contexts where it could be helpful to resort to mechanisms (administrative or judicial) aimed at enforcing the protection of rights directly violated by limitations on access to the internet. This might even include evaluating the admissibility—its residual nature notwithstanding—of an action for the protection of constitutional rights (*amparo* proceeding), provided there is a true and imminent violation or a threat of violation of the constitutionally protected content of a fundamental right or rights.

Lastly, these real limits to women's access to ICTs and the internet, and the lack of a response to this discrimination on the part of the legal system, once again reinforce the need to incorporate so-called "feminist legal methods" into a constitutional and human rights analysis. The fact is that social structures, accepted by law, subordinate women and put them at a disadvantage (Alvites 2011: 121). As such, they must be addressed by the state in compliance with its duty to guarantee the right to equality and non-discrimination. With the goal of identifying viewpoints whose absence in the law results in gender-based discrimination, and consequently establishing legal alternatives aimed at solving this problem, Bartlett maintains that it is necessary to use the following methods (2011: 24):

a) The "woman question," which asks about the gender implications of a social practice or rule: have women been left out of the consideration?
b) Feminist practical reasoning, which challenges the legitimacy of the legal norms or situations of those who claim to speak, through rules, for society or the community, when in fact what they are doing is reasserting power relations that, while not evident at first, result in injustices that affect women or place them at a disadvantage upon analysing the context. In our opinion, this method is especially relevant in the analysis of restrictions faced by women in their access to and use of ICTs and the internet.
c) The consciousness-raising method, an interactive and collaborative process of articulating women's own experiences and making meaning of them with others who also articulate their experiences.

We believe these methods can help to challenge the knowledge of legal norms and situations that require revisiting and reinterpretation based on the problems faced by women. The objective is to propose alternatives—with regard to women's access to ICTs and the internet—that lead to solutions, especially given the undeniable constitutional relevancy of these cases, as we have seen.

It goes without saying that cases involving conflicts of rights or restrictions on women's rights will require the application of the so-called balancing test, in order to weigh the special circumstances and needs faced by women and ensure the effective force of their fundamental rights. Examples of the importance of balancing, in the specific case of internet access, may include evaluating the proportionality of affirmative access measures that seek to guarantee women's rights, or the conflict that may arise in situations involving the right to internet access among minor females or males, since such circumstances also involve the application of the principle of the child's best interest, as established in the Convention on the Rights of the Child (Article 3) and in Law 27337—the Code on Children and Adolescents (Section IX, Preliminary Title). In any event, these situations will require a more detailed analysis on a case-by-case basis.

V. Final Considerations

We, as women, make up approximately half of the world's population, and yet—despite the undeniable advances made in recent decades—we are still fighting to guarantee the full force of our rights on an equal footing with men. This struggle has become particularly important in view of new technological and scientific breakthroughs.

The foregoing inevitably leads us to reflect on our duties as legal professionals committed to guaranteeing the real effectiveness of the constitutional rights of those—such as women—who continue to face situations of discrimination.

As such, there is a clear need to study this new issue, one that has still been insufficiently examined from a legal perspective, but which requires legal solutions to circumstances that the state has thus far failed to address. Indeed, the state's failure to act is all the worse considering its constitutional obligation to guarantee the fundamental rights of all persons, and especially those who—for a number of reasons—find themselves in a particularly vulnerable position. This obligation, it should be noted, includes the adoption of measures—including affirmative actions—for such purpose.

Even if we acknowledge the importance of a conscientious analysis that helps to guarantee women's effective access to new information and communications technology, we must not overlook the fact that this analysis will be insufficient unless it is accompanied by mechanisms, tools, and, more generally, public policies that contribute to its effective compliance and implementation, preventing the violation of women's fundamental rights by the state and private individuals alike. It must likewise be borne in mind that the eradication of the different expressions of discrimination against women, and their inclusion as true citizens, will doubtlessly have a positive effect on the country's political, economic, and social development.

We would like to reiterate here that the purpose of this paper has been to present the information gathered with regard to women's access to ICTs and the internet; and to foster discussion and reflection on a situation that is in urgent need of a serious and rational debate, a debate that ultimately leads to the eradication of gender discrimination against women, in view of the growing consciousness of the universality, indivisibility, and interdependence of human rights.

The ultimate purpose here is nothing but respect for fundamental rights, breaking down the legal system and rebuilding it as part of the process of the constitutionalization of law, in keeping with the requirements inherent to new scientific and technological advances. Because these advances must, without fail, be placed in the service of all persons (regardless of gender, age, cultural identity, or other such factors), respecting those principles that must serve as an inspiration for all constitutional and democratic states under the rule of law.

Bibliography

ALVITES, E. (2011). "Derecho constitucional y métodos feministas. La interpretación del derecho a la igualdad y a la no discriminación para la protección de los derechos de las mujeres." In *Métodos feministas en el Derecho*. Lima: Palestra.

BARTLETT, K. T. (2011). "Métodos Jurídicos Feministas." In *Métodos feministas en el Derecho. Aproximaciones críticas a la jurisprudencia peruana.* Lima: Palestra.

BOBBIO, N. (1991). *El tiempo de los derechos*. Madrid: Editorial Sistema.

CEDAW Committee 2010. *Proyecto de Recomendación general N° 28 relativa al artículo 2 de la Convención sobre la eliminación de todas las formas de discriminación contra la mujer*, CEDAW/C/GC/28. Available at:
http://www.acnur.org/t3/fileadmin/Documentos/BDL/2012/8338.pdf?view=1.

CEDAW Committee 2014. *Observaciones finales sobre los informes periódicos séptimo y octavo combinados del Perú*. CEDAW/C/PER/CO/7-8. Available at:
http://tbinternet.ohchr.org/_layouts/treatybodyexternal/Download.aspx?symbolno=CEDAW/C/PER/CO/7-8&Lang=Sp.

ECLAC (2016). *Estado de la banda ancha en América Latina y el Caribe*. Available at:
http://repositorio.cepal.org/bitstream/handle/11362/40528/6/S1601049_es.pdf.

GARCÉS PERALTA, P. C., and PORTAL FARFÁN, D. C. (2016). "La protección de los derechos fundamentales de las mujeres en la jurisprudencia del Tribunal Constitucional: ¿más limitaciones que avances?" *Pensamiento Constitucional*, No. 21, pp. 107-162.

IACHR (2013). *Libertad de Expresión e Internet.* Office of the Special Rapporteur on Freedom of Opinion and Expression. Available at:

http://www.oas.org/es/cidh/expresion/docs/informes/2014_04_08_internet_web.pdf.

IACHR (2016). *Estándares para una internet libre, abierta e incluyente*. Office of the Special Rapporteur on Freedom of Opinion and Expression. Available at: http://www.oas.org/es/cidh/expresion/docs/publicaciones/INTERNET_2016_ESP.pdf.

IACHR (2017). *Informe Anual de la Comisión Interamericana de Derechos Humanos 2016*. Available at: http://www.oas.org/es/cidh/expresion/docs/informes/anuales/InformeAnual2016RELE.pdf.

LANDA Arroyo, C. (2006). *Constitución y fuentes del Derecho*. Lima: Palestra.

ORGANIZACIÓN NO GUBERNAMENTAL PARA LA COOPERACIÓN SOLIDARIA (2012). "Guía Didáctica: La pobreza tiene rostro de mujer." Burgos: AMYCOS. Available at: http://amycos.org/admcms/wp-content/uploads/2012/04/Guia DidacticaMujer.pdf.

RUÍZ BRAVO LÓPEZ, P. (1999). "Una aproximación al concepto de género." In *Sobre Género, Derecho y Discriminación*. Lima: Defensoría del Pueblo and Pontificia Universidad Católica del Perú.

SALOMÉ RESURRECCIÓN, L. M. (2015). "La 'discriminación múltiple' como concepto jurídico para el análisis de situaciones de discriminación." Master's Thesis in Constitutional Law. Lima: Pontificia Universidad Católica del Perú.

SEARA, M. (30 mayo, 2015). "La feminización de la pobreza: ¿desigualdad de género reducida a la pobreza?" Available at: http://www.vocesvisibles.com/mujer-y-pobreza/la-feminizacion-de-la-pobreza.

UNITED NATIONS 1993. *Vienna Declaration and Programme of Action*. Vienna: United Nations.

UNITED NATIONS 2011. *Information and Communications Technology for Development*. A/RES/66/184. Geneva: United Nations.

UNITED NATIONS 2016. *Documento final de la reunión de alto nivel de la Asamblea General sobre el examen general de la aplicación de los resultados de la Cumbre Mundial sobre la Sociedad de la Información*. Available at: http://unctad.org/es/PublicationsLibrary/ares70d125_es.pdf.

UN-Women 2015. "La Declaración y la Plataforma de Acción de Beijing cumplen 20 años." Available at: http://www.unwomen.org/-/media/

headquarters/attachments/sections/library/publications/2015/sg%20report_synthesis-sp-fin.pdf?la=es&vs=3454.
UN-Women 2017. *Las mujeres en el cambiante mundo del trabajo—Algunos datos que debería conocer.* Available at: http://interactive.unwomen.org/multimedia/infographic/changingworldofwork/es/index.html.
UNDP. *Estrategia de igualdad de género*. Lima: PNUD Perú. Available at: http://www.undp.org/content/dam/peru/docs/Empoderamiento/Estrategia%20de%20Igualdad%20de%20Genero%20de%20PNUD%20Peru.pdf.
UNESCO 2014. *Tendencias Mundiales en Libertad de Expresión y Desarrollo de los Medios*. Montevideo: UNESCO. Available at: http://unesdoc.unesco.org/images/0022/002297/229704S.pdf.
UNESCO 2017. *Recommendations for Action: Bridging the Gender Gap in Internet and Broadband Access and Use*. Working Group on the Digital Gender Divide. New York: United Nations.
PERU CONGRESS OF THE REPUBLIC Law 30364—the Act for the Prevention, Punishment, and Eradication of Violence against Women and Family Members. Legal Norms Bulletin of the Official Gazette *El Peruano*. Lima, November 23, 2015.
PERU CONGRESS OF THE REPUBLIC Law 28983—the Act on Equal Opportunities for Men and Women (LIO). Legal Norms Bulletin of the Official Gazette *El Peruano*. Lima, March 16, 2007.
PERU CONGRESS OF THE REPUBLIC Law 27337—the Code on Children and Adolescents. Legal Norms Bulletin of the Official Gazette *El Peruano*. Lima, August 2, 2000.
DEFENSORÍA DEL PUEBLO [Peruvian National Ombudsman's Office] (2012). "Indicadores para la incorporación del enfoque de género en los presupuestos de los gobiernos regionales." Lima: Serie Documentos Defensoriales, Document No. 23.
INSTITUTO NACIONAL DE ESTADÍSTICA E INFORMÁTICA [Peruvian National Institute for Statistics and Computer Science] (INEI) 2016 A. "Perú: Brechas de Género, 2016: Avances hacia la igualdad de mujeres y hombres". Available at: http://www.inei.gob.pe/media/MenuRecursivo/publicaciones_digitales/Est/Lib1388/Libro.pdf.
INSTITUTO NACIONAL DE ESTADÍSTICA E INFORMÁTICA [Peruvian National Institute for Statistics and Computer Science] (INEI) 2016 B. "Encuesta Nacional de Programas Estratégicos 2011-2015." Available at:

http://www.inei.gob.pe/media/MenuRecursivo/publicaciones_digitales/Est/Lib1366/index.html, p. 75.

INSTITUTO NACIONAL DE ESTADÍSTICA E INFORMÁTICA [Peruvian National Institute for Statistics and Computer Science] (INEI) 2017 A. "Peru: Evolución de los indicadores de los objetivos de desarrollo del Milenio al 2015." Available at: http://www.inei.gob.pe/media/MenuRecursivo/publicaciones_digitales/Est/Lib1413/libro.pdf.

INSTITUTO NACIONAL DE ESTADÍSTICA E INFORMÁTICA [Peruvian National Institute for Statistics and Computer Science] (INEI) 2017 B. "Las Tecnologías de la Información y Comunicación en los Hogares. Estadísticas de las Tecnologías de Información y Comunicación en los Hogares." Technical Report No. 2, January/February/March 2017. Available at: https://www.inei.gob.pe/media/MenuRecursivo/boletines/02-informe-tecnico-n02_tecnologias-de-informacion-ene-feb-mar2017.pdf.

MINISTERIO DE TRANSPORTES Y COMUNICACIONES [Peruvian Ministry of Transportation and Communications] (2016). *Políticas Públicas de Acceso a las Tecnologías de la Información y la Comunicación. Experiencias internacionales*. Available at: https://www.mtc.gob.pe/comunicaciones/regulacion_internacional/publicaciones/Publicaciones/Pol%C3%ADticas%20Acceso%20TIC.pdf.

MINISTERIO DE LA MUJER Y POBLACIONES VULNERABLES [Peruvian Ministry for Women's Affairs and Vulnerable Populations] Supreme Executive Order (Decreto Supremo) 008-2016-MIMP—Supreme Executive Order approving the "National Plan against Gender Violence 2016-2021." Legal Norms Bulletin of the Official Gazette *El Peruano*. Lima, July 26, 2016.

MINISTERIO DE LA MUJER Y POBLACIONES VULNERABLES [Peruvian Ministry for Women's Affairs and Vulnerable Populations] Supreme Executive Order (Decreto Supremo) 004-2012-MIMP—Supreme Executive Order approving the "National Gender Equality Plan." Legal Norms Bulletin of the Official Gazette *El Peruano*. Lima, August 18, 2012.

TRIBUNAL CONSTITUCIONAL [Peruvian Constitutional Court] File No. 5652-2007-AA/TC (Gambini Vidal case). Judgment dated November 6, 2008. Available at: https://tc.gob.pe/jurisprudencia/2008/05652-2007-AA.pdf.

TRIBUNAL CONSTITUCIONAL [Peruvian Constitutional Court] File No. 047-2004-AI/TC (case of the law allowing for the appointment of professors who have passed the public examination). Judgment dated April 24, 2006. Available at: http://www.tc.gob.pe/jurisprudencia/2006/00047-2004-AI.html.

TRIBUNAL CONSTITUCIONAL [Peruvian Constitutional Court] Files No. 0025-2005-PI/TC and No. 00262005-PI/TC (case of the Colegio de Abogados de Arequipa [Arequipa Bar Association], et al.). Judgment dated October 28, 2005. Available at: http://www.tc.gob.pe/jurisprudencia/2006/00025-2005-AI%2000026-2005-AI%20Admisibilidad.html.

TRIBUNAL CONSTITUCIONAL [Peruvian Constitutional Court] File No. 00015-2008-PI/TC (case of the Provincial Municipality of El Callao). Judgment dated January 6, 2010. Available at: http://www.tc.gob.pe/jurisprudencia/2010/00015-2008-AI.html.

THEMATIC TABLE 6: STATE OF LAW IN THE FIGHT AGAINST CORRUPTION

A Global Anti-corruption Agenda and Alternatives for Domestic Normative Change

José Ma. Serna de la Garza[1]

I. Introduction

Mexico has a severe problem with corruption. This is evident through various studies that have been carried out over the past years by Mexican as well as international institutions. For example, according to the National Survey on Corruption and the Culture of Legality (2015), 92 per cent of those surveyed believed that there is corruption in Mexico, compared to 5.8 per cent who believe there is no corruption. Similarly, the majority of those surveyed (80.9 per cent) believe that insecurity is the number one problem in the country, followed by 70 per cent who believe that it is corruption, and 56.9 per cent who believe it is drug trafficking (Marván, 2015: 68-69). On the other hand, according to data from Transparency International, between 1998 and 2014 Mexico fell 48 spots in the Corruption Perceptions Index, going from the rank of 55th to 103rd out of 175 countries included in the survey, with an overall score of 35 out of 100 (Transparency International, 2014).

Independently of the data gathered in surveys, each day citizens witness material acts of corruption: in the illegal housing developments proliferating throughout Mexican cities; in the dysfunctional criminal justice system, which is pitted against the rights of the accused and of the victims of crime; in prisons controlled by the inmates themselves; in electoral processes where public funding is used to support one candidate or another; in quotidian contact with the preventative police and transit police; in licensing processes for public works and in government purchasing programs; to name but a few examples.

[1] Researcher at the Institute of Legal Research (IIJ) at the Autonomous National University of Mexico (UNAM).

In addition, corruption has an impact on various aspects of national life. For example, it is well known that high levels of corruption limit Mexico's economic development. The World Economic Forum has pointed out that corruption is the key factor that stifles increased competition in Mexico, with insecurity and the inefficiency of bureaucracy in second place (World Economic Forum, 2016).

Corruption is also related to the growth of organized crime. The complicity of and the protection offered by particular state agents make possible the creation, growth, and strengthening of networks dedicated to illegal activities like narcotics trafficking, kidnapping and human trafficking.

In addition, corruption impedes the full enjoyment of many human rights. This occurs as the rights of the accused as well as those of victims are trampled by the machinery of the so-called criminal justice system; as well as in the impossibility of enjoying the right to education, health care and a safe natural environment. In this sense, as Transparency International (TI) has pointed out (Transparency International, 2015: 3):

> ... 'free' education costs more than poor people can afford, the most vulnerable are sold counterfeit medicine, and women are trafficked by criminal networks that pay bribes for protection. TI has witnessed how corruption leads to the mismanagement of many of our planet's most precious resources, undermines progress towards the Millennium Development Goals, fuels wars and prevents state-building, erodes sustainability and denies future generations a fair chance, if any chance at all.

There are many links between corruption and human rights violations. In fact, introducing a human rights perspective within programs to combat corruption has become one of the most promising paths for fighting against this scourge (International Council on Human Rights, 2009).

It must be said that corruption is not only a national problem, nor is it an issue that is related only to administrative law or criminal law. Rather, it is a global problem, and it is a problem for human rights, and thus, of constitutional law. We find evidence that it is a global problem in normative international regimes that are dedicated to organizing collective action to combat corruption in the international community. We consider corruption a constitutional issue because of the impact that it has on the full enjoyment of a variety of human rights as well as on the legitimacy of democratic institutions.

The purpose of this essay is to combine these two dimensions, the global and the constitutional. We explain the existence of a diversity of international state and non-state groups, which create a language, a discourse, and a series of proposals aimed at states and social actors within those states, that have led to the creation of a truly global agenda against corruption. We will then identify what implications this agenda could have for constitutional change in Latin America, a region which today is faced with the enormous challenge of finding institutional and normative solutions to efficiently combat corruption.

In order to achieve our aims, in the remainder of this introduction we will allude briefly to the origins and *raison d'être* of the concept of global governance, so as to create a theoretical framework through which we can adequately explain which actors are involved and what instruments are being used to combat corruption today, in our globalized world. Next, in Section II, we will look at a diversity of global actors and their proposals to combat corruption. We will conclude with Section III, in which we carry out a series of final reflections in which we attempt to make a general evaluation of the context in which Latin American states and other social actors are attempting to fight corruption more efficiently in the world today.

We begin by affirming that intense interactions at the level of the international community, with the participation of both state and non-state actors, are part of a phenomenon which has relatively recently been named global governance. This term is increasingly present in research agendas and debates in the social sciences. However, it is not a straightforward concept. On the contrary, it is a polysemic concept which can be interpreted in diverse ways.

In addition, it tends to be used in various senses, sometimes descriptively, other times prescriptively.

For some, global governance refers to a collection of rules and institutions created over the last decades to organize collective action on a world scale, with the goal of attending to problems which are perceived as global (Finkelstein, 1995: 367-372). For others, global governance is part of a hegemonic discourse that is compatible with the dominant transformations taking place nationally and internationally, a discourse which contributes to legitimizing the market and private actors in areas previously understood to be part of the public sphere (Brand, 2005: 155-176).

We will not enter into this debate in depth here. However, for the purpose of this essay, I will identify some phenomena and processes which are elemental in all the analysis of this term, which require further academic research and reflection: 1) We are facing an unprecedented expansion in the formal and informal roles of international, multilateral institutions; 2) We are faced with a significant increase in the reach, density and level of influence that regulations generated internationally have on how national societies are organized; 3) We are witnesses to fundamental changes in the political, legal and ethical composition of state sovereignty and the relation between the state, citizens and the international community; 4) We can observe the formation of complex transnational networks of state and non-state actors that generate norms that regulate global issues and problems; 5) there is clear evidence that nation states are opening up to various international regimes, which have increasing relevance in the orientation of behaviors and social relations domestically, and finally; 6) We are witnessing a growing interpenetration of international law and national law, as between international institutions and national administrative apparata in diverse areas (Hurrell, 2002: 1-2).

Something about the way that collective actions are organized at a global level to attend to problems perceived as global has drawn the attention of social scientists, who seek an explanation, and also prescriptive guidance that allow us to organize these emerging systems of relations. Legal studies should not distance themselves from these issues.[2]

A true agenda of a global fight against corruption has emerged linked to this context called global governance, from which recommendations regarding regulatory change are directed at national governments as well as at a plurality of social actors active within them. Some of these changes have or can have a constitutional dimension, while others have a legal dimension. In the next section of this essay I will analyze some points of the said agenda, so as to link them to changes in legal and constitutional matters which have occurred or could occur in Latin America, in order to

---

[2] These are a few works that approach this problem from a juridical perspective: Goldmann, Matthias, "A Matter of Perspective: Global Governance and the Distinction between Public and Private Authority," *Global Constitutionalism*, vol. 5, Issue 1, March 2016, pp. 48-84; Laporta, Francisco, "Globalización e Imperio de la Ley. Algunas dudas Westfalianas," in Cancio Meliá, Manuel, *Globalización y Derecho. Anuario de la Facultad de Derecho de la Universidad Autónoma de Madrid*, no. 9, 2005, pp. 177-198; and Twining, William, "A Post-Westphalian Conception of Law," *Law and Society Review*, EUA, March 2003, Vol. 37, No 1, pp. 199-257.

combat corruption. The aim is to evaluate the possibility of incorporating some of the proposals put forward through this agenda in the fight against corruption in this region, although my investigation focuses specifically on the case of Mexico.

II. Global Actor and a Global Anti-Corruption Agenda

In this section, I will examine documents generated by a diversity of global actors, from which proposals or recommendations aimed at strengthening national strategies for fighting corruption are derived for nation states and social organizations within them.

Transparency International

For Transparency International,[3] stopping corruption means altering the old networks of power that control the rules of the game. It proposes centering the creation of legal frameworks that generate balances and counterbalances within institutions, as well as the creation of mechanisms that give voice to citizens. In this way, Transparency International suggests distinguishing between small-scale corruption (which affects access to basic public services for all citizens, but for the poorest in particular); and large-scale corruption (which strengthens powerful economic groups and contributes to perpetuating inequality). In addition, TI points out that there is interaction between national and international corruption, which manifests in numerous ways, "...ranging from transfers of stolen assets to opaque international business practices" (Transparency International, 2015: 7).

In terms of norms and regulations, TI emphasizes the necessity to increase transparency and access to information, the creation of mechanisms to fight impunity and corruption within police forces and in the justice system, and the advantages of implementing international standards through coordinated national efforts by public and private sector groups.

Taking these elements into account, we could well say that Mexico has experienced important reforms in terms of transparency and the public's access to information. This is the case of the reforms to Article 6 of the Mexican Constitution in 2007 and 2014, which established the public

[3] Transparency International is a non-governmental organization founded in 1993, which has as its objectives to promote transparency and access to public information, as well as fighting corruption.

character of all information in possession of public institutions, trusts, and public funds, as well as of any physical or moral person or union which receives public funding and executes public funds or realized acts of authority at the federal, state or municipal levels (the withholding of which can only be temporarily observed for reasons of public interest and national security, according to the terms set out in law). In addition, it was decided that the principle of maximum publicity should prevail in the interpretation of this right, and that those who are "obliged subjects" under the statutes on transparency should document every act that derives from the carrying out of their powers, responsibilities, or functions. Moreover, it was established that the information on one's private life and personal information are protected in the terms and with the exceptions fixed in the corresponding statutes; and that any person, without showing special interests or justifying its use, can have free access to public information regarding their personal records or to the rectification of their records. In addition, it was ordered that mechanisms of access to information and efficient procedures for reviewing the said information should be substantiated before autonomous, specialized and impartial organizations at the national and state levels.

The norms regarding transparency are there. However, we are faced with an important structural problem: there is a reduced social base using the system for requesting access to information. In Mexico, the system for requesting access to information is used by a small number of citizens: 10 per cent of requests are made by journalists, 20 per cent by NGOs and 30 per cent by businessmen. Specialists, men, and high-income people predominate among those who request information, which is to say, disadvantaged groups are those less likely to use the system (Consejo Internacional de Políticas de Derechos Humanos, 2011: 22).

In a review of how systems of access to information work in 14 countries carried out by the Open Society Justice Initiative,[4] it was shown that public officials are often more worried about *who* is requesting information than they are about *what* is being requested. Because of this, the Open Society Justice Initiative recommends that national governments clarify with public servants and other personnel involved in public organizations that

[4] The Open Society Justice Initiative is a program of Open Society Foundations, a private philanthropic organization in the United States founded in 1979 by millionaire George Soros, whose mission is to support the emergence of societies in which governments are accountable to citizens, to support democracy, the respect for human rights, human dignity, and the rule of law.

discrimination in the reception of requests and in the provision of information is unacceptable and will be met with disciplinary and potentially legal consequences. In addition, they recommend that civil society organizations should monitor freedom of information practices, investigate suspected incidents of discrimination, present legal cases when discrimination is detected, and attempt to impose sanctions as established in anti-discrimination laws (Open Society Justice Initiative, 2006: 176-180).

Similarly, in a 2009 report, the Carter Center indicated that asymmetry in Latin American societies exists to the extent that the most vulnerable groups possess less knowledge and less capacity to employ the mechanisms to access information, although they are often those who have the greatest need of obtaining the said information.[5] Due to this, the Carter Center recommended that governments in the region take specific measures to mitigate structural disadvantages, because otherwise many in society will be excluded from the potential benefits of access to information (Carter Center, 2009: 2).

Perhaps one of the key missing ingredients in Mexico is a greater participation by civil society, which is another aspect highlighted by TI. In this respect, TI points out that to advance in the fight against corruption, it is important that there should be strong pressure and a broad public commitment: "This commitment will reinforce the demand for solid institutions and give a strong mandate for political leaders to comply with the promises they have made" (Transparency International, 2015: 16).

It must be clarified, however, that in the recent creation of the National Anticorruption System (SNA) in Mexico, through constitutional and legal reforms approved between 2015 and 2016, the participation of organizations and well-known figures in civil society was crucial. This participation will remain key in the launch and maintenance of the new mechanisms of this system, which is just beginning to take shape nationally.

---

[5] The Carter Center is an organization funded by former U.S. President Jimmy Carter, which has as its mandate supporting human rights, democracy, freedom, improved health, conflict prevention and relief from human suffering. One of their programs is the Global Access to information Program. See more at their webpage: www.cartercenter.org.

Transparency Mexico

Transparency Mexico (TM) is linked with Transparency International, and was created in 1999 as a non-governmental organization with the objective of approaching the problem of corruption through a holistic perspective, shifting public policies and private attitudes to generate concrete changes which could have an impact on the institutional framework and on the culture of legality in Mexico.

Among the most important contributions of TM is the National Index of Corruption and Good Governance, which is the first historic study of corruption in the country, which allows for the evaluation of changes in terms of corruption in public services and administrative procedures in various years between 2001 and today.[6] TM also has a Program of International Anti-Corruption Conventions and Mechanisms, created in 2009, directed at measuring how Mexico is advancing in the implementation of international anti-corruption conventions through a series of metrics known as the Unique Indicators System (SUI).

TM also created the Initiative for the Strengthening of Institutionality in Social Programs, directed at reinforcing the protection of social programs, through a platform of public information which is neutral and independent, and which establishes a series of minimum attributes of institutionality in social policies. This institutionality comes about through the existence of a minimum of 20 attributes classified into four categories:

a. Rules of operation and other guidelines;
b. Mechanisms of transparency and accountability;
c. Mechanisms of control and supervision;
d. Mechanisms of civil society participation.

Spending on social programs is linked to the elaboration of public budgets and the execution of budgets. The overseeing of these processes on the part of civil society organizations has been considered a mechanism to combat corruption. In this sense, the International Budget Partnership

---

[6] Public services and administrative procedures include: paying taxes; receiving care during medical emergencies; obtaining military service cards, passports or proof of studies; requests for permission to open a business; vehicle verification; taking a case to court; or accessing basic public services, like drinking water, sewage, streetlights, and paving. See Transparency Mexico's website at: www.tm.org.mx.

(IBP)[7] launched an initiative called Open Budgets, with the aim of promoting public access to budget information and the adoption of responsible budget systems. Basically, what this Initiative does is generate methodologies, tools, and instruments to train civil society organizations in many countries so that these groups can carry out what Open Budgets calls monitoring and analysis of budget processes along all stages (formulation, approval, execution, evaluation and auditing).[8] The key premise of these activities is that when budget processes are closed and hermetic, the doors are opened for public administrators to fund programs which are unpopular and inappropriate, misspending public funds and fostering corruption. Therefore, civil society must demand openness and intervene in every step of all public budget processes.

In order to reach this goal, the IBP and its partners around the world combine high quality analysis, which is accessible and timely, with public awareness campaigns and the defense of rights, through intense work in coalitions and with formal and informal actors (governments, legislatures, auditors, civil society and the media). The IBP has produced conceptual tools like inclusive budget processes, a public finance accountability ecosystem; and citizen budgets,[9] and has created an Open Budget Index[10] via the Open Budget Survey,[11] through which what they call a global civil society movement for transparency, accountability and participatory budget processes.

Returning to our sketch of TM, which in 1999 created a Process Monitoring Unit, which has as its aim to make public information regarding economic development, and make known the particularities and conditions encountered in contracting or licensing procedures monitored

---

[7] The International Budget Partnership (IBP, created in 1997) came about from the activities of a civil society organization in India named Disha, which since the mid-1980s began to analyze public budgets in India so as to contribute to an improvement in public policies and the provision of services, especially for the poor.

[8] See their website at: www.internationalbudget.org.

[9] These are documents designed to present key information on public finances in a manner that is accessible to the general public.

[10] This measures transparency in the creation of public spending budgets worldwide.

[11] This is a broad and comprehensive analysis and survey that evaluates whether governments give the public access to information regarding the drafting of budgets and opportunities to participate in national level budget processes.

by TM.[12] It is worth noting that this monitoring system came about in the framework of a system created by TI linked to the concept of integrity pacts, which are an idea and tool for government authorities and bidding corporations, developed with the goal of reducing corruption and wasteful spending in public sector contracts. These instruments demand the collaboration of both parties to contracts, facilitated by a civil society organization and an independent monitoring group which contribute to supervising all of the phases of the contract to ensure the pact is honored.

This issue brings up a reflection that is linked to the constitutional and legal dimension, referring to the regulations for the adjudication of contracts for acquisition, rental, and public sector services, as in conventional international law, the regulation of public contracts and their connection with anti-corruption measures are relevant. In this essay, we will only point out that Article 9 of the United Nations Convention against Corruption establishes a series of norms relative to public contracts.

As is well known, corruption in public contracting processes happens both on the side of government and on the side of corporations. That is why it is also worth mentioning the Global Reporting Initiative,[13] whose mission is to support companies, governments and other organizations in understanding and communicating about the impact of corporations on the critical issues of sustainability, climate change, human rights, and corruption, among others. Through a system of reports, this institution has generated a global standard of guidelines for the elaboration of sustainability memos by companies who wish to evaluate their economic, environmental and social practices. In their reports, there are data about how companies act during public bidding processes.[14] This information makes it possible to make public (nationally and globally) when companies participate in acts of corruption during the said processes.

Global Integrity

Global Integrity is a non-governmental organization that seeks to promote transparency and accountability among governments worldwide, through

[12] In this monitoring scheme, TM designates "social witnesses," who are people who "adopt" (so to say) a public contracting process, in order to follow it through various stages and make public information related to the process.

[13] The Global Reporting Initiative is an international, non-governmental independent institution which is an official participant in the United Nations Program for the Environment.

[14] www.globalreporting.org.

cutting edge research and technologies that inform, connect and empower public and private organizations which are working to foster more open societies.[15] One of the projects in which Global Integrity is most involved is called the Open Government Partnership, which is a volunteer initiative that seeks to obtain concrete commitments from governments toward their citizens, to promote transparency, empower citizens, fight against corruption, and deploy new technologies to strengthen governance. This Alliance has developed an Independent Review Mechanism (MRI), which carries out bi-annual evaluations of each participant in the alliance.

Mexico began participating formally in the Alliance in 2011,[16] and by 2013 the first Progress Report (2011-2013) was published by the MRI. In this report the commitments of the Mexican government are listed (they are categorized under access to information, citizen participation, accountability, technology and innovation for transparency and accountability); there is a review of the level of compliance (which is either complete, in process, or unstarted); the timeliness of compliance to commitments is considered, and there is a review of the results of each commitment, identifying the important challenges in terms of public service, public integrity, public resources, secure communities, and corporate accountability (Open Government Partnership, 2013).

For example, one of the commitments (Number 23) is called Mining For All, and its objectives include: promoting more transparency and better accountability in the mining sector to jumpstart development and social wellbeing. This commitment seeks, at a minimum, to: 1) elaborate together with civil society a diagnostic of the existence, quality, accessibility or lack thereof of geographical, statistical, socio-environmental, fiscal, financial and administrative information related to the mining sector; 2) based on this diagnosis, guarantee access to information in an opportune and adequate manner, aligned with the concept of open data and within a regulatory framework valid from November 2013 to October 2015; and 3) build proposals to eliminate obstacles to transparency in the mining sector in a collective manner between government and civil society, identified through the diagnosis carried out from November 2013 to October 2015

---

[15] See this organization's website at: www.globalintegrity.org.

[16] Entering into the Alliance requires creating a Tripartite Technical Secretariat (STT) as a permanent and institutionalized space of dialogue and decision-making regarding processes of open government in Mexico. It includes one representative of the federal government (the head of the Secretariat of Public Service) a representative of the National Institute for Access to Public Information and the Protection of Personal Data, and a coalition of civil society organizations.

(Open Government Partnership, 2013: 71).

It is worth pointing out that commitments do not always translate into concrete actions. For example, in looking at the poor results of the Mining for All commitment, the Progress Report (2011-2013) noted the causes of this situation were the lack of willingness on the part of the three government agencies (the Secretary of Economy, the Secretary of Finance and Public Credit, and the Secretary of Agrarian Territorial and Urban Development) responsible for carrying out the proposals to improve transparency, including the pre-diagnosis carried out by civil society. In addition, this Report pointed to the lack of coordination between the said government agencies to work in favor of complying with the commitment, a failure which was never fully explained or accounted for (Open Government Partnership, 2013: 74).

Extractive Industry Transparency Initiative (EITI)

The above brings us to the Extractive Industries Transparency Initiative (EITI), which was formed as a global coalition of governments, companies and civil society organizations which works to improve openness and the responsible administration of revenues generated by natural resource extraction. In 2003, this coalition agreed to a Declaration of Principles to increase the transparency of payments and revenues in the extractive sector (EITI Principles) which, generally, proposes that the wealth generated from natural resources should benefit all citizens, and that this requires high standards of transparency and accountability.

Without going into detail, among the EITI's Declaration of Principles are: the importance of governments and corporations in the extractive industries in respecting transparency is highlighted, as is the need to improve the management of public finances and accountability; it is stated that improved transparency should be achieved within legal and contractual frameworks; and that financial transparency can improve conditions for national and international foreign direct investment, and thus, favor the principle and the practice of accountability by governments to all citizens with respect to revenue flows and public spending; in addition, it declares the desire to promote high levels of transparency and accountability in public life, governance and economic activity; and emphasizes the need for a broad, coherent and viable focus with respect to informing the public about payments, measures which should be easy to introduce and apply, and that the publication of payments in a given country should include all corporations in the extractive industries that are active there. Finally, the Declaration of Principles notes that all interested parties have important and pertinent contributions to make in the search for solutions; and that the interested parties include governments and government organizations, extractive industry companies, service companies, multilateral organizations, investors, and non-governmental organizations (Extractive Industries Transparency Initiative, 2013: 9).

In order to adhere to the EITI, governments must comply with a series of requirements, which implies the realization of important internal regulatory changes.[17] Whether governments adhere to the EITI standard or not, it is a guide for regulatory reform which seeks to increase transparency in the mining sector in Latin America. The EITI Principles constitute an agenda for social groups interested in promoting transparency in the mining sector of their own countries.

Global Organization of Parliamentarians Against Corruption

Founded in 2002 at the World Conference of Parliamentarians in Ottawa, the Global Organization of Parliamentarians Against Corruption (GOPAC), seeks to achieve accountability and transparency through efficient mechanisms against corruption, and promote participation and inclusive cooperation between parliamentarians, government, and civil society, as well as assisting and supporting parliamentarians in their work in pushing and legislating for government accountability and transparency.[18] There are two documents produced by this organization that are particularly relevant for this essay: the *Guidelines to Strengthen Oversight through Parliamentarian-Donor Collaboration* (GOPAC, 2013);[19] and another co-authored with the World Bank Institute, titled *Improving Democratic Accountability Globally* (World Bank Institute and GOPAC,

---

[17] The EITI has an International Council in charge of the EITI Standard, organized through a system of reports presented by participating states. This Council monitors and evaluates the progress of all the countries with respect to their compliance with the requirements of the Standard. All implementing nations must comply with the same global standard, and all are evaluated through a process called Validation. The Validation of the EITI examines the progress of the country with regard to EITI standards, analyzes its impact, and makes recommendations for strengthening the process and the improvement of governance in the sector. Depending on the result of the Validation, the country will be re-evaluated within a period of between three months and three years.

[18] Available at: http://gopacnetwork.org/es/.

[19] Available at: http://gopacnetwork.org/Docs/GOPAC_PN%20Guidelines_FINAL_ EN.pdf.

2013).[20] The first starts from the premise that parliamentarians have a key role to play in ensuring governments use their funds adequately, for defined ends, as well as in avoiding corruption and other forms of misuse of government reserves. The second is a manual that seeks to explain the instruments and tools that the legislative power can employ to oversee the government and contribute to the reduction of corruption in presidential systems. These tools are as follows:

> 1) formulating questions for the government; 2) questioning; 3) motions; 4) parliamentary commissions; 5) missions and reports; 6) Superior Auditing Institutions; 7) anti-corruption agencies;[21] and finally 8) advocacy groups.

Later, the manual refers to the contextual factors that determine the real functioning of the aforementioned tools, which include the type of government, the electoral system, political parties, social legitimacy, political culture, the administrative structure, external actors, sponsors, and interest groups. It concludes with the affirmation that the presence of a large number of oversight tools in and of itself is not enough to guarantee that oversight is carried out effectively, because it is possible that legislators do not use the tools at their disposal, or that they use them in an inefficient manner (World Bank Institute and GOPAC, 2013: 25).

III. Final Reflection

As I have examined elsewhere, one of the most important elements that characterizes the current phase of globalization is the emergence of a list of international problems or "global dangers," in the words of Beck, which cannot be solved by individual states, and whose solution will necessarily come from greater levels of interdependence: population explosion; environmental degradation; terrorism; water shortages; energy shortages and food shortages; epidemics; the use of deep sea resources; and corruption (Beck, 1998: 67-71). These are global problems that are urgent

---

[20] Available at: http://gopacnetwork.org/Docs/CO_Handbook_EN.pdf.

[21] In the Manual it is affirmed that in general, the effectiveness of organizations against corruption has been disappointing. Often—it is said—these organizations are captured by the government to protect their own leadership and/or to harass opposition leaders. "There have been no cross-country analyzes of the effectiveness of such agencies in curbing corruption. It can however be hypothesized that anti-corruption agencies are most effective when independent of government and free of political interference. In spite of the disappointing performance, anti-corruption agencies have become increasingly popular" (World Bank Institute and GOPA C, 2013: 17).

not just for national states, but that involve a wide diversity of organizations of varying kinds. In this essay, we have looked at what we have called global actors, as well as at their proposals. But it should be mentioned that there are already international regulatory regimes in regard to the fight against corruption. For example, there is the United Nations Convention against Corruption (General Assembly Resolution 58/4, October 31, 2003), the Inter American Convention Against Corruption, ratified by the 35 member-states of the Organization of American States (including Mexico and Peru), and the Organization for Economic Development and Cooperation (OECD) Convention on Combating the Bribery of Foreign Public Servants in International Business Transactions.

The global agenda of the fight against corruption is visible to everyone. There is also a diversity of actors and groups, internationally and nationally, state and non-state, who have ideas, suggestions, recommendations and proposals. In addition, they are all potential allies in the fight against the scourge of corruption that causes so much damage to society today.

I will end on a reflection of Lord Russell-Johnston (former President of the Parliamentary Assembly of the Council of Europe), in which it is clear that to fight corruption it is not enough to change regulations, rather, there is a need for strategies of deeper intervention in government and societies (Johnston, 2005: 71):

Since corruption is essentially an evasion of legislation, I could just say that it is not the law that counts so much as the way it is determined by the efficacy of the administrative and judicial structures through which it operates and the political and economic culture of the country in which it is applied. And when a country is deeply mired in corruption—when bribery is an accepted part of everyday living, a necessary part of the income of police and officials—extrication is hugely difficult.

Bibliography

BRAND, Ulrich (2005). “Order and Regulation: Global Governance as a Hegemonic Discourse of International Politics?” *Review of International Political Economy*, vol. 12, No. 1.

CARTER CENTER. *Americas Regional Findings and Plan of Action for the Advancement of the Right of Access to Information*, Americas Regional Conference on the Right of Access to Information, April 28-30, 2009.

CONSEJO INTERNACIONAL DE POLÍTICAS DE DERECHOS HUMANOS (ICHRP) (2011). *La Integración de los Derechos Humanos en la Agenda de combate a la Corrupción: Retos, Posibilidades y Oportunidades*. Geneva.

EXTRACTIVE INDUSTRIES TRANSPARENCY INITIATIVE (2013). *El Estándar del EITI*, Secretaría Internacional del EITI, Norway, July 11, 2013.

FINKELSTEIN, Lawrence (1995). "What is Global Governance?" *Global Governance*, vol. 1, no. 3.

GOLDMANN, Matthias (2016). "A Matter of Perspective: Global Governance and the Distinction between Public and Private Authority," *Global Constitutionalism*, vol. 5, Issue 1, March 2016.

GOPAC (2013). *Guidelines to Strengthen Oversight through Parliamentarian-Donor Collaboration*. Ottawa, Ontario, November 2013.

HURRELL, Andrew (2010). "Emerging Powers, Global Order and Global Justice", Lecture delivered at the IILJ International Legal Theory Colloquium, Spring 2010, *The Turn to Governance: The Exercise of Power in the International Public Space*, New York University Law School, January 20, 2010.

INTERNATIONAL COUNCIL ON HUMAN RIGHTS (2009). *La Corrupción y los Derechos Humanos, Estableciendo el Vínculo*, International Council of Human Rights Policies, Technological Institute and Higher Education of Monterrey, Versoix, Switzerland and Monterrey, Nuevo León, Mexico, 2009.

JOHNSTON, Russell (2005). "The legislative approach to fighting corruption", United Nations Office against Drugs and Crime, *Global Action Against Corruption: The Mérida Papers*, United Nations, Vienna, 2005.

LAPORTA, Francisco (2005). "Globalización e Imperio de la Ley. Algunas dudas Westfalianas", in Cancio Meliá, Manuel. *Globalización y Derecho. Anuario de la Facultad de Derecho de la Universidad Autónoma de Madrid*, no. 9.

MARVÁN Laborde, María *et al.* (2015). *La Corrupción en México: percepción, prácticas y sentido ético, Encuesta Nacional de Corrupción y Cultura de la Legalidad*, in the collection *Los Mexicanos vistos por sí mismos, Los Grandes Temas Nacionales*, UNAM, Mexico.

OPEN GOVERNMENT PARTNERSHIP (2013). *Mecanismo de Revisión Independiente (MRI): México, Informe de Avance 2011-2013*. Washington, DC.

OPEN SOCIETY JUSTICE INITIATIVE (2006). *Transparencia y Silencio, Encuesta sobre Leyes y Prácticas del Acceso a la Información en Catorce Países*, *Open Society Institute*, Nueva York.

Transparency International, *Corruption Perception Index 2014: Results*, 2014. Available at: https://www.transparency.org/cpi2014/results.

TRANSPARENCY INTERNATIONAL, *Strategy 2015*, Berlin, Germany, 2015. Available at: https://www.transparency.org/files/content/ourorganisation/TI_Strategy_2015.pdf.

TWINING, William (2003). "A Post-Westphalian Conception of Law", *Law and Society Review*, EUA, Vol. 37, No. 1. March 2003.

WORLD BANK INSTITUTE and GOPAC (2013). *Improving Democratic Accountability Globally: A handbook for legislators on congressional oversight in presidential systems*, November 2013. Available at: http://gopacnetwork.org/Docs/CO_Handbook_EN.pdf.

WORLD ECONOMIC FORUM (2016). Global *Competitiveness Report 2015-2016*. Available at: http://reports.weforum.org/global-competitiveness-report-2015-2016.

The Constitutional Anti-corruption Principle and the Office of the Comptroller General of the Republic

Erika García-Cobián Castro[1]

I. Introduction

Corruption is a topic of concern for constitutional law, given its harmful effects on fundamental rights—especially on the rights of society's most vulnerable individuals or groups—as well as its destructive impact on the core principles of a constitutional and democratic state under the rule of law.

In acts of corruption, the exercise of the state's power is abused and diverted to satisfy personal or private interests, ignoring the limits placed on this power by the Constitution and the rest of the legal system, and thus undermining the conceptual foundations and the legitimacy of a state limited by law, and particularly by constitutional law.

For this reason, the checks and balances among government branches and constitutional entities—as one of the defining principles of the constitutional state—must fine-tune the quality and effectiveness of their instruments, including the governmental control exercised by the National Control System and the Office of the Comptroller General of the Republic,

[1] Erika García Cobián, Master in Constitutional Law graduated from the Pontificia Universidad Católica del Perú, and Master in Fundamental Rights graduated from the Universidad Carlos III in Madrid, Spain. Master in Latin American Studies graduated from the Universidad de Salamanca, Spain. Currently pursuing her Doctor of Law degree at the Pontificia Universidad Católica del Perú. Teacher in the Constitutional Law area at the Pontificia Universidad Católica del Perú and a member of the Constitutional Law and Fundamental Rights Research Group at the same university. Senior Advisor to the Governance sector of the German Agency for International Cooperation (GIZ).

as its governing body, for the purpose of protecting the public budget and the state's resources.

In such context, this paper seeks to address a problem that has proven especially critical in Peru this year, and which may be summed up as a kind of skepticism with regard to the role that the Office of the Comptroller General of the Republic—as a constitutionally autonomous entity with direct competencies in the control of public spending—should play in the fight against corruption, and its contributions to the enforcement of the constitutional anti-corruption principle.

Expressions of this skepticism can be found, for example, in the survey of the Peruvian population conducted by *El Comercio* newspaper and IPSOS-APOYO regarding the institutions in which Peruvians trust, published on October 1, 2017. In this survey, the Office of the Comptroller General ranks twenty-sixth out of a total of thirty-two institutions. The survey also shows that 33% of the people interviewed trust this institution, while 55% do not (2017).

Elsewhere, we have the statements made by the current president of Transparency International, who says that if the Peruvian Office of the Comptroller General "has been notable for anything, it is for decades of total inability and ineffectiveness in the prevention and punishment of public corruption" (Ugaz, 2017).

It has become commonplace to hold the Office of the Comptroller General of the Republic at fault for the inactivity or inhibition of government officials, under the argument that the supervisory entity's controls and intervention constitute obstacles to public management.

On the other hand, note should also be made of the questions raised by a group of administrative law scholars and litigation attorneys regarding the bill that sought to broaden the powers of the Office of the Comptroller General, allowing it to investigate, rule on, and punish public officials for their functional administrative responsibilities. These challenges were based on a supposed excess of power on the part of the Office of the Comptroller General that might affect the state under the rule of law and the statutes applicable to public officials. There were also questions regarding the very makeup of the sanctioning powers included in the bill, with critics arguing that these powers allegedly violated the principles of legality, due process, *non bis in idem*, and proportionality, among others (Danós, 2010). With regard to these sanctioning powers, it should be noted that there is currently a challenge of unconstitutionality being heard against Law 29622, which amended Law 27785—the Organic Act on the National Control System and the Office of the Comptroller General of the Republic, and broadened the Office's powers in sanctioning proceedings involving functional administrative responsibility.

In light of the foregoing, the objective of this article is to present a series of elements for the analysis—from a constitutional law standpoint—of the role of the Office of the Comptroller General of the Republic in the fight against corruption. This analysis seeks to help form a critical and constructive judgment with regard to the Office's institutional potential and performance in enforcing the anti-corruption principle contained in the Peruvian Constitution, within the framework of a constitutional state, and ultimately to the benefit of fundamental rights.

II. The Constitutional Anti-Corruption Principle

The anti-corruption principle in a constitutional state presupposes a concept of corruption that—in the words of Bustos—must be useful to constitutional law in at least three senses. It must explain the importance of the relationship between corruption and the force of the Constitution; it must make it possible to analyze those constitutional problems that stem from corruption; and it must inspire criteria of interpretation and action against corruption to diminish the threat of violation, or the actual violation, of the Constitution and the fundamental rights contained therein (2010: 72).

It is thus important to review the concept of corruption established in the most recent National Plan for the Fight against Corruption 2012-2016. This Plan defines corruption as the "undue use of power to obtain an irregular benefit, whether of an economic or non-economic nature, through the violation of a duty to comply, to the detriment of the legitimacy of authority and the person's fundamental rights" (Peruvian Prime Minister's Office, December 9, 2012).

It is clear that the concept established by the Plan lays bare the relationship between corruption and the Constitution, by noting the harm that corruption does to fundamental rights, as well as the legitimacy of authority. Nevertheless, in an effort to further highlight corruption's impact on the Constitution, the phrase "to the detriment of the legitimacy of authority and the person's fundamental rights" might be substituted with "to the detriment of the contents of the Constitution, thus incurring a violation of human rights and the legitimacy of the exercise of power in the constitutional state."

In a similar vein, Fernández coincides with Bustos, arguing that:

> (…) public corruption is not only the problem of the ruler whose legitimate mandate has been infringed upon by the greed of the dishonest public official. Rather, it is one of the most significant pathologies that may befall a social democratic state under the rule of law, since it not only limits the ability of public administrations to meet citizens' demands, but it also directly violates the principles that govern social coexistence, contravening its ethical and legal rules, and even going so far—in the most serious of cases—as to pose a threat to the very survival of the democratic regimen. (2011: 46-47)

As part of this approximation to the concept of corruption, the jurisprudential line developed on the matter by the Peruvian Constitutional Court (PCC) also offers an important supplementary framework. The Constitutional Court's jurisprudential doctrine has revealed a process in which increasing value is placed on the fight against corruption as an important right that must be protected by the Constitution.

In earlier cases, the Court's rulings emphasised the seriousness of acts of corruption, equating them with terrorism and drug trafficking, and thus situating the fight against corruption as one of the primary objectives of the state's criminal policy. The Court stated that "(…) the Constituent Assembly (had) noted a particularly harmful aspect of acts of corruption, given the magnitude of the damage they caused to the substantive group of values recognised by the Constitution." In light of this, it urged the branches of government to be especially diligent in fighting corruption, in accordance with the ethical values that must prevail in any social democratic state under the rule of law (PCC, July 21, 2005, legal merits: 59 and 65).

Later on, in a second phase of development, the Constitutional Court reinforced the obligation established in the Constitution with regard to the fight against corruption, assigning it the force of a mandate derived from the Constitution, specifically Sections 39 and 41, which establish that "all public officials and employees are in the service of the Nation," and that the term for the running of the statutes is longer in the case of "crimes against the public administration or government property." As a result, compliance with this mandate was deemed legally enforceable (PCC, April 23, 2007: 11).

In a third and subsequent phase, the Constitutional Court introduced the anti-corruption principle as a constitutional principle. The Court ruled that the body of constitutional law required all forms of corruption to be fought using mechanisms of parliamentary political review (Sections 97 and 98 of the Constitution), ordinary judicial control (Section 139 of the Constitution), constitutional judicial control (Section 200 of the Constitution), and administrative control, among others. It declared that this principle

> (…) is binding for the traditional branches of government, to which we must add the Constitutional Court, which must act in compliance with its duty of concentrated and diffuse constitutional jurisdiction, taking concrete constitutional measures to strengthen democratic institutions and prevent avoid a direct attack against the social democratic state under the rule of law, as well as the integral development of the country. (PCC, August 29, 2007: 54-55)

In this third phase, the Court insisted that the fight against corruption is a right deserving of constitutional protection, based on the democratic order clause contained in Section 43 of the Constitution, together with Sections 39 and 41, which hold that "[a]ll public officials and employees are in the service of the Nation"; and that they are thus in the service of the greater good and subject to responsibility for their actions (PCC, May 3, 2012: 16).

With regard to the *constitutionalization* of the fight against corruption, note should be made of the *constitutionalization* of a positive dimension of the anti-corruption principle: the so-called principle of "good management," implicitly constitutionalized, according to the Constitutional Court's interpretation, in Title I, Chapter IV of the Constitution: "On Public Duty," as well as Section 39 of the Constitution (PCC, November 14, 2005; May 3, 2012). The Constitutional Court additionally makes reference to Section 44 of the Constitution, establishing that the obligations contained in this precept "are basic duties of the state: to defend national sovereignty; to guarantee the full force of human rights; to protect the population from threats to its safety; *and to promote the general wellbeing, which is rooted in justice and in the integral and balanced development of the Nation*," and that these duties also apply to public officials and servants (May 3, 2012: 15).

The Constitutional Court's jurisprudence highlights the constitutional relevance of the fight against corruption, as well as its enshrinement as a constitutional principle.

Indeed, the Court has used the anti-corruption principle as a parameter for the objective validity of norms, public policies, or acts by public entities or officials in a range of cases that it has examined. The constitutional anti-corruption principle has become a factor in weighing decisions, when the force of this right comes into conflict or interrelates with certain other fundamental rights or constitutionally protected rights (Montoya, 2016).

These two constitutional functions of the anti-corruption principle must also be taken into account when analyzing the legal configuration and actions of the Office of the Comptroller General of the Republic, along with other bodies of governmental control, in terms of the role they are obligated to play in the fight against corruption.

III. Office of the Comptroller General of the Republic: External Control of Public Spending

It is vital to the very concept of the Constitution to have a constitutional body, vested with autonomy and independence, which is assigned the mission of controlling the implementation of the state's budget, or public spending under state management, given the constitutional relevance of the public budget.

The public budget is a tool used to achieve the state's purposes by establishing public revenues and spending, as well as a concrete budget distribution and allocation, based on the state's priorities, objectives, and goals (Petrei, 1997: 17; Kresalja and Ochoa, 2009: 682). This is particularly important in view of the public budget's social facet, as well as its direct relation to the realization of fundamental rights.

Thus, for example, Section 77 of the Political Constitution of Peru establishes that *"[t]he budget equitably allocates public resources. Its programming and implementation are based on criteria of efficiency in basic social needs and decentralisation."*

Accordingly, any control of budget management must seek to ensure that the economic and financial exercise of the public administration is carried out with respect for the will of the Parliament, and in compliance with the formal and substantive legal conditions necessary to achieve the objectives set forth when formulating the approved public budget (Vallès, 2003: 29-30), as well as to meet the population's basic social needs, ultimately acting with respect for the people's fundamental rights.

In comparative law and democratic systems, the high degree of specialization now required for the duties involved in the implementation of the budget by the public administration has given rise to the need to create specialized entities. These entities are responsible for aiding the legislative branch in the exercise of its duty to oversee the administration's economic/financial management, providing processed, technical information on the implementation of the budget. These entities are bodies for the external control of public spending, also known as Courts of Auditors (Vallès, 37) or Offices of Comptrollers General, or by their standardized denomination as Supreme Audit Institutions (SAIs).

A "Supreme Audit Institution" is defined as the public agency that, by virtue of its legal powers, exercises the most important duties in the public auditing of the state—regardless of what it is called, or how it is created or organized (INTOSAI). Its typical duty is to "verify, audit accounts, review, supervise, control, (or) inspect" (INTOSAI) the use and management of public resources in the state, as an expression of the necessary control of public spending by the administration in a constitutional state.

Under Peruvian constitutional law, the Office of the Comptroller General of the Republic (CGR, for its acronym in Spanish) is an autonomous constitutional entity and the governing body of the National Control System, responsible for supervising the lawful implementation of the state's budget, public debt operations, and all acts by those institutions subject to its control (Political Constitution of Peru, 1993: Section 82). The Constitution is supplemented by Law 27785—the Organic Act on the National Control System and the Office of the Comptroller General of the Republic, which specifies that the CGR governs all structured and functionally integrated agencies for control, standards, methods, and procedures, which have been created to conduct and carry out governmental control.

Governmental control is defined in the Organic Act on the National Control System as all preventive or corrective supervision of the acts and results of public management, including the evaluation of systems for administration, management, and control, based on criteria of efficiency, effectiveness, economy, transparency, legality, and faithfulness to policy guidelines and action plans, on a decentralized basis.

Government control may take the form of control of legality or management, financial control, evaluation of internal controls, or other forms of control deemed useful, depending on the entity and the subject matter in question. Governmental control must also *"aim its operations at strengthening and ensuring transparency in the management of entities, as well as promoting values and responsibility among public officials and servants"* (Law 27785, 2002: Section 16). The foregoing is directly tied to the obligation to contribute to and promote transparency, public ethics, and the fight against corruption in the state, its agencies, and its officials.

IV. Contributions by the Office of the Comptroller General of the Republic in Guaranteeing the Force of the Anti-Corruption Principle in a Constitutional State

As noted above, the constitution of a constitutional state imposes the obligation to fight all forms of corruption, as a prerequisite for the enduringness of democratic institutions that guarantee a responsible, citizen-oriented public management. Among the different mechanisms and institutions at the disposal of the state in order to control corruption is the mechanism of administrative control, as exercised by the CGR in its role as the governing body of the control system (Landa, 2006: 364 ff.; PCC, August 29, 2007).

The institutional configuration of the CGR, as designed in Peruvian constitutional law, is a response to the theoretical and institutional developments with regard to Supreme Audit Institutions and their role in the fight against corruption.

In the Santiago Declaration of 2013, the Organization of Latin American and Caribbean Supreme Audit Institutions (OLACEFS, for its acronym in Spanish) acknowledged that

> the role played by SAIs in the fight against corruption, by virtue of their legal powers, results in the strengthening of their own legitimacy and citizens' trust in them. (…) In this respect, it should be borne in mind that the different international anti-corruption conventions currently in force have reconfigured the role played by SAIs in the promotion of integrity, including awareness of the fact that corruption is a violation of human rights. (emphasis ours.)

In light of the foregoing, OLACEFS declares that it will "continue taking on the challenges posed by the highest demands citizens may make of their public authorities, particularly in matters of the fight against corruption, the development of a culture of transparency, and the active inclusion of citizens in processes of public deliberation" (2013).

For its part, the Evaluation and Control Office of the Oversight Commission of the Supreme Audit Institution of Mexico performed a comparative study of Supreme Audit Institutions around the world (2005),[2] concluding that these institutions were called on to play a predominant role in the fight against corruption, in a globalized context in which this phenomenon has increased in complexity, specialization, and effectiveness. The study finds that Supreme Audit Institutions are able to contribute—via their duties, attributes, and supervision and control mechanisms—to the achievement of the state's modernization and to government accountability, as strategic guidelines in the current fight against corruption (2005: 18).

It is interesting to note here that in Peru, the CGR has the specialized duty to control compliance by the state's entities and officials with their legal obligations related to the management and implementation of public resources. As part of this duty, the CGR is responsible for issuing technical decisions on whether or not national, regional, and local entities have complied with their statutory obligations. These duties on the part of the CGR are aligned with what is known as the control of legality and are aimed at protecting public resources and the proper functioning of state administration, as well as preventing and fighting against corruption, in turn helping to meet people's needs and guarantee their fundamental rights.

If, during its control of legality in the use of public resources and the public budget, the Office of the Comptroller General of the Republic identifies the irregular handling of the public budget, likely violations, or acts entailing alleged criminal, civil, or administrative liability, the CGR shall then bring legal actions in an effort to determine all applicable responsibilities.

The CGR must report cases of alleged criminal and civil liability to the Government Attorney General's Office and carry out actions before the judicial branch, in defense of the state's interests with regard to the protection of the public budget, the prohibition of corruption, and good public administration. Ultimately, such actions are aimed at helping to

---

[2] The investigation included the study of Supreme Audit Institutions in the following countries: Argentina, Australia, Bangladesh, Canada, Chile, Colombia, Costa Rica, Denmark, the United States, Great Britain, Iceland, New Zealand, Peru, Thailand, Venezuela, Germany, Brazil, Spain, France, Holland, Uruguay, China, South Korea, and Japan.

clarify and determine all responsibilities through the system in place for the administration of justice.

In terms of criminal liability, there has been a gradual and quite significant increase in positive results achieved through control reports filed with the judicial branch. Thanks to a diagnosis performed with the support of German cooperation, implemented by GIZ in 2008, it was found that just 7% of all control reports resulted in a guilty verdict in the court system against those accused of acts of corruption (Perú 21, May 10, 2010). As of February 2017, control reports resulting in a guilty verdict in the court system for acts of corruption had jumped to 87%.[3]

Meanwhile, in criminal proceedings underway against regional governors accused of serious crimes of corruption between 2014 and 2017, the CGR has submitted reports and documents to the Government Attorney General's Office and the judicial branch, based on the Office's investigations into twenty-two regional governors (CGR 2017a).

On the other hand, starting in 2011—the year that the CGR was granted sanctioning powers to determine functional administrative responsibility and impose the respective sanctions, in accordance with Law 29622 and its Regulations, approved by Supreme Executive Order (Decreto Supremo) 023-2011-PCM—all alleged administrative responsibilities detected in audits conducted by the CGR and by institutional control offices must now be investigated and ruled on in a sanctioning administrative proceeding handled by the CGR and the Superior Administrative Responsibilities Tribunal, which reports to the said Office.

Since 2011, a total of 999 public officials have been found administratively responsible, and sanctions have been imposed for administrative offences committed in the implementation of the public budget (CGR 2017b).

---

[3] A positive result in the judicial branch is understood to mean the issuing of at least one guilty verdict in a criminal proceeding in which there may be more than one defendant. Source: Peruvian State Prosecutor's Office. Office of the Comptroller General of the Republic.

The Challenge of Unconstitutionality Filed against Law 29622—the Act Amending the Organic Act on the National Control System and the Office of the Comptroller General of the Republic, and Expanding Powers in Sanctioning Proceedings Involving Matters of Functional Administrative Responsibility

As noted in the introduction to this paper, there have been several challenges to the expansion of the CGR's sanctioning powers in matters of functional administrative responsibility involving public officials and servants under the scope of its control who have been accused of alleged irregularities, as established in a Control Report.

By way of background, it should be recalled that prior to the passage of Law 29622, a number of institutions and attorneys specializing in administrative law had asserted the alleged unconstitutionality of Bill 4210/2010-CGR, which sought to expand the powers of the CGR in sanctioning proceedings involving matters of functional administrative responsibility. These critics claimed that the bill established a framework of supervisory powers that exceeded the CGR's scope; that the powers for internal control and the implementation of disciplinary sanctions against public officials and servants were vested in the heads of each specific entity; that the bill would affect the state under the rule of law and the statutes applicable to public officials; and that it violated the principles of legality, due process, *non bis in idem*, and proportionality, among others (Government Attorney General's Office, 2010; Danós, 2010).

Following a debate in the Audit and Control Commission, the bill was passed by a Plenary Session of the Congress of the Republic, on the first vote, on November 18, 2010. The bill was signed on December 6 of the same year, becoming Law 29622—the "Act Amending Law 27785—the Organic Act on the National Control System and the Office of the Comptroller General of the Republic, and Expanding Powers in Sanctioning Proceedings Involving Matters of Functional Administrative Responsibility." The law was published the following day in the official gazette "El Peruano."

On August 20, 2015, a challenge of unconstitutionality was filed with the Constitutional Court against Section 1 of Law 29622 by the Bar Association of Arequipa, claiming the alleged violation of the right and principle of independence and impartiality in jurisdictional functions. The challenge argues that the sanctioning body is not independent from or impartial to the examining body's pronouncements in the sanctioning administrative proceeding, given that both bodies belong to the same institution, i.e. the Office of the Comptroller General of the Republic. As such, the challenge objects to the amendment made to Section 51 of the Organic Act on the National Control System and Office of the Comptroller General of the Republic, which was modified to read as follows:

> FIFTY-ONE: The sanctioning proceedings regarding the functional administrative responsibility of the offenders referred to in this Act consist of (2) levels.
>
> The first level, under the responsibility of the Office of the Comptroller General of the Republic, consists of an examining body and a sanctioning body. Both enjoy technical autonomy in their actions. The examining body carries out the investigations and proposes a ruling on the offences and sanctions to the sanctioning body. The latter issues a well-reasoned resolution, either imposing or dismissing the proposed sanctions.
>
> The second level, under the responsibility of the Superior Administrative Responsibilities Tribunal, rules on appeals against the decisions issued by the sanctioning body.

The challenge asserts that:

> (The sanctioning body) will exercise its sanctioning powers in favour of the proposals issued by the examining body, for the simple reason that if it were to dismiss the proposed sanction, this would lay bare mistakes in the investigation and the violation of due process by the Office of the Comptroller General itself. It is thus clear that both the examining body and the sanctioning body has the same interests [sic], that is, to conserve the credibility of all the actions it carries out, which therefore proves its lack of objectivity.

An exhaustive analysis of the constitutionality of the problem set forth and the challenges raised to it exceeds the scope of this paper. It should be noted, however, that the arguments referred to herein cannot be considered either exclusive or exclusionary in an analysis of the constitutionality of Law 29622. As we have argued throughout this paper, the anti-corruption principle must be taken into account as one of the constitutional principles in play, both as an objective value for the validity of laws and acts in the legal system, and as a form of weighing situation involving conflicts or confluence with other constitutionally protected rights.

It is thus necessary to bear in mind that the CGR, by virtue of its constitutional mission within the state—that is, to supervise the lawful implementation of the state's budget, public debt operations, and all acts by those institutions subject to its control—has significant potential to contribute to the normative force of the constitutional anti-corruption principle.

The CGR's sanctioning administrative power—as regulated in the Organic Act on the National Control System and the Office of the Comptroller General, amended by Law 29622, whether exercised in response to acts that hamper governmental control, or a failure to comply or violation of legal norms regulating public duties by the parties subject to its control—is, in principle, constitutionally legitimate in view of the need to contribute to the effective external control of public spending, administrative honesty in the handling of public resources, the principle of good management, and the constitutional anti-corruption principle, all of which are constitutionally legitimate purposes.

This power is not incompatible with Peru's body of constitutional law—even if there is no such power expressly provided for in the Constitution—if we consider the fact that the constitutional state allows for the legal recognition of "implicit powers" on the part of constitutional bodies, defined as powers that are not expressly included in the Constitution, but which are absolutely necessary in order for a constitutional body to effectively carry out the duties attributed to it by virtue of the Constitution (PCC, March 13, 2003).

It should be recalled here that, prior to the passage of Law 29622, there were proven instances of weakness in the effective control of actions by public officials and servants, when sanctioning powers regarding functional administrative responsibility remained exclusively in the hands of the heads of the public institutions to which the said officials and servants belonged.

The opinion issued on the bill expanding the CGR's sanctioning powers, written during the process for its approval in the Congress of the Republic, included the following information on the results of the control body's recommendations:

> The bill is primarily a response to the failure to implement the recommendations established in the control reports, which determine the functional administrative responsibility incurred by those entities which are the subject matter of the said reports. Indeed, these entities often refuse to define individual responsibilities, thus making it impossible to apply the corresponding sanctions. According to the Office of the Comptroller

> General of the Republic, out of a total of 466 recommendations made by that entity between 2001 and 2010, for example, just 34% have resulted in sanctioning administrative proceedings, with 27.04% currently underway and the rest pending. (…) The Office of the Comptroller General notes that this situation is due to a variety of factors, including: a) the absence of a standardised procedure for defining responsibilities, since there are multiple employment regimens in force in the public administration; and b) the fact that each entity is itself responsible for sanctioning its own personnel. (Congress of the Republic, 2010b)

As for the argument set forth in the challenge of unconstitutionality filed against Law 29622, on the other hand, it should be noted that while the guarantees of due process—which include the principles of independence and impartiality[4]—are applicable in sanctioning administrative proceedings, the jurisprudence of the Inter-American Court of Human Rights[5] and the Constitutional Court (PCC, November 14, 2005: 18; PCC, August 7, 2008: 33) has established that because administrative authorities are bound by the Constitution and the fundamental rights contained therein, the application of these guarantees must be adapted to the characteristics inherent to the administrative sphere, taking into account that "final and binding administrative resolutions can be appealed through a contentious administrative suit," in accordance with Section 148 of the Constitution.

The principles of judicial independence and impartiality referred to in the challenge are supplemented by the General Administrative Proceedings Act, which establishes that "[a]dministrative authorities shall act without any type of discrimination against the subjects they supervise, granting

---

[4] "The right to be tried by an independent and impartial judge or tribunal is a fundamental guarantee of due process." Constitutional Court judgment kept in File No. 00156-2012-PHC/TC (Tineo case): 49.
Article 8.1 of the American Convention states that, "Every person has the right to a hearing, with due guarantees and within a reasonable time, by (…) [an] independent and impartial judge or tribunal, (…) in the substantiation of any accusation of a criminal nature made against him or for the determination of his rights and obligations of a civil, labour, fiscal, or any other nature."

[5] "(…) when the Convention refers to the right of everyone to be heard by a 'competent judge or tribunal' to 'determine his rights,' this expression refers to any public authority, whether administrative, legislative, or judicial, which, through its decisions determines individual rights and obligations. For that reason, this Court considers that any State organ that exercises functions of a materially jurisdictional nature has the obligation to adopt decisions that are in consonance with the guarantees of due legal process in the terms of Article 8 of the American Convention." Inter-American Court of Human Rights. *Constitutional Court v. Peru*. Merits, Reparations, and Costs. Judgment dated January 31, 2001: 71.

them equal treatment and protection in the proceedings, and ruling in accordance with the legal system, in keeping with the greater good" (Section IV, 1.5).

Section 252 of the General Administrative Proceedings Act, on the other hand, establishes that:

> To exercise sanctioning powers, it is first mandatory to follow the legal or reglementary procedure in force, characterised by:
>
> 1. **A structure that differentiates between the authority that conducts the investigative stage, and that which rules on the application of the sanction** (emphasis ours).

The principle of impartiality in administrative proceedings is defined in the General Administrative Proceedings Act, which holds that administrative authorities are prohibited from acting in a discriminatory manner toward the subjects they supervise in an administrative proceeding, and must grant them equal protection and treatment.

With regard to this matter, there is a general understanding that:

> The guarantee of an impartial authority ensures people that their disputes will be decided by an entity that has no personal interest in or relation to the matter in dispute, and that said entity will maintain an objective position when ruling on it. Consequently, the guarantee of impartiality means that those authorities that hear any type of proceeding shall have no preconceived opinions on how they will rule on it, commitments to any of the parties, etc. This guarantee likewise binds the authority not to allow itself to be influenced by the news or public opinion regarding its actions. (as cited in Ministry of Justice, 2013: 25)

In the sanctioning administrative proceedings carried out by the CGR, the sanctioning body has no personal interest in, nor any preconceived opinion with regard to, the ruling on the case, nor any commitment to the investigating body. Likewise, the sanctioning body does it appear to be subject *"to influence, incentive, pressure, threat, or interference, whether direct or indirect, acting solely and exclusively in accordance with—and at the behest of—the law"* (PCC, August 8, 2012: 51).

Both the investigating body and the sanctioning body are technically autonomous, in accordance with Section 51 of the Organic Act on the National Control System and the Office of the Comptroller General's Office of the Republic, as well as Sections 110 and 113 of the Regulations on the Organization and Functions (ROF) of the Office of the Comptroller

General of the Republic. They are two distinct or differentiated bodies, in accordance with the provisions of the ROF of the CGR (Sections 108 and 112), and there are no aspects of hierarchy or interference in their decisions, in accordance with the design of the proceeding that connects them.

Furthermore, the sanctioning administrative proceedings under the responsibility of the CGR include a Superior Administrative Responsibilities Tribunal, *"which constitutes the court of last administrative resort in the sanctioning proceeding. It is a collegiate body that reports to the Office of the Comptroller General, with technical and functional independence in the matters under its competence, and autonomy in its decisions"* (Law 27785, 2002: Section 56). The Tribunal's design guarantees the principles of independence and impartiality in a structure characterized by the clear differentiation and autonomy of its bodies.

Finally, guarantees of due administrative process—by the very nature of their scope of application, i.e., within a single public entity—cannot always be applied with identical content nor with the same intensity that characterizes such guarantees in the judicial system, where jurisdictional proceedings involve two or more constitutional bodies vested with full independence and autonomy from one another.

V. Final Reflections

Constitutional doctrine has had relatively little to say about the Office of the Comptroller General of the Republic and its function of controlling the state's implementation and management of public resources. This situation has been addressed instead in other spheres, given the high degree of specialization in matters of budgeting, accounting, and auditing inherent to the oversight activities constitutionally attributed to these types of entities (Vega, 1999: 215-240).

Nevertheless, the scope of the CGR's powers and its status as an autonomous constitutional entity are an important manifestation of the constitutional state and its principle of the separation of powers. This entity is distinguished by the control actions it performs on the implementation of the state's public budget, and its contribution to the protection of constitutional principles such as the legality of budget implementation and public resources management, the "efficiency of social needs," good management by the state, and the prohibition of corruption, among others.

Although this institution shares many of the same problems as the public sector as a whole, with regard to institutional weakness and inefficiency in carrying out its constitutional purposes, the fact is that an absolutely skeptical stance toward the CGR's performance—which is frequently expressed in the disparagement of the very concept of the institution—threatens to reinforce corruption in our state, with the consequent harm to fundamental rights that this would entail.

As such, we propose a critical analysis and assessment of the Office of the Comptroller General as part of the state's compliance with its obligations in the fight against corruption. Such an analysis, conducted from a constitutional law standpoint, will enable us to identify constitutionally relevant problems in the exercise of the CGR's constitutional duties and obligations, as well as in the relationships of control and collaboration established with other constitutional bodies and government branches as part of the fight against corruption.

Special attention will be given, for example, to the CGR's actions in the implementation of public works tied to the company Odebrecht and its collaboration in determining the applicable criminal responsibility in the justice system; proposals for the constitutional reform of the National Control System and the Office of the Comptroller General of the Republic, as proposed by the recently appointed Comptroller General; problems linked to the appointment and removal of a Comptroller; the freezing of regional and local government accounts due to indications of corruption in their management, at the request of the CGR, and other matters.

It is important to highlight these problems, submit them to public debate and citizen oversight, and propose lines of functional action or correction that will help to strengthen the anti-corruption principle, in order to ultimately forge a state that plays a more significant role in the lives of ordinary citizens, with a focus on meeting their needs.

Bibliography

DANÓS, Jorge, et al. (2010). "Observaciones al proyecto de Ley Nº 4210/2010-CG."

El Comercio newspaper (2017). "Encuesta: ¿en qué instituciones confían los peruanos?" Available online at http://elcomercio.pe/politica/encuesta-instituciones-confian-peruanos-noticia-462214.

FERNÁNDEZ AJENJO, José Antonio (2011). *El control de las administraciones públicas y la lucha contra la corrupción: especial referencia al Tribunal de Cuentas ya la Intervención General de la Administración del Estado*. Navarra: Aranzadi.

BUSTOS GISBERT, Rafael (2010). "Corrupción política: un análisis desde la teoría y la realidad constitucional." *Teoría y realidad constitucional* (25), 69.

INTERNATIONAL ORGANISATION OF SUPREME AUDIT INSTITUTIONS (INTOSAI). *INTOSAI Online Glossary of Audit Terminology*. Available at http://www.intosaiglossary.org/Main.aspx. Last retrieved on March 19, 2012.

KRESALJA, Baldo, and OCHOA, César. (2009). *Derecho constitucional económico*. Lima: Fondo Editorial de la Pontificia Universidad Católica del Perú.

LANDA ARROYO, César. (2006). *Constitución y fuentes del derecho*. Lima: Palestra.

MONTOYA, Yvan (September 30, 2016). "La Constitucionalización del control y represión de la corrupción." Paper presented at the Jornada Nacional de Derechos Fundamentales (First International Symposium on Fundamental Rights). Lima: Facultad de Derecho Pontificia Universidad Católica del Perú, Themis.

ORGANISATION OF LATIN AMERICAN AND CARIBBEAN SUPREME AUDIT INSTITUTES (OLACEFS) (2013). "Santiago Declaration on Governance, the Fight against Corruption, and Public Trust." Santiago, Chile.

PERÚ 21 NEWSPAPER (May 10, 2010). *"Apenas 7% de las denuncias de corrupción terminan en sentencia"*. Available at http://archivo.peru21.pe/noticia/479534/apenas-denuncias-corrupcion-terminan-sentencia. Last retrieved on October 8, 2017.

PERU DEMOCRATIC CONSTITUENT CONGRESS (Congreso Constituyente Democrático) *Political Constitution of Peru* (1993).

PERU CONGRESS OF THE REPUBLIC (Congreso de la República) Law 27444—the General Administrative Proceedings Act. Legal Norms Bulletin of the Official Gazette "El Peruano," Lima. April 11, 2001.

PERU CONGRESS OF THE REPUBLIC (Congreso de la República) (2010a). Law 29622—the Act Amending Law 27785—the Organic Act on the National Control System and the Office of the Comptroller General of the Republic, and Expanding Powers in Sanctioning Proceedings Involving Matters of Functional Administrative

Responsibility. Legal Norms Bulletin of the Official Gazette "El Peruano," Lima. December 7, 2010.

PERU CONGRESS OF THE REPUBLIC (Congreso de la República) (2010b). Opinion issued on Bill No. 4210/2010-CGR, which proposes an Organic Act on the National Control System and the Office of the Comptroller General of the Republic, and the Expansion of Powers in Sanctioning Proceedings Involving Matters of Functional Administrative Responsibility. Legal Norms Bulletin of the Official Gazette "El Peruano," Lima. March 21, 2001.

PERU CONGRESS OF THE REPUBLIC (Congreso de la República) Law 27785—the Organic Act on the National Control System and the Office of the Comptroller General of the Republic. Legal Norms Bulletin of the Official Gazette "El Peruano," Lima. July 23, 2002.

OFFICE OF THE COMPTROLLER GENERAL OF THE REPUBLIC (Contraloría General de la República) (2017). "Regulations on Organisation and Functions" Comptroller General's Resolution No. 028-2017-CG.

OFFICE OF THE COMPTROLLER GENERAL OF THE REPUBLIC (Contraloría General de la República) (2017a). "Regional presidents (governors) involved in control documents issued during the period between 2014 and 2017 (April 2017)." Unpublished.

OFFICE OF THE COMPTROLLER GENERAL OF THE REPUBLIC (Contraloría General de la República) (2017b). "Registry of sanctioned parties with a sanction still in force, within the scope of the sanctioning powers of the Office of the Comptroller General of the Republic" (second half of 2017). Available at http://www.contraloria.gob.pe/wps/wcm/connect/ca86aa58-5372-40a2-95e4-61caa1156f4e/RW_2Trim2017.pdf?MOD=AJPERES&CACHEID=ca86aa58-5372-40a2-95e4-61caa1156f4e. Last retrieved on October 8, 2017.

MINISTRY OF JUSTICE (Ministerio de Justicia) (2013). "Guide for the Application of the Principle/Right of Due Process in Administrative Proceedings." Lima: Ministry of Justice and Human Rights.

GOVERNMENT ATTORNEY GENERAL'S OFFICE (Ministerio Público) (2010). Official Letter No. 730-2010-MP-FN, dated October 6, 2010. Opinion on Bill No. 4210/2010-CGR. Lima.

PRIME MINISTER'S OFFICE (Presidencia del Consejo de Ministros) Supreme Executive Order (Decreto Supremo) 023-2011-PCM, approving the Regulations on Law 29622.

PRIME MINISTER'S OFFICE (Presidencia del Consejo de Ministros) Supreme Executive Order (Decreto Supremo) 119-2012-PCM, approving the National Plan for the Fight against Corruption 2012-2016. Legal Norms Bulletin of the Official Gazette "El Peruano," Lima. December 9, 2012.

CONSTITUTIONAL COURT (Tribunal Constitucional) File No. 013-2002-AI/TC (Case on the Law Reinstating Terminated Magistrates). Judgment dated March 13, 2003. Available online at https://tc.gob.pe/jurisprudencia/2003/00013-2002-AI.html.

CONSTITUTIONAL COURT (Tribunal Constitucional) File No. 2235-2004-AA/TC (Grimaldo Saturnino Case). Judgment dated February 18, 2005. Available online at http://www.tc.gob.pe/jurisprudencia/2005/02235-2004-AA.pdf.

CONSTITUTIONAL COURT (Tribunal Constitucional) File No. 03741-2004-AA/TC (Salazar Yarlequé Case). Judgment dated November 14, 2005. Available online at https://tc.gob.pe/jurisprudencia/2006/03741-2004-AA.pdf.

CONSTITUTIONAL COURT (Tribunal Constitucional) File No. 00019-2005-AI/TC (Wolfenson Case). Judgment dated July 21, 2005. Available online at https://tc.gob.pe/jurisprudencia/2005/00019-2005-AI.pdf.

CONSTITUTIONAL COURT (Tribunal Constitucional) File No. 0006-2006-CC/TC (Casinos and Slot Machines Case). Court Order dated April 23, 2007. Available online at http://cdn01.pucp.education/idehpucp/wp-content/uploads/2017/06/30185900/jurispnactc02.pdf.

CONSTITUTIONAL COURT (Tribunal Constitucional) File No. 8495-2006-PA/TC (Valdivia Cano Case). Judgment dated August 7, 2008. Available online at http://www.justiciaviva.org.pe/nuevos/2008/agosto/21/sentencia_devaldivia.pdf.

CONSTITUTIONAL COURT (Tribunal Constitucional) File No. 0009-2007-PI/TC and File No. 0010-2007-PI/TC (joinder of the APCI and NGOs Cases). Judgment dated August 29, 2007. Available online at http://www.tc.gob.pe/jurisprudencia/2007/00009-2007-AI%2000010-2007-AI.html.

CONSTITUTIONAL COURT (Tribunal Constitucional) File No. 0017-2011-PI/TC (Case of Crimes of Collusion and Unjust Enrichment). Judgment dated May 3, 2012. Available online at http://www.tc.gob.pe/jurisprudencia/2012/00017-2011-AI.pdf.

CONSTITUTIONAL COURT (Tribunal Constitucional) File No. 00156-2012-PHC/TC (Tineo Case). Judgment dated August 8, 2012. Available online at http://www.tc.gob.pe/jurisprudencia/2012/00156-2012-HC.pdf.

PETREI, Humberto, and PETREI, Romeo (1997). *Presupuesto y control: pautas de reforma para América Latina* (No. 351.72).

UGAZ, José Carlos (July 3, 2011). "La increíble y triste historia del cándido contralor y el gobierno desalmado." *El Comercio* newspaper. Available online at http://elcomercio.pe/opinion/columnistas/increible-triste-historia-candido-contralor-gobierno-desalmado-jose-ugaz-439195.

EVALUATION AND CONTROL OFFICE (Unidad de Evaluación y Control). Oversight Commission (Comisión de Vigilancia) of the Supreme Audit Institution of the Federation (2005). "Fiscalización superior comparada. Una aproximación al estudio de los modelos de fiscalización superior en el mundo." Mexico City: Biblioteca de Fiscalización Superior.

VEGA BLÁZQUEZ, Pedro de (1999). "La configuración constitucional del tribunal de Cuentas de España. Cuestiones Constitucionales (001)." Available online at http://www.juridicas.unam.mx/publica/rev/cconst/cont/1/art/art8.htm. Last retrieved on October 10, 2017.

VALLÈS VIVES, Francesc (2003). *El control externo del gasto público: configuración y garantía constitucional*. Madrid: Centro de Estudios Políticos y Constitucionales.

THEMATIC TABLE 7: CONSTITUTIONAL CONTROL AND CONVENTIONAL CONTROL

Inter-American Conventionality Control at the National Level: A Concept Still Under Construction

David Lovatón Palacios[1]

I. Introduction

Ever since its first judgment in Velásquez Rodríguez vs. Honduras, the Inter-American Court has consistently applied conventionality control—even if it has not specifically referred to it as such—as legal grounds for determining Member States' international liability for internal acts or norms that violate the rights enshrined in the American Convention on Human Rights (ACHR).[2]

In other words, the essence of the jurisdictional labor carried out by the Inter-American Court has always been to determine the compatibility (or incompatibility) of internal acts or norms with the fundamental rights established in the inter-American *corpus juris*. In recent years, that function has been baptised with its own name (i.e., conventionality control), attempts been have made to establish a conceptual framework, and new legal consequences have arisen, such as this concept's application by national judges and courts, or the *erga omnes* effect of the Inter-American Court's jurisprudence.

Let it be noted here that we support the tool of conventionality control, in view of the contributions it has made to the force and validity of inter-

---

[1] Attorney at law, Master of Constitutional Law, and Doctor of Law. Full professor of law at the Pontificia Universidad Católica del Perú (PUCP) and consultant for the Due Process of Law Foundation (DPLF).

[2] Conventionality control "consists of verifying the alignment of internal legal norms (…) with the American Convention on Human Rights (…) and the interpretative standards set forth by the Inter-American Court of Human Rights" (BAZÁN, 2012: 17-18).

American law at the national level in Latin America.[3] At the same time, the critical voices raised with regard to this matter—although we may not entirely share their views—have helped to see beyond the enthusiasm generated by one part of the doctrine and identify certain aspects still pending construction or further precision, as well as to adjust or refine some of its legal consequences.

II. Recent Developments in Conventionality Control

The most recent developments in conventionality control, as it currently stands, are as follows: i) its identification and conceptual demarcation; ii) the *erga omnes* effect of inter-American jurisprudence; and iii) its application by national judges and courts.

While the expression "conventionality control" has only recently come into use in the judgments of merit issued in the cases of Almonacid Arellano vs. Chile and Dismissed Congressional Employees vs. Peru in 2006, it was Sergio García Ramírez, the President of the Inter-American Court at that time, who originally coined the term for this innate function of the Court in his concurring opinion in the case of Myrna Mack Chang vs. Guatemala in 2003.[4]

In the judgments of merit in the case of Almonacid vs. Chile, the Court further laid the foundations for conventionality control in two ways. On the one hand, it used this specific name to refer to a review of the internal legal system's alignment with the inter-American *corpus juris*. On the other, it established the judicial branch's obligation to exercise such

[3] César Landa reminds us that, in the case of Peru, conventionality control was applied for the first time—and indeed, was pioneered in Latin America—by judge Antonia Saquicuray in 1995, when she ruled that the Self-Amnesty Act passed by the then-president Alberto Fujimori was unenforceable (2014: 230).

[4] "At the international level, it is not possible to divide the State, to bind before the Court only one or some of its organs, to grant them representation of the State in the proceeding—without this representation affecting the whole State—and excluding other organs from this treaty regime of responsibility, leaving their actions outside the 'conventionality control' that involves the of the international court" (IA Court of HR, 2003, paragraph 27). The aforementioned judge would again use the term "conventionality control" in his opinions in the cases of Tibi vs. Ecuador in 2004, López Álvarez vs. Honduras in 2006, and Vargas Areco vs. Paraguay in 2006 (BAZÁN, 2012: 25-26).

conventionality control over norms or decisions that are incompatible with the inter-American *corpus juris*.[5]

In that same year, in the case of Dismissed Congressional Employees vs. Peru, the Court added that the organs of the judicial branch have a duty to exercise conventionality control *ex officio*, although it clarified that this must always be done "within the scope of their respective competence."[6] This clarification has become very important in light of the criticisms that we will discuss further below.

The Court's line of jurisprudence was consolidated in the cases of La Cantuta vs. Peru, Boyce vs. Barbados, Heliodoro Portugal vs. Panama, and Gomes Lund vs. Brazil. In the case of Gomes Lund vs. Brazil, the Court also made two new jurisprudential advances with regard to conventionality control. On the one hand, it specified that judicial decisions—and not only norms such as amnesty laws—were also subject to conventionality control. On the other hand, it explicitly established itself as the final or ultimate interpreter of the American Convention.[7]

---

[5] "The Court is aware that domestic judges and courts are bound to respect the rule of law, and therefore, they are bound to apply the provisions in force within the legal system. But when a State has ratified an international treaty such as the American Convention, its judges, as part of the State, are also bound by such Convention. This forces them to see that all the effects of the provisions embodied in the Convention are not adversely affected by the enforcement of laws which are contrary to its purpose and that have not had any legal effects since their inception. In other words, the Judiciary must exercise a sort of 'conventionality control' between the domestic legal provisions and the American Convention on Human Rights. To perform this task, the Judiciary has to take into account not only the treaty, but also the interpretation thereof made by the Inter-American Court, which is the ultimate interpreter of the American Convention" (IA Court of HR, 2006a: paragraph 124).

[6] "(…) the organs of the Judiciary should exercise not only a control of constitutionality, but also of 'conventionality' *ex officio* between domestic norms and the American Convention; evidently in the context of their respective spheres of competence and the corresponding procedural regulations" (IA Court of HR, 2006b: paragraph 128).

[7] "On numerous occasions, the Court has held that ascertaining whether the State violated its international obligations, by means of its actions before its judicial organs, can lead to this Court examining the particular domestic procedures, eventually including the decisions of the higher courts, so as to establish the compatibility with the American Convention. (…) The Judicial Power must take into consideration not only the treaty, but also the interpretation that the Inter-

Conventionality control over administrative decisions or interpretations, for its part, was established by the Court in the case of López Mendoza vs. Venezuela, in the ruling dated September 1, 2011; and the case of Atala Riffo and Daughters vs. Chile, in the ruling dated February 24, 2012, in which the Court ratified the duty of "alignment of judicial and administrative interpretations and judicial guarantees with the principles established in the jurisprudence of the Inter-American Court of Human Rights ('IA Court of HR')" (Bazán, 2012: 31).

Later, the Court's jurisprudence took two leaps forward in consolidating conventionality control in the case of Gelman vs. Uruguay. On the one hand, it established that it was not only judges and courts at all levels of the justice system that have the obligation to exercise conventionality control, but "any public authority" (IA Court of HR, 2011: paragraph 239). On the other hand, the Court ruled that even an amnesty law (known as the "Ley de Caducidad," or the "Expiry Law of the State," in the case of Uruguay) that had been approved by popular vote on not one, but *two* occasions, was not immune to conventionality control.[8]

In terms of the expansion of the subjective sphere of conventionality control to include "any public authority," this is one of the most frequently criticized aspects of this concept at present. We cannot help but agree that it is not a good idea—and may even be counterproductive—to try and extend the power of conventionality control to any and all "public authorities" (a phrase that is perhaps overly broad), especially considering that not even constitutional control has undergone such an expansion, instead being limited to judges and courts.[9]

As such, it would be best for the jurisprudence of the Inter-American Court to explain or specify, on the one hand, that conventionality control is reserved for national judges and courts—just like constitutional control, in

---

American Court, as the final interpreter of the American Convention, has given it" (IA Court of HR, 2010: paragraphs 49 and 176).

[8] "The fact that the Expiry Law of the State has been approved in a democratic regime and yet is ratified or supported by the public, on two occasions, (…) does not automatically or by itself grant legitimacy under International Law" (IA Court of HR, 2011: paragraph 238).

[9] In the case of Peru, the jurisprudence of the Constitutional Court (PCC) originally extended the power of diffuse constitutional control to collegiate administrative tribunals nationwide. The PCC later amended this jurisprudential criterion, and once again limited the exercise of constitutional control exclusively to the judges and courts of the judicial branch.

those national legal systems that include the concept of diffuse or mixed constitutional control—and that, on the other hand, the obligation of any public authority to act in accordance with the inter-American *corpus juris* is not an expression of conventionality control, but rather an effect of Article 2 of the ACHR, which establishes the international obligation of the States Parties to adopt "*legislative and other provisions*" to enforce the rights enshrined by the inter-American system. "Other provisions," it should be noted, may be understood here to include administrative measures.

With regard to the conventionality control of norms that have been democratically approved, we believe the Court consolidated its jurisprudential doctrine on the matter in the case of Barrios Altos vs. Peru, wherein it ruled that democratic legitimization by majority opinion does not suffice to ensure a norm's compatibility with international human rights standards. Rather, it is also essential for such norms to respect internationally acknowledged fundamental rights.[10]

In the face of this new inter-American legal panorama set forth by the Court's jurisprudence, some high courts in the Americas (including those of Argentina, Colombia, Mexico, Peru, etc.) have displayed a growing tendency toward not only exercising conventionality control, but also establishing that such control is now a legal obligation of national courts. Víctor Bazán divides the evolution of the Inter-American Court's jurisprudential doctrine on the matter into two aspects: i) the expansion of those parties bound to exercise conventionality control at the national level; and ii) those measures subject to the said control (Bazán, 2012: 31).

For several years now in Peru, the jurisprudence of both the Constitutional Court (PCC) and the Supreme Court, in criminal matters, has been applying conventionality control to laws that have ultimately been declared unconstitutional, incorporating human rights treaties and the jurisprudence of the Inter-American Court into the body of constitutional

---

[10] "The democratic legitimacy of specific facts in a society is limited by the norms of protection of human rights recognised in international treaties, such as the American Convention, in such a form that the existence of a true democratic regime is determined by both its formal and substantial characteristics, and therefore, particularly in cases of serious violations of nonrevocable norms of International Law, the protection of human rights constitutes an impassable limit to the rule of the majority, that is, to the forum of the 'possible to be decided' by majorities in the democratic instance, those who should also prioritise 'control of conformity with the Convention'" (IA Court of HR, 2011: paragraph 239).

law, as a parameter based on which the PCC can conclude whether or not laws are constitutional:

> (…) under the rule of the constitutional canon that this Court is sworn to uphold, there is an additional duty for which all public powers are responsible; namely, the compulsory observance of human rights treaties ratified by Peru, as well as the interpretation of such conventions made in all proceedings by international courts established as per treaties to which Peru is a party. (2006b: paragraph 14)

In short, we believe that—despite the critical comments that we will examine herein below—conventionality control is one of the most important expressions of the process of "inter-Americanization" of the constitutional state in Latin America. Nowadays, it is not only the Inter-American Commission and Court, but national judges and courts, too, that evaluate whether judicial or administrative norms or decisions are—or are not—aligned with the human rights standards enshrined in the inter-American *corpus juris*.

III. Conventionality Control and Constitutional Control

With the incorporation of conventionality control into the internal sphere, we are faced with questions regarding the relationship between conventionality control and constitutional control. We are of the opinion that, although many countries in Latin America now incorporate international human rights law into their body of constitutional law, conventionality control and constitutional control are not entirely identical.

We posit that the main difference between conventionality control and constitutional control lies in the fact that, ultimately, conventionality control can be exercised on constitutional norms. Indeed, a constitutional norm may be *constitutional*, for all effects and purposes, but this does not necessarily mean it is compatible with the inter-American *corpus juris*. Therefore, it may be subject to conventionality control.

In the case of *The Last Temptation of Christ* vs. Chile, the Inter-American Court ruled that Section 19.12 of the Chilean Political Constitution of 1980—which established a system of censorship for the exhibition and advertisement of film productions—was incompatible with the American Convention (IA Court of HR, 2001: paragraph 88), and thus ordered the Chilean State to amend its laws, including the Chilean Constitution itself (IA Court of HR, 2001: Operative Point 4).

From our point of view, there can be no doubt that the Inter-American Court has the power—occasionally and on an exceptional basis—to deem a constitutional norm incompatible with the inter-American *corpus juris*. What *is* subject to debate is whether national courts and judges can—or cannot—exercise conventionality control over constitutional norms. While the Inter-American Court's jurisprudence clearly establishes the obligation of national judges and courts to exercise conventionality control—even *ex officio*—on internal decisions or norms, it has not specified whether this control also includes constitutional norms. It almost seems as if, when the Court extended conventionality control to include the domestic sphere, it failed to take into account this possible legal consequence. As such, we will proceed to take a position on the matter here.

Ariel Dulitzky argues that the judicial power to declare a constitutional norm incompatible with the inter-American *corpus juris* should be expressly included in the Constitution (2014: 541-542). We coincide with this interpretation, given that the Inter-American Court's own jurisprudence has repeatedly held that conventionality control at the national level must be exercised "in accordance with the competence" of the internal jurisdictional organs.

For this very reason, Sergio García Ramírez, the creator of conventionality control himself, has proposed filtering or tempering this power or prerogative vested in all national judges and courts with the creation of a kind of "exception of conventionality," by virtue of which the conventionality control exercised by judges and courts in those States with diffuse control would require a mandatory review by the higher courts (Supreme Courts or Constitutional Courts).[11] In a certain way, he proposes that conventionality control at the national level be refocused (García Ramírez, 2011: 151-152).

Since its very inception, the Inter-American Court has exercised a kind of focused conventionality control at the inter-American level. With the cases of Almonacid vs. Chile and Dismissed Congressional Employees vs. Peru, however, the Court decided to extend this conventionality control to national judges and courts. The intention appears to have been to create a kind of diffuse conventionality control, but with the important condition

[11] Similarly, Ariel Dulitzky suggests the review of a preliminary ruling, although done directly by the Inter-American Court: "A mechanism must be established that allows for cases pending before the national courts to be submitted for the consideration of the Inter-American Court. In this sense, we might follow the model of the European Union" (2014: 562).

that it be exercised only in those countries where this form of constitutional control has been established by law.

Those countries that have only focused control should be subject to the jurisprudence of the Inter-American Court, wherein it states that conventionality control must be exercised at the national level in accordance with the competence of the internal jurisdictional organs, and following the procedures established for such effect. This would mean that conventionality control over constitutional norms can only be exercised by the higher courts vested with focused control.

In the case of Peru, the Constitution establishes a mixed system. On the one hand, it grants the judges and courts of the judicial branch the power of diffuse constitutional control (Section 138, Paragraph 2); while on the other, it attributes the Constitutional Court with a focused constitutional control (Section 202). Under the constitutional procedural laws currently in force, however, the decisions of the Constitutional Court prevail over the decisions of the ordinary judges and courts, i.e., focused control prevails over diffuse control.[12]

We are thus of the opinion that, in the Peruvian legal system, although all judges and courts have the power to exercise conventionality control on an exceptional basis, even over constitutional norms, this control must be reviewed by the Constitutional Court, in accordance with the provisions established in the constitutional procedural laws in force.

IV. Conventionality Control and the Hierarchy of Human Rights Treaties

It is often mistakenly believed that the prevalence of the inter-American *corpus juris* over national law is based on the principle of hierarchy. The hierarchical position of human rights treaties in the system of sources of each internal legal system is not, however, the main basis of conventionality control. A national constitution may—or may not—establish a hierarchical position for these treaties, but this has no effect on whether conventionality control can be applied.

[12] "Judges cannot fail to apply a norm whose constitutionality has been upheld in an action alleging unconstitutionality or a public interest suit" (Preliminary Title, Section VI, Paragraph 2 of the Code of Constitutional Procedure).

As we know, in international public law, the principle of *pacta sunt servanda*—as enshrined in Articles 26 and 27 of the Vienna Convention—establishes States' obligation to honor and comply with the treaties and conventions they have ratified. Consequently, no State can "invoke the provisions of its internal law as justification for its failure to perform a treaty."[13]

Thus, as we see it, the prevalence of human rights treaties over national law—whether it be the constitution or laws—in the case of conflict, stems from the international obligation assumed by national States when—acting freely and sovereignly—they sign or ratify the said treaties. This prevalence is not rooted in the constitutional hierarchy (or lack thereof) granted to treaties and conventions by our system of sources of law, but in the obligation that the State has assumed under international public law.

Therefore, for the effects of international human rights law (IHRL) and its relationship to internal law, we do not deem it essential to grant a hierarchical position to human rights treaties within a national system of sources. This does not mean that the hierarchical position that a specific national legal system confers upon human rights treaties is irrelevant; but we must insist that the most important thing here is the international obligations that the States have acquired; in this case, under the inter-American human rights system.

In Peru, Section 55 of the Constitution establishes that "[t]he treaties entered into by the State and currently in force form part of national law," without indicating a normative hierarchy for treaties in general, and human rights conventions in particular. In keeping with the arguments we have just set forth, if a constitutional norm and a human rights convention are found to be incompatible, we maintain that the latter should prevail—not because of any considerations with regard to normative hierarchy, but rather, in compliance with the international obligation to honour those treaties that have been ratified by Peru.

V. Some Criticisms of Conventionality Control

In the Latin American doctrinal debate over conventionality control, authors such as Ariel Dulitzky (2014; 2013; 2012), Karlos Castilla (2014; 2013), and Alfredo Vitolo (2013) have raised their critical voices.

---

[13] Article 27 of the Vienna Convention on the Law of Treaties.

The main criticisms levelled against the inter-American doctrine of conventionality control, as developed by the Court and much of the Latin American doctrine, essentially revolve around the following issues: i) whether the conventionality control extended to include national judges and courts should (or should not) be considered a truly new prerogative, or if it is simply an attempt to assign a new name to a previously existing legal duty; ii) whether the *erga omnes* effects of the judgments of the Inter-American Court also include those States that are not party to such proceedings; iii) the complexity and relative inaccessibility of inter-American jurisprudence for national judges and courts; and iv) the absence of the Inter-American Commission (IACHR) in the development and application of conventionality control.

Is Conventionality Control a New Prerogative for National Judges and Courts?

According to Karlos Castilla, conventionality control is in fact a "false conventionality control" (2014: 151 and 161), in the sense that it is merely "(…) a way that the Inter-American made up to demand greater compliance with the American Convention, mainly by national judges. However, this erroneous and sloppy use of the term 'conventionality control' has created problems where there were none before" (2014: 162). Accordingly, he argues, it is simply a specification of international human rights obligations, for which Castilla proposes the name "guarantee of treaties" (2013: 91-92; 2014: 162).

In regard to this criticism, we believe it is necessary to take into account two aspects. Firstly, we have made it clear throughout this paper that conventionality control has inarguably been present since Velásquez Rodríguez vs. Honduras, the very first case on which the Inter-American Court ruled, in the sense that the Court is inherently competent to determine whether internal decisions or norms are—or are not—compatible with the inter-American *corpus juris*.

In other words, it is true that conventionality control is not a new and original idea in the Court's jurisprudence, but rather, a consequence or development of its previously established conventional competence, as part of a process of internationalization of the protection of fundamental rights. Even Sergio García Ramírez, the creator of the term "conventionality control," is quick to admit that it "is an expression or aspect of the systematised and organised reception, at the national level, of the international (or supranational) conventional juridical order" (2011: 127).

Consequently, we do not share the critical spirit of this conclusion that conventionality control is nothing new or original, since it is just that, a conclusion, which all of us share and which must be understood in the context of the evolution of international human rights law in general, and the inter-American *corpus juris* in particular.

Secondly, Karlos Castilla argues that through this notion of conventionality control, the Inter-American Court has overreached in its prerogatives and gone beyond conventional limits. While Castilla agrees that international human rights law must be enforced and applied at the national level, he does not agree that it was necessary or advisable to create this particular concept. Rather, the State's duty to comply with its obligations would have been sufficient, including, as it does, national judges and courts:

> I would like to reiterate here that I am in favour of national judges (and all national authorities) ensuring that the effects of the American Convention on Human Rights (ACHR), and human rights treaties in general, are not attenuated by the application of laws contrary to the Convention's purpose and goals, but this should not be done through legal precepts that alter or impose national systems that are onerous to implement. (…) Rather, the content and authorised interpretations of these treaties must be incorporated into the everyday tasks of the national courts: *not so as to prevail in all cases, but so that they may always be taken into account, and—if they are found to provide broader and better protection of human rights—applied without any reservation whatsoever* (Castilla, 2013: 55, emphasis ours).

Thus, according to Castilla, a national judge or court is not necessarily required to impose or apply inter-American law. In some cases, national law must prevail when it is more favorable than inter-American law. In regard to this argument, we believe that the author falls into two conceptual inaccuracies: i) the duty to honor international obligations does not necessarily presuppose—as we have already shown—the hierarchical superiority of human rights treaties over internal law; and ii) the primacy of inter-American law does not rule out the possible application of internal law, when the latter is more favorable.

With regard to the primacy of inter-American law and its supposed incompatibility with the application of a national norm that is more favorable to fundamental rights, we likewise find ourselves obligated to refute Castilla's criticisms, given that the application of the most favorable norm is a principle of international law, whereby international norms act as a minimum level upon which national law is free to improve the contents of rights.

It is a mistake to claim that the primacy of inter-American law always presupposes, regardless of the circumstances, that an international norm shall be applied to the detriment of the national decision or norm. Such cases apply only when the latter includes a narrower content of the right(s) in question. Therefore, only *in peius* situations will trigger the mechanism of conventionality control over internal decisions or norms. If the internal decisions or norms are more favorable than their inter-American counterparts, then international law itself establishes that they shall prevail.

Does the Jurisprudence of the Inter-American Court Have *Erga Omnes*, or Only the *Inter Partes* Effect?

Some authors have questioned the *erga omnes* effect of the Inter-American Court's judgments, arguing that the American Convention only establishes the *inter partes* force of such judgments, meaning that they are only binding upon the States party to a given proceeding. According to Dulitzky:

> Nowhere in the text of the convention does it state that the Court's jurisprudence is binding for the States Parties to the Convention that were not party to the suit, or that national courts must respect this jurisprudence. Using the theory of conventionality control, the Court is transforming international law into a system of precedents, similar to common law. (…) Article 68.1 clearly states that the "States Parties to the Convention undertake to comply with the judgment of the Court in any case to which they are parties," but not in cases to which they are not parties (2014: 547-548).

Along these same lines, Alfredo Vitolo argues that:

> This criterion established by the Inter-American Court violates the consent granted by the States when, by virtue of the American Convention, they created the Court and determined its attributes, limiting their own sovereignty by granting the Court a certain sphere of competence. It is precisely for this latter reason that the attributes of the Inter-American Court cannot be interpreted in an extensive manner, going beyond what the States could have intended and construed upon entering into the Convention (2013: 365).

We, on the other hand, believe that the Inter-American Court can, in fact, interpret its attributes in an extensive manner. Indeed, it has done so all these years by broadening the contents of the fundamental rights enshrined in the inter-American instruments, or by establishing other, new rights derived from those original rights, such as the right of access to public information, the right to the truth, or the rights of indigenous peoples.

Of course, this extensive interpretation must be exercised with caution by the Court, establishing its limits or even correcting the said interpretation after listening to the criticisms and concerns that authors such as those cited above have raised with regard to this and other matters. We must reiterate, however, that—in our opinion—the Court can indeed make an extensive interpretation of its competence, given that the intention of the States that approved the ACHR should not be the sole criterion of interpretation taken into account; it is also necessary to consider the principle of human dignity, the expansive nature of human rights, etc.

Furthermore, the literal terms of the ACHR reveal the fact that it was drafted based on the human rights challenges faced at that moment in history—as could only be expected—and that it is thus up to the bodies responsible for interpreting and applying it, such as the Court and the Commission, to develop and update the Convention.

A similar interpretation has been advanced regarding the *erga omnes* effect of the judgments of the European Court of Human Rights (ECHR). According to García Roca, the sustained jurisprudential development of the ECHR has exceeded the literal meaning of Article 16.1 EC—which contemplated only the *inter partes* effect of its judgments—and has imbued them with an *erga omnes* effect:

> The ECHR (…) seems to have no doubt of the *erga omnes* effect of its decisions, as is inevitable in a system of collective guarantee, as opposed to one based on mere reciprocity. But there is always someone, without fail, who continues to challenge their binding force. It is no coincidence that Article 16.1 EC, when recognising the binding force (or *force obligatoire*) of the judgments, establishes the States' obligation to "respect" (…) the final and binding judgments, but restricts this to "the suits to which they are a party." A restrictive wording, exceeded by the reality of the jurisprudence. (2012: 221-222)

Complexity and Insufficient Accessibility of Inter-American Jurisprudence

Another criticism raised against conventionality control is the complexity it has reached and the inaccessibility of inter-American jurisprudence for national judges and courts, thus making it difficult to apply this concept internally. Worse yet, this circumstance poses a risk of a defective or misguided application of conventionality control.

In regard to this matter, Karlos Castilla argues that:

> If the IA Court of HR wants to make great demands of the internal courts, it must also hold itself to a higher standard, transmitting clear and cognisable messages to all recipients (…) establishing the way in which its jurisprudence should be used, and creating an overview or summary of this jurisprudence, such that anyone who wishes to familiarise him or herself with it and apply it is not required to read several thousand pages in order to decipher it (2013: 94).

We find this criticism valid, given the duty to observe not only human rights treaties, but also all inter-American jurisprudence with *erga omnes* effects. In the case of the Inter-American Court, one must review not only the judgments on preliminary exceptions, merits, reparations, and costs, but also resolutions monitoring the compliance with the aforementioned judgments, the provisional measures it issues from time to time, and its advisory opinions.

Furthermore, as we will discuss in the following section, when speaking of inter-American jurisprudence, we often think only of the Court and neglect the Inter-American Commission. As the other body in the inter-American system, the Commission's reports and decisions must also be taken into account when exercising conventionality control: admissibility and inadmissibility reports, merits reports, precautionary measures, duly approved friendly settlements, responses to inquiries submitted by the States, country reports, thematic reports, and annual reports.

As we can see from this brief overview, the inter-American *corpus juris* has become rather voluminous and complex. As such, its correct application at the national level, in the form of conventionality control, requires complete knowledge of this body of law on the part of national judges and courts, something that is still the exception to the rule at this point in time. Only some of the national high courts in Latin America could be said to generally have a handle on and knowledge of the inter-American *corpus juris*, but the same does not hold true for other judicial levels (with certain commendable exceptions, as always).

This circumstance does make it impossible to apply conventionality control at the national level, but it *does* pose a serious problem that—if not addressed—may cause undesirable consequences, such as a demagogical or distorted application of conventionality control. In response, authors such as Dulitzky have asserted that "the Court needs to develop a systematic policy so that judges and attorneys (…) can gain an up-to-date knowledge of the latest jurisprudential developments in Latin America that apply the Convention" (2014: 567).

This systematic policy should include, among other specific measures, a substantial improvement in access to inter-American jurisprudence through more user-friendly websites for both the Inter-American Commission and the Court. The Court has made some inroads here, but the Commission has lagged behind. Additionally, in alliance with other international organizations or national high courts, training plans on international law should be implemented, aimed at judges, district attorneys, public defenders, and national attorneys. Finally, the Commission and the Court should set up a quick and easy alert system—using social media—regarding their decisions and jurisprudential criteria.

Absence of the IACHR in the Development and Application of Conventionality Control

We agree with the criticism that the Inter-American Commission on Human Rights (IACHR)—the other body in the inter-American system, along with the Court—is not typically taken into account in the reflection and debate over conventionality control. The Court itself has contributed to this situation (not in bad faith, of course) by referring only to its own jurisprudence as a parameter for conventionality control, and by confusing its own status as *final* interpreter with that of *only* interpreter of the ACHR in the Americas.[14]

[14] With regard to this matter, Dulitzky argues that the Court "must carry out a much more serious analysis of the value of the Inter-American Commission's decisions. At the very least, the Court must address questions such as: What is the interpretative value of the IACHR's practice? What is the degree of deference to be granted? When must these decisions be followed and when can a dissenting position be taken? Especially at this point in time, after the Commission has changed its role from representative of victims' interests to protector of the inter-American public order, the Court must be much more serious in considering the arguments of its inter-American peer. And above all, it must stipulate that the Convention, as interpreted by the Court *and* the Commission, is the parameter for conventionality control" (2014: 566).

Nowhere, however, does the American Convention establish that the Inter-American Court is the only official interpreter of the inter-American *corpus juris*. Quite the contrary, the ACHR clearly designed a "bifrontal" system (Dulitzky, 2014: 551) of inter-American interpretation; that is, a system with two heads—the Court and the Commission—with no hierarchical relationship between them. According to Dulitzky:

> On the one hand, the Commission is one of the two organs entrusted with the task of monitoring the Convention (Art. 33) and a consultative organ of the Organisation specialising in human rights (Art. 106, Charter of the OAS). Together with the Court, the Inter-American Commission also has assigned functions in specific cases, and is vested with the power to set forth "conclusions" regarding alleged violations of the Convention (Arts. 50 and 51). As an organ with multiple functions and powers—some of them quasi-judicial—the Commission does not issue judgments, per se. From this perspective, then, it can be correctly stated that it does not establish jurisprudence. The Convention does not, however, assign a particular hierarchical rank to the final decisions of the Court and the Commission, nor does it establish a single final interpreter of the Convention. (…) Indeed, it allows for a final decision of the Commission, by virtue of Art. 51; or of the Court, by virtue of Art. 61, *et seq.* As such, the Convention creates two possible final decisions or interpretations. In light of the foregoing, the value of both organs' interpretations, as expressed in cases, must be considered of equal importance (2014: 549-550).

We agree with Dulitzky's argument that the ACHR does not establish the Inter-American Court as the only—and certainly not the "official"—interpreter of the inter-American *corpus juris*. Rather, there are two organs that interpret this body of law—the Court and the Commission—and there is no hierarchical relationship between them.

Having said this, however, we must differ with Dulitzky on two points. On the one hand, we take issue with his argument that the Commission exercises "quasi-judicial" functions. As we see it, something either *does* or *does not* have a given juridical nature or quality; there is no room for "quasi" or "almost." We therefore find it necessary to determine more precisely whether the Commission does, or does not, have jurisdictional functions; and if not, what kinds of function it fulfils, in such case.

On the other hand, although we concur that there is no hierarchical relationship between the Court and the Commission, and that the Commission's decisions must be incorporated into the parameter of conventionality control, we remain unconvinced that the decisions of both organs—in the individual petition system—necessarily have the same legal value in all cases.

With regard to the first aspect, the question must be raised: What is the juridical nature of the Commission? Judicial? Pre-trial? Political? Mixed? Technical? It is not a judicial organ, because it is not called a tribunal or a court, and it does not issue judgments, only reports (recommendations). It is thus clear that the only judicial body in the inter-American system is the Court. It cannot reasonably be argued that the ACHR created two jurisdictional organs.

On the other hand, we are of the opinion that the Commission carries out important non-jurisdictional activities, such as *in loco* country visits, press releases condemning or welcoming a range of developments pertaining to human rights throughout the Americas, public hearings, advisory to the States or the OAS when so requested, and more.

Furthermore, while the Commission is the gateway to the individual petition system, and thus plays a fundamental role, we do not believe that such functions are judicial in nature. Rather, they are pre-trial functions, i.e., prior to a possible judicial proceeding before the Court. It is interesting to note here that the amendment of the Court's Rules of Procedure in January of 2009 assigned the Commission the role of guarantor of the inter-American "public interest,"[15] which some attorneys at the Executive Secretary's Office of the Commission have coincided in calling the "inter-American public order."[16]

It might therefore be concluded that the Commission fulfills mixed functions, i.e., both technical and pre-trial functions, in its capacity as guarantor of the "inter-American public order." We are well aware, however, that this reflection on the juridical nature of a *sui generis* body

---

[15] "(…) the Commission, in its capacity as guarantor of the public interest under the American Convention, shall represent the alleged victims in order to ensure that they enjoy legal defence" (Article 34.3 of the Rules of Procedure of the Inter-American Court).

[16] "One final point to be noted is that involving the aspect of 'inter-American public order.' The regulatory reform of the IA Court of HR, and especially its statement of purpose, makes reference to the modification of the IACHR's role in proceedings before the court. It also states that the Commission, as an organ of the IAHRS, shall assume the defence of the inter-American public order involved in the cases" (SERRANO, 2012: 328-329).

such as the Commission remains underdeveloped, and is deserving of further, unhurried reflection.

As for our second discrepancy with Dulitzky's arguments, we do indeed agree with the criticism that the Commission's decisions should also be taken into account as inter-American parameters in the exercise of conventionality control. Our question, however, is whether that part of the inter-American *corpus juris* always has the same legal value or force as the jurisprudence of the Inter-American Court.

There are two aspects based on which we are inclined to believe that they do not, in fact, always have the same value, and that the Court's "jurisprudence" enjoys a greater weight with regard to those cases and matters on which it pronounces. On the one hand, the general lack of familiarity with the decisions of the Commission is much greater than in the case of the Court. We therefore believe it is also necessary to take into account the greater or lesser degree of legal certainty in determining the parameters to be applied in conventionality control.

On the other hand, although Dulitzky is right in pointing out that a petition, upon being processed, may end up in the Court or in the Commission, and that both final decisions must be complied with by the States, it is also true that there is a possibility that the Commission will "submit" the petition to the Court. Thus, in our opinion, this "bifrontal" inter-American system also includes a possible encounter in which the Commission decides, autonomously, that the Court shall have the final word.

If this latter point is true—especially following the amendment of the Regulations of the IACHR in 2001, by virtue of which the Commission no longer decides, with absolute discretion, which cases will be sent to the Court and which will not—then we hold that the Court's judgments—in those cases in which the Commission brings a suit before it—should be assigned greater force than the decisions of the Commission. Of course, with regard to those cases or matters on which there has been no Court pronouncement, only decisions by the Commission—for example, when a petition ends with a Final Merits Report pursuant to Article 51 of the ACHR—we believe that the Commission's inter-American criteria carry the same weight as those of the Court.

Nevertheless, these discrepancies do not diminish our agreement with the main thrust of this point, which is that there is still an outstanding debt owed to the IACHR, a body that stands on equal footing with the Court as part of the inter-American system. For this reason, its decisions must also be closely considered when applying conventionality control at the national level.

VI. Final Reflection

Conventionality control has been, and continues to be, a valuable tool for the growing relevance of the inter-American *corpus juris* at the national level, placed at the disposal of the judges and courts of Latin America. At the same time, it is still a concept under construction, with conceptual boundaries that require further refinement, precision, and even correction through the jurisprudence of the Court and the reports of the Commission.

Bibliography

ALBANESE, Susana (coord.) (2008). *El control de convencionalidad.* Buenos Aires: Ediar.

BAZÁN, Víctor. (2012). "El control de convencionalidad: incógnitas, desafíos y perspectivas." In BAZÁN, Víctor; NASH, Claudio (eds.), *Justicia constitucional y derechos fundamentales: el control de convencionalidad 2011*, 17-55. Bogota: Centro de Derechos Humanos de la Facultad de Derecho de la Universidad de Chile/Konrad Adenauer Foundation.

CASTILLA, Karlos. (2013). "¿Control interno o difuso de convencionalidad? Una mejor idea: la garantía de tratados." *Anuario Mexicano de Derecho Internacional*, No. XIII: 51-97. Available at: http://www.revistas.unam.mx/index.php/amdi/article/view/35524/32349. Last retrieved on March 28, 2016.

CASTILLA, Karlos. (2014). "Control de convencionalidad interamericano: una mera aplicación del derecho internacional." *Derecho del Estado*, No. 33: 149-172. Available at: http://revistas.uexternado.edu.co/index.php/derest/article/view/3960/4261. Last retrieved on March 28, 2016.

DULITZKY, Ariel E. (2012). "Twenty Reflections on the Reflection Process." *Aportes DPLf: Magazine of the Due Process of Law Foundation (DPLF)*, Vol. 5, No. 16, Mar.: 11-13. Washington, DC. Available at: http://dplf.org/sites/default/files/1332509827.pdf. Last retrieved on October 1, 2015.

DULITZKY, Ariel E. (2013). "An Inter-American Constitutional Court? The Invention of the Conventionality Control by the Inter-American

Court of Human Rights." *Texas International Law Journal*, Vol. 50, No. 1: 45-93. Available at: https://law.utexas.edu/faculty/adulitzky/69-inter-amer-constitutional-court.pdf. Last retrieved on March 21, 2016.

DULITZKY, Ariel E. (2014). "El impacto del control de convencionalidad. ¿Un cambio de paradigma en el Sistema Interamericano de Derechos Humanos?" In RIVERA, Julio César; ELÍAS, José Sebastián; GROSMAN, Lucas Sebastián; LEGARRE, Santiago (dirs.), *Tratado de los derechos constitucionales*, 533-569. Buenos Aires: Abeledo Perrot, 2014. Available at: https://law.utexas.edu/faculty/adulitzky/67-Impacto-del-Control-de Convencionalidad.pdf. Last retrieved on March 28, 2016.

GARCÍA RAMÍREZ, Sergio (2011). "El control judicial interno de convencionalidad." *Ius*, Vol. V, No. 28: 123-159. Available at: http://www.scielo.org.mx/pdf/rius/v5n28/v5n28a7.pdf. Last retrieved on March 21, 2016.

GARCÍA ROCA, Javier (2012). "El diálogo entre el Tribunal Europeo de Derechos Humanos y los Tribunales Nacionales Constitucionales en la construcción de un orden público europeo." *Teoría y Realidad Constitucional*, No. 30: 183-224. Spain: UNED. Available at: http://revistas.uned.es/index.php/TRC/article/view/7005/6703. Last retrieved on March 21, 2016.

IA COURT OF HR (2001). Case of *The Last Temptation of Christ* (Olmedo Bustos *et al.*) vs. Chile. Judgment on merits dated February 5, 2001. Available at: http://www.cidh.oas.org/relatoria/showDocument.asp?DocumentID=10. Last retrieved on October 1, 2015.

Case of Myrna Mack Chang vs. Guatemala. Judgment dated November 25, 2003 (Merits, Reparations, and Costs). Available at: http://www.corteidh.or.cr/docs/casos/articulos/seriec_101_esp.pdf. Last retrieved on October 1, 2015.

Case of Almonacid Arellano *et al.* vs. Chile. Judgment dated September 26, 2006a (Preliminary Exceptions, Merits, Reparations, and Costs). Available at: http://www.corteidh.or.cr/docs/casos/articulos/seriec_154_esp.pdf. Last retrieved on October 1, 2015.

Case of Dismissed Congressional Workers (Aguado Alfaro *et al.*) vs. Peru. Judgment dated November 24, 2006b (Preliminary Exceptions, Merits, Reparations, and Costs). Available at: http://www.corteidh.or.cr/docs/casos/articulos/seriec_158_esp.pdf. Last retrieved on March 23, 2016.

"Rules of Procedure of the Inter-American Court of Human Rights," dated January 29, 2009. Available at: http://www.corteidh.or.cr/sitios/reglamento/ene_2009_esp.pdf.

Case of Gomes Lund, *et al.* (Guerrilha do Araguaia) vs. Brazil. Judgment dated November 24, 2010 (Preliminary Exceptions, Merits, Reparations, and Costs). Available at: http://fueromilitar.scjn.gob.mx/Resoluciones/seriec_219_esp.pdf. Last retrieved on March 23, 2016.

Case of Gelman vs. Uruguay. Judgment dated February 24, 2011 (Merits and Reparations). Available at: http://www.corteidh.or.cr/docs/casos/articulos/seriec_221_esp1.pdf. Last retrieved on October 1, 2015.

LANDA, César (2014). "El impacto del control de convencionalidad en el ordenamiento peruano entre la época de la dictadura y la consolidación de la democracia constitucional." In CASTAÑEDA, Susana (coord.), *Constitucionalismo y democracia en América Latina: controles y riesgos*, 219-254. Lima: Asociación Peruana de Derecho Constitucional/Instituto Iberoamericano de Derecho Constitucional.

PERUVIAN CONSTITUTIONAL COURT. File No. 2730-2006-PA/TC (Arturo Castillo Chirinos case). Judgment dated July 21, 2006. Available at: http://www.tc.gob.pe/jurisprudencia/2006/02730-2006-AA.html. Last retrieved on March 23, 2016.

SERRANO, Silvia. (2012). "Sometimiento de casos ante la Corte Interamericana de Derechos Humanos por parte de la Comisión Interamericana de Derechos Humanos." *IIDH*, Vol. 56. Available at: http://www.corteidh.or.cr/tablas/r30354.pdf. Last retrieved on April 1, 2016.

VÍTOLO, Alfredo M. (2013). "Una novedosa categoría jurídica: el 'querer ser.' Acerca del pretendido carácter normativo erga omnes de la jurisprudencia de la Corte Interamericana de Derechos Humanos. Las dos caras del 'control de convencionalidad.'" *Pensamiento Constitucional*, No. 18, 2013. Available at: http://revistas.pucp.edu.pe/index.php/pensamientoconstitucional/article/viewFile/8961/9369. Last retrieved on March 21, 2016.

Thematic Table 8: New Fundamental Rights

CONSTITUTIONALLY PROTECTED CONTENT OF THE FUNDAMENTAL RIGHT TO DRINKING WATER AND THE STATE'S POSITIVE OBLIGATIONS IN GUARANTEEING IT

JUAN CARLOS DÍAZ COLCHADO[1]

I. Introduction

A recent constitutional amendment (Law 30588) incorporated Section 7-A into the text of the Peruvian Constitution, recognizing the fundamental right to drinking water in the following terms:

> The State recognises the right of every person to gain progressive and universal access to drinking water. The State guarantees this right, prioritising human consumption over other uses.
>
> The State promotes the sustainable management of water, which is recognised as an essential natural resource, and as such, constitutes a public good and property of the Nation. Its domain is inalienable and imprescriptible.

This newly incorporated constitutional provision recognizes two aspects of water: as a fundamental right (drinking water) and as a natural resource (public good and property of the Nation).

It should be added here that the subjective dimension of drinking water—which is the focus of this paper—is insufficient, recognizing as it does only one part of its content: progressive and universal access to drinking water. Furthermore, it recognizes only one obligation on the part of the

[1] Master of Constitutional Law, graduated from the Pontificia Universidad Católica del Perú. Professor at the Graduate School of the same university, and at the Universidad Nacional del Santa School of Law.

State: to guarantee access to drinking water, prioritizing human consumption.

While there is international precedent—such as General Comment No. 15 of the UN Committee on Economic, Social, and Cultural Rights (2002) and Resolution 64/292 of the UN General Assembly (2010), on the recognition of the right to water as a human right;[2] as well as the jurisprudential developments of the Inter-American Court of Human Rights (IA Court of HR) (in the cases of Yakye Axa vs. Paraguay, Xámok Kásek vs. Paraguay, Saramaka People vs. Suriname, Vélez Loor vs. Panama, and Pacheco Teruel vs. Honduras) and the Peruvian Constitutional Court (PCC) to that same effect (judgments kept in File No. 06534-2006-PA/TC and File No. 6546-2006-PA/TC)—the reflection on drinking water as a fundamental right in Peru is still a pending task. Indeed, its constitutional recognition proves as much.

As a fundamental right, drinking water has a constitutionally protected content that imposes a series of positive obligations upon the State (the objective, institutional, or social dimension of the right). It likewise involves a series of limits, since—like all fundamental rights—drinking water is not, on the one hand, an absolute right, given that it is also subject to certain conditioning factors related to its scarcity as a resource;[3] while, on the other hand, its exercise may enter into conflict with other rights, which must be analyzed on a case-by-case basis, using the proportionality test.

In the present paper, we will address the constitutionally protected content of the right to drinking water, as well as the obligations that arise from this content. We will then examine—briefly, at least—some of the limits to this right. Lastly, we will review the jurisprudential practice of the PCC with regard to the right in question.

---

[2] On the precedents for the recognition of the right to drinking water in other international instruments, see Blanco (2017: 206-210); Ubajoa (2016: 27-37); and Bernal (2015: 184-185).

[3] Although water is abundant on our planet (over 70% of which is covered by oceans), the water that is put through the purification process is not taken from the oceans, but from freshwater sources. As such, just 2.53% of all water on our planet can be used for human activities (Salmón 2012: 245)

II. Constitutionally Protected Content of the Right to Drinking Water

The determination of the precise constitutionally protected content of a right must necessarily start with the constitutional recognition of the right itself. As we have seen, the Peruvian Constitution of 1993 recognizes and guarantees the right of universal and progressive access to drinking water. However, based on an interpretation aligned with the international instruments that recognize human rights and the jurisprudence developed on the matter by the bodies responsible for the control and oversight of those instruments,[4] we will expand upon the said content. For this purpose, we will essentially make use of General Comment No. 15 of the UN Committee on Economic, Social, and Cultural Rights.

It should be noted here that the content of the fundamental right to drinking water encompasses *at least* the following three minimum rights:[5]

Minimum Rights[6]	Specific Content
Right of access to the supply of drinking water	Universal and progressive access to the supply of drinking water. Prohibition of unjustified exclusion from access (prohibition of discrimination). Reasonability of rates, such that they can cover the cost of providing the service. This does not exclude the possibility of subsidies (such as those currently provided).

[4] The interpretation—in accordance with human rights treaties—of constitutional provisions recognising rights is established in the Fourth Final and Temporary Provision of the Constitution of 1993, and in the Preliminary Title, Section V of the Code of Constitutional Procedure.

[5] Without prejudice to the foregoing, the PCC has established that the minimum content of the right to drinking water includes access, quality, and sufficiency (judgment kept in File No. 6534-2006-PA, Santos Eresminda Távara Ceferino case, Merits 22 to 24).

[6] This tripartite structure has been used by the PCC in other cases involving pensions, such as the judgment kept in File No. 00050-2004-AI (constitutional amendment of the pension regime set forth in Decree Law (Decreto Ley) 20530) and the judgment kept in File No. 1417-2005-PA (Anicama Hernández case, involving the essential content of the right to a pension).

Right to a minimum supply of drinking water	The service must be provided continually, which does not exclude the use of a system for rationing its supply. The water supplied must be sufficient to cover basic needs for personal consumption and hygiene. The water supplied must meet adequate health conditions (quality) to make it apt for human consumption.
Right not to be arbitrarily deprived of the supply of drinking water	Prohibition against the State or private third parties from arbitrarily interrupting, suspending, or cutting off supply of the service.

These minimum rights, taken as a whole, impose a series of positive obligations with which the State must comply.

III. Positive Obligations of the State with regard to the Constitutionally Protected Content of the Fundamental Right to Drinking Water

Broadly speaking, the State's positive obligations are to satisfy access to the progressive supply of drinking water for the entire population; to guarantee that the water supplied meets certain conditions that ensure it is apt for human consumption; and to protect individuals in case of arbitrary deprivation of the supply.

Delving into further detail now, it can thus be established that in terms of access,[7] the State must implement the infrastructure—whether directly or indirectly (through private concessionaires)—that conveys the water to its recipients. Specifically, the State must ensure that:

---

[7] According to the Ministry of Housing, Construction, and Sanitation, 93.4% of Peru's population has access to drinking water in urban areas; but only 63.2% in rural areas. Of the annual volume used, 87.7% goes to agriculture, 9.9% to supplying water to the population, 0.9% to industry, and the remaining 1.5% to mining (Peruvian Ombudsman's Office 2015: 11).

- The drinking water services and facilities are physically present at those places where individuals reside, work, study, etc., or at places near to them.
- The water, the services, and the facilities must be completely accessible in economic terms. In other words, their cost must be affordable for all, except in those cases where, due to the upgraded or specialized nature of the service offered, a higher investment was required to make it available.
- In accordance with the preceding rule, no type of discrimination or distinction shall be permitted, to the detriment of equal conditions in the supply of water. The State shall provide preferential protection to the most vulnerable sectors of the population.
- The State shall promote a policy of ensuring that information is permanently available on water use, as well as the need to protect it as a natural resource.

In regard to the minimum provision of the service, this requires the State to guarantee its continuous supply. While ideally, a permanent supply would be offered twenty-four hours a day, this is unreasonable due to the scarcity of water (Arbulú, 2014: 127), which has been accentuated by climate change, the pollution of water sources, and extractive activities (such as mining). In view of the foregoing, we do not believe that the right would be violated if the State were to guarantee a rationed supply of drinking water services (supply during certain hours of the day, restrictions on the use of drinking water involving administrative sanctions, i.e., only for human consumption, avoiding any unnecessary use). Such measures should ultimately help to achieve greater levels of coverage in the service for those who do not yet have access to it.

The State is also responsible for guaranteeing that drinking water can be dispensed in quantities that are sufficient, at a minimum, to meet elemental or basic personal needs, such as personal and domestic use; or even health needs, given that each individual's very existence depends on these needs being met. The WHO has established this minimum quantity at 50 litres per person per day (Ubajoa, 2015: 56), which may vary depending on the specific circumstances of each case.

Finally, the State must guarantee the quality of the drinking water, ensuring that it fully meets the applicable health standards. This includes the implementation of an adequate purification process, maintaining optimal conditions in the services and facilities through which it is supplied, and constantly monitoring the water's microbiological conditions.

For such purposes, the State must adopt the preventive measures necessary to keep the water from being contaminated with harmful microorganisms or substances, or even by industrial processes that are detrimental to it as a natural resource. Similar criteria must be employed for the services or facilities used to supply water. Indeed, the natural wear and tear of such services or facilities cannot be used as an excuse for any inadequate conditions in the water. Once their natural period of useful life has elapsed, these services and facilities shall be replaced with others that offer equal or better quality standards.

Water, in other words—as an asset whose existence must be guaranteed—cannot and must not be dispensed under conditions that are clearly incompatible with the basic needs of each person.

Finally, the prohibition against the arbitrary deprivation of drinking water supply imposes upon the State the obligation to create a legal, institutional, and procedural (administrative and judicial) framework that enables any person who believes his or her rights have been affected to seek the restitution of such rights by the competent authorities.

IV. Limits on the Fundamental Right to Drinking Water

The limitations on the right to drinking water stem from problems encountered when attempting to achieve universal access. This is because there are not enough resources to implement the infrastructure needed to convey the water supply to the entire population. In Peru, this impossibility is also linked to the geographic conditions under which the drinking water networks must be built, or, in some cases, the lack of water sources (rivers, lakes, melt-off from mountain peaks).

Another supply-side problem is the contamination of water sources, which requires an outlay of resources to purify the water. This ultimately leads to a higher cost for the population, paradoxically leading to exclusion, since not everyone is able to afford the rates.

The supply of drinking water is an essential public service. However, like all public services, its enjoyment involves a cost, and this cost can either be covered through taxes or through rates charged for the provision of the service. In this regard, problems may arise due to the privatization of water and the establishment of rates that are too high, to the detriment—in terms of access—of the lower-income sectors of the population. Therefore, if we are to promote a system of public-private partnerships in an effort to guarantee universal access, special attention must be paid to the design of the projects (contracts), since recent experience shows that this system has been used to engage in corruption, on the one hand; and has increased the cost of public services and fostered exclusion, on the other, a situation experienced more acutely among those sectors that have historically been left behind.

In any case, it is the State's responsibility to make sure that the rates charged for the supply of drinking water are reasonably proportional to the cost involved in building and maintaining the networks, plus the cost of purifying the water. Alternately, the State can establish a system of subsidies, such as the one currently in force in Peru.

Finally, and solely for the purposes of illustration, the right to drinking water may come into conflict with other constitutionally protected rights. For example, it may clash with the right to the free development of one's personality, given that some sectors of the population, during the hot summer months, use water in their Carnival games or set up portable pools in the street. It may conflict with the right to property, in those cases where it becomes necessary to expropriate private property so as to improve or expand the water supply infrastructure. It may be at odds with the right to freedom of contract, since the water supply is granted based on a contract, by virtue of which the temporary or permanent suspension of the supply may be implemented as a contractual punishment in the case of failure to pay the established rates (indeed, such cases have already been addressed in the jurisprudence, as we will see in the following section). Or it may conflict with the regime for the promotion and protection of foreign investment and arbitration, given that many disputes with investors in large-scale infrastructure projects involve the protection of water sources (Bohoslavsky and Bautista, 2011).

V. The Jurisprudence of the Constitutional Court with regard to the Fundamental Right to Drinking Water

The table below contains a summary of those cases ruled on by the PCC that involve the right to drinking water, following the recognition of this right from 2006 through to 2013, according to the ruling database search function available on the Court's website.

Summary of cases ruled on by the constitutional court involving the fundamental right to drinking water (2006-2013)

No.	File No.	Relevant Facts of the Case	Resolution and *Ratio Decidendi* of the Case, According to the Constitutional Court	Aspect of the Right to Drinking Water Infringed upon in the Case
1	06534-2006-PA	Santos Eresminda Távara Ceferino filed a petition against SEDAPAL, seeking to have the water service in her apartment restored. The service was suspended by the respondent by virtue of a contractual clause which stated that if any of the apartment owners in the building were more than two months behind on their bill payments, the water supply would be cut off to all of the apartments in the building, an event that had effectively occurred in this case. The petitioner, however, was up-to-date on her payments.	In this case, the Court concluded that although SEDAPAL's response may be considered suitable, it was also unnecessary, given that it was disproportionate to suspend the water supply of someone who was up-to-date with their bill payments. The PCC also used this case to formally recognize drinking water as a fundamental right, based on the unenumerated rights clause (Section 3 of the Constitution), and to establish the essential characteristics of this right.	Recognition of the right to drinking water. Right not to be arbitrarily deprived of access to drinking water.
2	06546-2006-PA	César Augusto Zúñiga López filed a petition against the drinking water service provider in Lambayeque, seeking to have his drinking water service restored. The respondent alleged that his petition was inadmissible, because the prior account owner still owed money. The petitioner stated that he had filed an appeal via administrative channels. However, as of the date on which the petition was filed, the administrative appeal was still awaiting a ruling.	The PCC declared the petition inadmissible, given that the administrative appeals body had ruled on the appeal, ordering the company to issue a new decision in the case. As such, the PCC found that all prior legal channels had yet to be exhausted. Without prejudice to the foregoing, the Court recognized the right to drinking water as a fundamental right, and established the content of the said right.	Recognition of the right to drinking water and its essential content.

3	03668-2009-PA	Hermegilda García Salgado filed a petition against the company Blue Hill SAC, seeking to force the company—in its capacity as drinking water and electricity service provider for the Fundo San Hilarión in Cañete, where the petitioner's property is located—to restore her utility services. According to the petitioner, the respondent had cut off the supply of the utilities in question for no reason whatsoever. For its part, the respondent company claimed that it was the new owner of the estate, for which reason it was not responsible for assuming any charges, including the consumption of electricity and water by the petitioner. The respondent demanded that the petitioner vacate the property.	The PCC declared the petition well founded, since it was proven in this case that the petitioner's utilities had been cut off arbitrarily, without any justification whatsoever, considering that the petitioner had not refused at any point to pay the cost of the services provided. The PCC further stated that the sudden cut-off of the services, including drinking water, was an abuse of the cause of action, given that it is prohibited to take justice into one's own hands, and especially to use basic services as a means of coercion to force the tenant to vacate the property, when there are other legal means available in accordance with law.	Right not to be arbitrarily deprived of access to drinking water.
4	05657-2009-HC	Guillermo Maura Beramendi filed a petition seeking a writ of habeas corpus in favour of Julio César Salinas Saavedra, against the Head of the Villa El Salvador Commercial Office of SEDAPAL. In this case, the petitioner argued that on June 18, 2009, the respondent ordered the beneficiary's drinking water supply to be cut off, which infringed on his right to drinking water, in connection with the	The case was dismissed in the first and second instance, because it did not involve the constitutionally protected content of any right protected by habeas corpus. However, the PCC did state that "in the abstract, the suspension of water services may have a concrete, negative impact, whether as a threat or a violation, on an individual's psychosomatic wellbeing. It is thus	Right not to be arbitrarily deprived of access to drinking water.

		right to personal wellbeing.	necessary to order the admission of the petition in question for processing, in order to evaluate the subject matter of the dispute regarding the alleged violation of the right to drinking water, in connection to the right to personal wellbeing" (Merit 4).	
5	03030-2010-PA	Edmer Trujillo Mori filed a petition against the SUNAT, challenging the proceeding for coercive enforcement brought by the entity against EPS Moquegua S.A. The petitioner argued that the collection of the debt (in excess of 11 million soles) would pose a risk to the provision of the drinking water supply service.	All instances, including the PCC, found that the right to drinking water would not be affected.	There is no connection with the right to drinking water.
6	01985-2011-PA	Eduardo Malca Vásquez filed a petition against the Sanitation Services Management Board (JASS) of Santa Rosa de Lima-Mollepampa (Cajamarca), seeking the restoration of his water supply. The respondent argued that the supply was being provided by virtue of a contract, due to the fact that the SEDACAJ had not yet expanded its drinking water supply network to the area. As such, the members of the Santa Rosa Housing Cooperative had authorized the provision of the water supply service to people who were not members of	The PCC declared the petition unfounded, given that the petitioner was not a member of the Santa Rosa Housing Cooperative, to which the respondent is obligated to supply drinking water. Supplying drinking water to the petitioner was in fact a violation of the authorization granted by the Irrigation District Technical Management of the Cajamarca Regional Directorate of Agriculture, since it was only authorized to provide a water supply to the members of the said Cooperative, of which the petitioner	Right not to be arbitrarily deprived of a drinking water supply.

		the cooperative, among them the plaintiff.	does not form part. Therefore, the cutting-off of the supply is not a violation of the right to drinking water. In this case, it was verified that the petitioner, acting through his daughter, had asked the SEDACAJ to provide the drinking water supply service, and a meter had been installed, although it had yet to be activated because the installation cost had still not been paid.	
7	02428-2011-PA	José Jorge Díaz Arrascue filed a petition against the District Mayor of Huambos for ordering the suspension of his water supply service. In this case, there is proof of an order to suspend service due to an illegal connection that was installed by the plaintiff.	The PCC declared the petition inadmissible, stating that there was a need for further evidence in the case, and that it could not be determined based on the evidence found in the case file whether the suspension of the service involved a legal or illegal connection. As such, the PCC left unharmed the petitioner's ability to seek the protection of his rights via other channels.	Right not to be arbitrarily deprived of a drinking water supply.
8	00001-2012-PI	The Public Prosecutor's Office challenged Regional Ordinance 036-2011-GR.CAJ-CR, which declared the Conga mining project inviable.	The PCC admitted the complaint, arguing that, according to the competence test, large-scale mining activities such as those of the Conga project are the competence of the national government, and not the regional governments. It was therefore up to the National Water Authority (ANA), and not the Regional Government of	This case involves water's dimension as a natural resource, although it also indirectly involves the right of access to drinking water.

			Cajamarca, to declare the intangibility of the headwaters located within the area of the Conga mining project.	
9	00753-2012-PA	Octavio Dávila Pucllas filed a petition against the Municipal Mayor of the Populated Centre of Huachipa, claiming that the respondent had cut off his drinking water supply in an attempt to evict him from his property. He thus sought the annulment of Manager's Resolution No. 051-2009-GDUC/MCPSMH, which denied the request to issue a certificate of possession and ordered that the petitioner be removed from the taxpayers' registry.	The petition was dismissed *in limine* by the judicial branch, because the case did not involve a violation of any fundamental right. In any case, it would require an evidentiary stage that does not exist in a proceeding for the protection of constitutional rights (*amparo*). Even so, the PCC stated that there was an aspect of the right to drinking water that should be addressed by the constitutional judges, for which reason the Court ordered the petition to be admitted for processing.	Right not to be arbitrarily deprived of access to drinking water.
10	01573-2012-PA	The Asociación Pro Vivienda Las Lomas, in the city of Pisco, filed a petition against EMAPISCO S.A., stating that the entity in question had been refusing to provide the association with drinking water via the installation of four fountains. The petitioners further claimed that it was public knowledge that they had possessed—peacefully, without interruption, and in good faith, for more than five years—a plot of land adjacent to the property of the Ministry of Agriculture, for which they hold	The petition was admitted, and the respondent was ordered to provide water using tank trucks. The PCC ruled that access to drinking water is not conditional upon proof of ownership of the land where the users live, but instead is based on their need for access to this resource for their day-to-day activities. Furthermore, the installation of infrastructure and the cost entailed therein cannot be considered an obstacle to the provision of water. As such, appropriate temporary measures may be implemented to	The right of access to a drinking water supply.

		certificates of possession issued by the District Municipality of San Andrés.	meet the petitioners' need for drinking water.	
11	03333-2012-PA	Cruz Mario Rodríguez Velásquez filed an appeal for the protection of constitutional rights (*amparo*) against EPSEL S.A., asking the Court to order the said entity to restore his connection to the public drinking water network. The respondent alleged that the service had been cut off because the petitioner had an outstanding debt for the services provided.	The petition was declared inadmissible, in view of the fact that it was an abuse of the fundamental right to drinking water to seek the continued supply of the service in question when the petitioner had a past-due debt, especially considering that he had already appealed the said debt before the competent administrative entities and it had been upheld.	Right not to be arbitrarily deprived of a drinking water supply.
12	05856-2013-PA	Teodomira Pizango Vda. De Vílchez filed a petition against SEDAPAL, claiming that the entity had refused to install a drinking water meter in her name, despite the fact that she had met all the requirements established for such purpose. She stated that in 2007, her name was taken off the utility bill by her husband's co-heirs, and that SEDAPAL had denied her request because there was a lawsuit underway regarding the ownership of the property where she lives.	The case was thrown out by the judicial branch. For its part, the PCC ordered that the petition be admitted for processing, summoning the respondents to appear before it, given that the jurisprudence has established that an individual cannot be stripped of the right to drinking water by a third party (prohibition against taking justice into one's own hands); and that the right of access to drinking water does not depend on proof of ownership (which, in this case, was currently being litigated). For such reason, SEDAPAL's arguments had no legal grounds.	Right not to be arbitrarily deprived of a drinking water supply by a third party, as well as the right of access to drinking water.

Source: Constitutional Court rulings database search function (www.tc.gob.pe)
Prepared by: The author
Note: The search term used was "right to drinking water." The search function found a total of fourteen (14) rulings (including both orders and judgments). Of these, two were discarded: a) the judgment kept in File No. 3052-2009-PA/TC,

because it involved the arbitrary dismissal of the employees of a water and sanitation service provider; and b) the judgment kept in File No. 00666-2013-PA/TC, tied to the right to sanitation.

As we can see, the cases ruled on by the Peruvian Constitutional Court are mainly tied to the right not to be arbitrarily deprived of the supply of drinking water, except for two cases, which involve the right of access to a drinking water supply. As such, these cases involve the obligations of the State (and third parties) not to arbitrarily deprive people of the right to drinking water, and to guarantee access thereto.

In our opinion, the foregoing content of the right to drinking water has been successfully judicialized due to the fact that no exceptional difficulties were encountered in terms of proving harm to the said right. When it comes to other aspects of the right's content—such as water quality or the reasonability of rates, for example—the protection thereof would require the production of evidence, a procedure that cannot be accommodated in proceedings for the protection of constitutional rights (*amparo*), since their very legal design omits any such stage. In view of the foregoing, it may be necessary to consider designing a special judicial process to guarantee *all* of the constitutionally protected content of the right to drinking water.

VI. And What of the Right to Sanitation Services?

The right to sanitation services has been recognized at the international level as being complementary to the right to drinking water (UN General Assembly Resolution No. 64/292 of 2010). This is because the satisfaction of the right to drinking water is just one component within a broader process, since its use entails the generation of wastewater that must then be adequately treated so it can be reincorporated into the water cycle.

In spite of the foregoing, Peru's constitutional amendments have not introduced this right into the Constitution. It thus remains an implicit constitutional right, under the unenumerated rights clause contained in Section 3 of the Constitution.[8] On such grounds, the PCC has already

[8] Constitution of 1993, Section 3. The enumeration of the rights established in this chapter does not exclude those others guaranteed by the Constitution, nor others of an analogous nature or those based on the dignity of man, or on the principles of popular sovereignty, the democratic State under the rule of law, and the republican form of government.

recognized the right to sanitation in connection with the right to drinking water.

In the judgment kept in File No. 00663-2013-PA—following the same lines of argumentation set forth in the judgments kept in File No. 6534-2006-PA and File No. 6546-2006-PA—the Peruvian Constitutional Court recognized the fundamental right to sanitation services based on Section 65 of the Constitution, which establishes the right to the protection of consumers' and users' rights; and Section 58, which imposes upon the State—within the framework of a social market economy—the duty to act, in matters of public services, to guarantee effective and continuous access thereto and provision thereof to users, in sufficient quantities and without discrimination. Sanitation is thus closely tied to the protection of the right to health and the realization of an adequate and dignified standard of living (Merit 5).

In this specific case, a petition had been filed against the water and sanitation service provider in the city of Arequipa (SEDAPAR), seeking a court order for the installation of a connection to the sewerage networks along the stretch between the Quinta Residencial Don Carmelo Housing Association and the Entel Perú No. II Cayma Housing Association. The petitioner claimed to meet all the requirements necessary to be granted the requested connection. The respondent, however, argued that the petitioner needed the authorization of the Entel Perú No. II Cayma Housing Association in order for SEDAPAR to proceed to install the connection.

Ultimately, the PCC ruled that the respondent's arguments were baseless, given that such authorization is not among the requirements established in Law 26338—the Sanitation Services Act, for granting the connection. In any event, it was the responsibility of the respondent—and not the petitioner—to obtain the easement. As such, the Court declared the petition founded and concluded that:

> (…) SEDAPAR has abdicated its duty to represent the State and achieve the purposes for which it was established, that is, to guarantee the right of access to sanitation services, in view of its erroneous interpretation of Law 26338. Furthermore, it is arbitrary and injurious to the right of access to sanitation services to require that the petitioner carry out the procedure to establish the access easement, when this is in fact the obligation of SEDAPAR.

VII. Conclusions

Based on the arguments set forth herein, we may reach the following conclusions:

a) The constitutional amendment that introduced the right to drinking water as a fundamental right into the Constitution of 1993 has fallen short of its purpose. It also failed to include the recognition of sanitation as a complementary part of the right to drinking water, as acknowledged at the international level.
b) As such, the provisions contained in Section 7-A of the Constitution must be interpreted in accordance with international human rights instruments, as well as the interpretations made thereof by the bodies responsible for the control and oversight of the said instruments. With regard to the fundamental right to drinking water, General Comment No. 15 on the right to water and UN General Assembly Resolution No. 64/292 are of particular relevance.
c) The constitutionally protected content of the right to drinking water includes three minimum rights: the right of access to the supply of drinking water; the right to a minimum provision of the service (which meets the conditions of continuity, sufficiency, and quality); and the right not to be arbitrarily deprived of such supply.
   This content gives rise to a series of positive obligations on the part of the State, which has the duty to satisfy, guarantee, and protect the fundamental right in question.
d) Drinking water as a fundamental right is subject to a series of limits, tied to the scarcity of this resource, which thus affects its accessibility for the population. As such, this right may come into conflict with certain other constitutional rights. The principle of proportionality shall be used to resolve such conflicts, taking into account the circumstances of each individual case.
e) The PCC's jurisprudence mainly involves cases seeking the protection of the right to drinking water against the arbitrary deprivation from supply.
f) The right to sanitation has been recognized in the PCC's jurisprudence as a complementary right to that of drinking water.

Bibliography

ARBULÚ, A. (2014). "El derecho al agua bajo análisis: distintos enfoques sobre un tema que nos compete a todos." *Revista Virtual del Centro de Derechos Humanos de la Facultad de Derecho de la Universidad San Martín de Porres*, No. 1: 116-132. Last retrieved on October 7, 2017. Available at: http://www.derecho.usmp.edu.pe/cedh/revista/archivos/007.pdf.

BERNAL, C. (2005). "La protección del derecho fundamental al agua en perspectiva internacional y comparada." *Revista de Teoría del Derecho de la Universidad de Palermo*, Vol. 2, No. 1. Last retrieved on October 6, 2017. Available at: http://www.palermo.edu/derecho/pdf/teoria-del-derecho/n3/TeoriaDerecho_08.pdf.

BLANCO, C. (2017). "El derecho humano al agua: apuntes sobre avances recientes en mecanismos internacionales de derechos humanos." In GUEVARA, A., URTEAGA, P., and Frida SEGURA (2017). *El derecho humano al agua, el derecho de las inversiones y el derecho administrativo*, 205-226. Cuartas Jornadas de Derecho de Aguas. Lima: Departamento Académico de Derecho, CICAJ, INTE-PUCP.

BOHOSLAVSKY, J. and J. BAUTISTA (2011). *Protección del derecho humano al agua y arbitrajes de inversión.* Santiago, Chile: CEPAL/GIZ.

CENICACELAYA, M. (2015). "La justiciabilidad de los derechos económicos, sociales y ulturales: el caso del derecho al agua en la jurisprudencia argentina." *Dixi*, Vol. 17, No. 22: 71-85. Last retrieved on October 4, 2017. Available at: https://revistas.ucc.edu.co/index.php/di/article/view/1243.

COMMITTEE ON ECONOMIC, SOCIAL, AND CULTURAL RIGHTS (2002). *General Comment No. 15: The Right to Water (Articles 11 and 12 of the International Covenant on Economic, Social, and Cultural Rights).*

MITRE, E. (2012). "La protección del derecho al agua en el derecho constitucional comparado y su introducción en los criterios de tribunales internacionales de derechos humanos." *Pensamiento Jurídico*, No. 35: 231-252. Last retrieved on October 4, 2012. Available at: https://revistas.unal.edu.co/index.php/peju/article/view/38414/pdf_222.

PERUVIAN OMBUDSMAN'S OFFICE (2015). *Conflictos sociales y recursos hídricos. Informe No. 001-2015-DP/APSCG.* Lima: Defensoría del Pueblo. Last retrieved on October 5, 2017. Available at: http://www.iproga.org.pe/descarga/conflictosagua-1.pdf.

SALMÓN, E. (2012). "El derecho humano al agua y los aportes del sistema interamericano de derechos humanos." *Universitas. Revista de Filosofía, Derecho y Política*, No. 16: 245-268. Last retrieved on October 5, 2017. Available at: http://universitas.idhbc.es/n16/16-11.pdf.

UBAJOA, J. (2016). *El derecho humano al agua en el derecho jurisprudencial de la Corte Constitucional de Colombia*. Bogota: Universidad Externado de Colombia.

THEMATIC TABLE 9: CONSTITUTIONALIZATION OF LAW

THE CONSTITUTIONALIZATION OF THE PERUVIAN JURIDICAL ORDER: ADVANCES AND OBSTACLES TO THE PROCESS

ELENA ALVITES*

I. Introduction

According to Guastini and Favoreu, the constitutionalization of juridical orders consists of a process characterized primarily by the expansion of the normative force of the constitution in the interpretation and application of the different branches of law; that is, "*a process involving the transformation of a body of law, after which said body is totally 'impregnated' by constitutional norms*" (Guastini, 2009: 49; Favoreu, 2001: 40). Nevertheless, as we will see, the constitutionalization of a juridical order is not only a process, but can also be understood as a result, as a kind of consolidation of the democratic, constitutional state, in which relationships occurring in the community, between the community and the state, and relationships among the bodies of the state, are based principally on the text of the constitution. The effort to obtain this result does not necessarily represent what has come to be known as "aspirational constitutionalism," based above all on the imprimatur and political unity surrounding constitutions (García Villegas, 2012: 93-94). Without ignoring the political facet of the constitution, we also believe that the different constitutional provisions are normative mandates subject to

* Doctor of Law graduated from the Universidad de Alicante and attorney at law graduated from the Pontificia Universidad Católica del Perú. Advanced Studies Diploma in the Constitution and Fundamental Rights from the Universidad de Alicante. Ms. Alvites was previously the head of the Decentralization and Good Governance Program at the Peruvian Ombudsman's Office. She is currently an associate ordinary professor at the Pontificia Universidad Católica del Perú (PUCP) School of Law. She is also a teacher and researcher with the Constitutional Law and Fundamental Rights Research Group (GIDCYDEF), recognized by the PUCP Vice-Rector's Office for Research.

interpretation and application by judicial operators, and that this is a form of engaging in politics—but through the constitution (Häberle, 2017: 124).

The purpose of this text is to present some of the advances made and the obstacles encountered in the process of the constitutionalization of the Peruvian juridical order, based primarily on cases heard by the Constitutional Court, with the occasional case involving the Peruvian Supreme Court. This overview seeks to identify the strengths of this process, in broad strokes, while also identifying and reflecting—based on two recent cases—on the limits of constitutionalization, as a process and as a result, in political relationships and decision-making.

This document is organized into four parts. In the first, we examine the general framework of the constitutionalization of law, looking at some of the characteristics of this process as it occurs in a constitutional state. The second part presents some examples of the process of constitutionalization of the Peruvian juridical order, involving the protection of fundamental rights by the Peruvian Constitutional Court ("CC," hereafter) and the Supreme Court.

The third part of this text presents two recent cases that demonstrate how the process of constitutionalization of the juridical order adds contemporary nuances to the tension and debate between the principle of democracy—on which the legitimacy of the state's legislative body is founded—and the principle of constitutionality—in defense of which the judges of the Constitutional Court seek to act. This tension is rooted in the fact that the court's decisions raise *"questions regarding the displacement of political decisions, especially those of the democratic legislature, by the decisions of the constitutional jurisdiction"* (Häberle, 2017: 122).

Within this schema, one of the cases examined here involves the protection that the CC has sought to guarantee, on up to three occasions, for the right to collective bargaining to which the employees of the Peruvian government are entitled. The other case, meanwhile, involves the protection of congresspersons' right to freedom of thought against equally legitimate legislative measures intended to discourage—and, if necessary, punish—"defections" by members of congress.

Based on the examination of these two cases, the final part of this text will offer a few brief conclusions, which—as always, in the academic sphere—are intended to foster discussion.

II. How to Understand the Constitutionalization of Legal Orders: Context, Process, and Result

The constitutionalization of law is understood as a process in which the constitution, as the supreme norm of a juridical order, displaces the law from the said position, from both a formal and substantive point of view; in such a way that the interpretation of constitutional provisions ultimately redefines the contents of the law, its interpretation, and its application (De Cabo, 2000: 79-82); and, in general, the juridical concepts and categories inherent to the different areas of law. This process is driven by the need to implement the mandates, prohibitions, and permissions—the margins, in short—derived from the different constitutional provisions (Alexy, 2003: 54 *ff.*).

The assertion of the constitution's supremacy, in its status as the founding norm, and, at the same time, a framework for the life of the community, *"is not limited to the organisation of state life. Its norms also encompass [....] the bases for the organisation of non-state life"* (Hesse, 1992: 16). Thus, the normative force of constitutional provisions is asserted so that their effects may extend to social life, given that the constitution brings together the set of values and principles inherent to the interests of the different social sectors that form part of the community (Häberle, 2002: 109).

As such, the constitutional texts of twenty-first-century constitutional states contain not only a design for the structure, organization, and competencies of state bodies; their provisions also contain the principles and values of the community to be governed. These texts encompass a significant axiological content that largely coincides with the catalogue of fundamental rights, the effects of which are vertical and horizontal (Bastida et al., 2004: 179-195; Prieto Sanchís, 2004: 58-61). From this standpoint, the constitutional state can be seen as an improvement upon the state under the rule of law, given that it conserves many of the elements of the latter, while also incorporating new subtleties that make it more all-inclusive, now that constitutional law has become more a law of principles than of rules (De Cabo, 1997: 304; Fioravanti, 2004: 28-29); while the normative force of its contents is materialized through the interpretation of the constitution by the different judicial operators, and particularly the judges of the constitutional court (Häberle, 1997: 64-71; Zagrebelsky, 2002: 16-17).

Within this frame of reference, the constitution sits at the top of the constitutional state's system of sources of law, where it regulates the production and interpretation of other sources of law, while itself acting as a source from which the rights and obligations of citizens and public powers alike are directly derived. Thus, the text of the constitution possesses direct normative force (Hesse, 1992: 57-58), while simultaneously constituting a fundamental norm and program used to guide state policy, which—in a constitutional state—must be constitutional policy (Gomes Canotilho, 2003: 23; Zagrebelsky, 2002: 13).

Because the text of the constitution occupies this position, its provisions must be used to orient the formation of all other legal norms, while also conditioning the contents thereof, as well as the interpretation of the different legal institutions that form the other branches of the juridical order. In this way, the constitutional provisions serve as formal and substantial limits on both the legislature and the interpreters of the law, which must not be trespassed upon (Guastini, 2000: 241-243; Fioravanti, 2004: 38). As noted by Zagrebelsky, the interpretation of legislation is conditional upon a *"relation of adaptation, and thus subordination, to a higher stratum of law established by the Constitution"* (2002: 34). Thus, the constitutional state is likewise founded on the rationalist ideal of the limited exercise of power and the protection of individuals, given that the state's actions in people's private lives, the relationships between persons, and the relationships between bodies of the state must all be guided by the interpretation and application of constitutional norms, and not by arbitrariness.

In view of the foregoing, the constitutional state becomes the dialectical organization of the different constitutional values and principles that have imbued the different stages in the evolution of constitutional thought with their content (Baldassarre, 1994: 30). It is not merely a prescriptive model, but also the product of a process involving the integration of cultural and normative elements (Smend, 1985: 132 *ff.*) that give content to a substantive constitutional text that is at the same time pluralistic and open to interpretation. Therefore, the constitutionalization of the juridical order can also be understood as a result or a goal to be attained, in view of the fact that it brings the legal categories of the different areas of law up to date, imbuing them with a certain dynamism thanks to the constitution's open clauses, without neglecting to guarantee the ultimate objective of constitutionalism—that is, the rationalization of power and people's fundamental rights.

The constitution's status as a directly applicable and justiciable norm has changed its relationship not only with the law, but also with jurisdiction. The constitution forms part of the normative material that must be applied by judges, and the effects of its axiological content extend to the different branches of law. As such, the work done by constitutional justice—whether imparted by a constitutional tribunal or by the entire group of judges who make up the judicial branch—in specific cases, as well as in unconstitutionality proceedings, is a form of materializing the constitution.

It should not be forgotten, after all, that the constitution is an unfinished text, always open to interpretation so that it can respond to the ongoing, living processes of the community that it seeks to regulate, except with regard to the fundamental principles of the constitutional order (Hesse, 1992: 23-25). As such, the interpretation given to constitutional provisions by operators of constitutional justice and the argumentative techniques they apply to the solution of specific cases must bear in mind that the constitution is simultaneously a guarantee of the protection of personal rights, and the protection of flexibility as a sign of openness to social changes. As Landa points out, *"the concept of 'constitution' is rendered an interpretative concept* par excellence, *where the creation of law is not something that comes predetermined or previously concluded by the norm, but is instead the product of a constructive interpretation"* (2013: 71).

Some authors who have addressed the constitutionalization of juridical orders maintain that the guarantee of the constitution, through constitutional judges, is an indispensable condition for all processes of constitutionalization. Indeed, they go so far as to assert that without the functioning of the constitutional jurisdiction, it would be impossible to speak of the constitutionalization of the juridical order (Guastini, 2009: 50; Carbonell and Sánchez, 2011: 34). The role played by constitutional judges in the interpretation and application of these constitutional texts is essential, given that they are the ones who profess the binding force of the constitution, applying it directly to specific cases and interpreting the legislation in accordance with constitutional provisions (Guastini, 2009: 52-56; Carbonell and Sánchez, 2011: 345-37). Constitutional justice might even be called the architect behind the *hyper-constitutionalization* of the juridical order, interpreted, in the critical view of De Cabo, as *"the extension of rights and liberties until practically all matters are understood to be impregnated therewith"* (2000: 80).

Nevertheless, this impregnation or substantive constitutionalization of the juridical order remains a goal or result yet to be achieved, in terms of the influence of the constitution and fundamental rights on political relations (Guastini, 2009: 58). It is here, in this space, that we can truly substantiate whether the expansion of the constitution's contents—and fundamental rights, in particular—have had any direct effect on the public powers (Alexy, 2003: 47). As Aguiló maintains, the constitution influences the political debate and the political process, as a result of which, among other things, "*a) political actors exhibit a marked tendency to resort to constitutional norms when arguing and defending their approach to politics and government; b) political conflicts and/or disputes between bodies from different levels of government tend to be settled jurisdictionally, applying constitutional norms; and c) judges tend not to display attitudes of self-limitation or self-restriction when it comes to so-called political matters*" (2007: 667). In other words, this process is in some ways the materialization of the traditional aspiration of constitutionalism, which—to a greater or lesser extent, and always with the particular nuances of any given case—seeks to ensure that "[*t*]*he guarantee of fundamental rights is the ultimate purpose of constitutionalism. This involves the existence of limited government, thus excluding any form of absolute or authoritarian government, and includes, among other institutions, the separation of powers*" (Salarzar, 2008, p. 91). It is precisely this aspect that is most problematic in the process of the constitutionalisation of the Peruvian juridical order, as we will see at the end of this essay.

III. Some Examples of the Process of Constitutionalization of Law in Peru

As noted in the above, constitutional jurisdiction is the protective mechanism incorporated into constitutions to guarantee their supremacy and integrity, and the normative force of their provisions, since the function of constitutional jurisdiction, as Häberle puts it, "*consists of the limitation, rationalisation, and control of state and social power; it is a substantive collaboration with the basic consensus; it resides in the new protection of minorities and the weak, and in the prompt reaction to new threats to human dignity, with a not entirely apolitical character of guidance and response*" (2003: 154). It can thus be said that constitutional justice is capable of facilitating the balance among the different divergent forces in society, collaborating with the process of political integration based on the values and principles established by the authors of the constitution (Montilla, 2002: 96).

As such, constitutional justice—through its jurisprudence—has taken on significant weight in the legal and political life of constitutional states (Hart Ely, 1997: 66 *ff.*; Aja, 1998: XXIV-XXVIII), particularly due to its role as a guarantor of fundamental rights, thus consolidating its legitimacy and acceptance by the population (Rousseau, 1992: 129 *ff.*). The Peruvian CC has been no stranger to this process, in its role as guarantor of the constitution's contents, especially from 2001 onward, when it revitalized itself as a body of constitutional defense and the last resort in the defense of fundamental rights. It is this latter aspect, in particular, that has been a driving force in different areas of law. As noted by Landa, the constitutionalization of Peruvian law has found in the guarantee of constitutional supremacy, and in the protection of fundamental rights—from both a subjective and objective standpoint—the basis for its institutionalization and functioning, particularly through the CC (2013: 34-35). Indeed, the CC's jurisprudence has made notable advances, and has also been the subject matter of analysis by various Peruvian authors in the different areas of Peruvian law. The following paragraphs contain a short and concise mention of some examples of how—from the standpoint of the interpretation of fundamental rights—progress has been made in the constitutionalization process in Peru.

In the area of **private law**, constitutionalization in Peru is tied to the protection of fundamental rights in relationships between private individuals and the limits on freedom of contract (Landa, 2014). Thus, the effect of fundamental rights has been asserted in legal relationships between private parties (the horizontal effect) as true mandates and limits on freedom of contract. Without delving too deeply into the debate or the problems at the root of this complex issue (Mendoza, 2009: 15 *ff.*), the assertion of the horizontal effect of fundamental rights and the limits that this supposes for private autonomy has not led to the elimination of this autonomy, but only an adjustment thereof and a reappraisal of private law. With regard to this matter, the CC has argued on several occasions that:

> *Fundamental rights have a horizontal or* inter privatos *effect (see Constitutional Court Judgment (STC) 1124-2001-PNTC, among others). Such effect is derived, on the one hand, from Section 38 of the Constitution, which establishes that all Peruvians have the duty to 'respect' and 'comply' with the Constitution; and, on the other, from the principle of dignity (Sections 1 and 3 of the Constitution), since a person's intrinsic value means that his fundamental rights also have regulatory effects within the scope of society and private autonomy. The dignity of the person thus entails a universal extension of fundamental rights to encompass all types of recipients, such that there is no social ambit that is exempt from their*

> *normative and regulatory effect. Indeed, if there were any such exempted area—no matter how exceptional it might be—this would signify a negation of the normative value of the principle of dignity itself.* (STC 06730-2006-PA/TC: 9; STC 00607-2009-PA/TC: 3-4)

Accordingly, private autonomy and freedom of contract are also subject to limits imposed by other fundamental rights, and *"private law is no longer aimed solely at individual self-determination, but also social justices. It could thus be said that a new facet has developed [...] making it—more than was previously the case—less of a protective law, and more of a demarcating law, which provides guarantees against abuse, and it is with this task in mind that we now address other areas of law,"* such as constitutional law (Hesse, 2001: 73). Indeed, the protection of fundamental rights "*cannot be omitted in those ambits regulated by private law where 'private powers' are particularly harmful to fundamental rights"* (Mendoza, 2009: 14; De Vega, 2002: 694-695). This is the understanding expressed by the CC in multiple judgments, wherein it has adjusted the scope of freedom of contract, noting that it is not an absolute right and that contracts entered into in the exercise thereof must not violate fundamental rights:

> *The defence of fundamental rights [...] is a requirement derived from the Constitution itself, which, in its Section 103, emphatically states that the abuse of rights is constitutionally inadmissible.*
>
> *[...] Contractual agreements, including those entered into in the exercise of individuals' private autonomy and freedom of contract, cannot violate other fundamental rights, given that, on the one hand, the exercise of freedom of contract cannot be considered an absolute right; and, on the other, all fundamental rights, as a whole, constitute [...] a substantive order of values on which the entire Peruvian juridical order is based.*
>
> *[...] It is particularly evident in those situations where, despite having entered into agreements between private parties, one of the parties has accepted certain contractual terms which—if there had not been a need to obtain a good or the provision of a service, among other cases—said party would not have agreed to, given that such condition constitutes an obviously unreasonable self-restriction on the exercise of his fundamental rights [...].* (STC 0858-2003-AA/TC: 22-23)

The CC also extends this limitation of private autonomy to matters that cannot be taken to arbitration even when the parties incorporate them into the contract, given their relation to other fundamental rights. In this regard, the court has argued that:

> *Individuals cannot be stripped of their right to have their disputes or disagreements aired* prima facie *before the ordinary jurisdiction. Thus, only in exceptional situations, arising from the individual's own will, shall the exercise of arbitral jurisdiction be permitted. [...] Even when this arbitral jurisdiction is derived from the consent of the parties to a contractual relationship, such consent shall in no way justify the redirection of matters to the arbitral jurisdiction when said matters, by their very nature, cannot be dispensed with by the subjects party to said relationship. This is the case, for example, with fundamental rights—which, as we know, cannot be subject matter of any negotiation whatsoever, not even in those cases where a party has stated his express intent to rid himself of them or alter their content, in whole or in part. This is also true, among other cases, for criminal matters, or even tax matters, with regard to which the state cannot waive its capacity of oversight and punishment.* (STC 4972-2006-PA/TC: 19-20)

The CC has even asserted that the normative force of the constitution and fundamental rights has such regulatory weight that *"the statutory norms of private entities and the acts of their governing bodies must be in full compliance with the Constitution, and in particular, with fundamental rights*" (STC 06730-2006-PA/TC: 9). In addition to unfair contract terms, freedom of contract and private autonomy are also limited by the right to equality and non-discrimination, the prohibition of arbitrariness, and due process, among other fundamental rights (STC 6167-2005-PHC/TC: 20-23; STC 00142-2011-PA/TC: 20-21 and 26; STC 0729-2003-AA/TC: 2-4; STC 0362-2002-HC/TC: 2; STC 00481-2000-AA: 4). Constitutionalization thus becomes evident as a process in which, as Landa states, "*we must aid all persons and even the state, in order to enforce the clauses of our model of a social and democratic state under the rule of law*" (Landa, 2014: 327).

The constitutionalization of private law has also manifested itself in the so-called **right to family life**. In response to widows' pension requests filed upon the death of a male cohabitant, the CC initially expressed a traditional position on the social protection of the matrimonial family, despite the fact that Section 5[1] of the Constitution recognizes and offers protection to de facto unions. Specifically, the CC asserted that:

---

[1] Political Constitution of Peru. Section 5: Common-law Partnerships. The stable union of a man and a woman, free from impediments to marriage, who form a de facto household, shall give rise to community property subject to a joint ownership regimen, as applicable.

> *Equal treatment cannot be given to marriage and de facto unions. Given that they are dissimilar situations, they must be treated unequally. While no one can be forced to marry, neither can he or she be forced to assume the pension-related rights and responsibilities inherent to marriage. The Constitution is intended to foster marriage, which is presented as a constitutional institution. It is true that the Constitution protects the family and its members in the varying states of need in which they may find themselves, as set forth in Section 4 of the Constitution. But this cannot be automatically applied to the figure of de facto unions. It is precisely for this reason that we must determine what the pension laws have to say about the conditions for the granting of pensions.* (STC 03605-2005-AA/TC: 5)

The court also concluded that the Constitution seeks to promote marriage, and that the protection offered to de facto unions—a living situation that is quite common in Peru—is of a property-related nature and did not give rise to pension rights, since these rights, according to the corresponding laws, are based on the existence of a bond of matrimony (STC 03605-2005-AA/TC: 7). Thus, the CC never expressly declared which kind of family is guaranteed by the Constitution. The court's arguments regarding social protection in the matter of widows' pensions revealed its favoritism toward matrimonial families. The court later reconsidered this position, however, finding that both the Constitution and the Civil Code define de facto unions *"as those intended to perform duties similar to matrimony; that is, a man and a woman as a couple, who share equal considerations, rights, duties, and responsibilities, bound to support the household that they have formed with the mutual obligation of nourishment, faithfulness, and assistance, providing said union has lasted at least two (2) years"* (STC 09708-2006-P A/TC: 1). Thus, according to the court's definition of a de facto union as the basis for a household or family, when one of the partners dies, the other has the right to a widow/widower's pension.

This change in the CC's jurisprudential line was consolidated in subsequent judgments, where the CC argues that the Constitution neither adopts, nor attempts to protect, a single model of family. In other words, it does not provide protection only to matrimonial families. On the contrary, the mandate of constitutional protection of the family is open to time and social changes. This protection therefore applies to family structures other than the traditional model, such as those based on a de facto union, single-parent families, and even so-called reconstituted or blended families (STC 09332-2006-PA/TC: 8-10), as well as families out of wedlock (STC 06572-2006-PA/TC: 7-11; STC 09332-2006-PA/TC: 4-7). However, in this last case, the CC asserts that the constitutional protection offered to de facto unions applies only if the de facto union is compliant with constitutional values, in order to ensure its compatibility with the other norms of the juridical order. Consequently, this protection requires that the persons forming part of the union have matrimonial capacity—that is, that they are free to enter into marriage, if they so wish; that it is a monogamous and heterosexual union; that it is permanent, for a period of at least two (2) years; and that it has the appearance of a public conjugal life (STC 06572-2006-PA/TC: 12-19).

The protection that the state is obligated to provide to the different types of family does not mean that the state can neglect the mandate set forth in Section 4 of the Constitution, according to which it shall promote matrimonial families, which, in the opinion of the CC, *"involve greater stability and security for children."* It also states, however, that the family cannot be conceived of as an institute destined for procreation. Rather, families form essential nuclei of the community that serve to *"transmit ethical, civic, and cultural values"* (STC 06572-2006-PA/ TC: 10-11). In this auspicious context set forth by the CC, it comes as no surprise that, on December 21, 2016—in a proceeding for constitutional protection (*amparo* proceeding) brought against the Peruvian National Vital Statistics Office (RENIEC, for its acronym in Spanish), which had refused to recognize the marriage of a same-sex couple entered into in Mexico City, where such marriages are regulated by law—the Seventh Constitutional Tribunal of the Superior Court in and for Lima ordered the RENIEC to register the marriage as valid in Peru, given that such recognition is based on the fundamental rights of equality and non-discrimination, and the right to the free and full development of personality, as established in the Peruvian Constitution, the Universal Declaration of Human Rights, and the international human rights conventions to which Peru is a party, in accordance with the Fourth Final and Temporary Provision of the Constitution itself[2] (File 22863-2012-0-1801-JE-CI-08: 23-24, 35). The court also found it unconstitutional that the Peruvian juridical order lacked:

> *any institution whatsoever, whether it be same-sex marriage, civil union, or another, similar institution, that protects or guarantees the right of same-sex couples to enter into a union subject to recognition by the juridical order, thus acknowledging their right to form a family, gain*

---

[2] Political Constitution of Peru. Four: Interpretation of Fundamental Rights. Norms on the rights and freedoms recognized by the Constitution shall be interpreted in accordance with the Universal Declaration of Human Rights, and with the international conventions and treaties on the same matters ratified by Peru.

> *rights of inheritance, and a whole sequence of rights that* are *enjoyed by heterosexual couples. For this reason, there is a whole sector of the population that, as of this date, is left unprotected and subject to constant discrimination, because their rights have not been recognised, when the fact of the matter is that such couples exist and cohabitate, and that they wish to protect one another.* (File 22863-2012-0-1801-JE-CI-08: 25)

This is one example of how the constitutionalization of family law in Peru is currently being constructed not only by the CC, but also by other judges in the Peruvian judicial branch.

With regard to **mercantile law**, it is also possible to observe signs of the process of constitutionalization of the Peruvian juridical order in the actions of the CC. This facet of the process of constitutionalization is also interesting because, as Landa points out, it has occurred over the last two decades in Peru *"based on the growth of the country's economy, which has led to the legal development of a series of commercial acts, such as the creation, transformation, and dissolution of corporations; the execution of mercantile acts and agreements; capital increases and reductions, with effects on pre-emptive rights and the rights of minority shareholders; as well as securities, public access to mercantile records, and corporate privacy, among other aspects. These have warranted pronouncements by the Constitutional Court, not* ex officio, *but* ex parte*"* (Landa, 2015: 192). We are interested here in highlighting two relevant aspects of this process. The first involves how the CC has identified and enunciated the constitutional principles of mercantile law, while the second is tied to consumer protection.

When it comes to the constitutional principles of mercantile law, the CC has ruled that economic freedoms—such as free enterprise and free individual initiative—are exercised within the framework of the principle of the social market economy, as set forth in Section 58[3] of the Constitution. This principle, according to the CC, is consistent with

> the constitutional values of liberty and justice, and is thus compatible with the axiological and teleological foundations that inspire a social and democratic state under the rule of law [...], where competition is guaranteed, along with the transformation of individual productivity into social progress, to the benefit of all. [...] A social market economy stands

---

[3] Political Constitution of Peru. Section 58: Social Market Economy. The individual initiative is free. It is exercised in a social market economy. Under this system, the state guides the country's development, and acts primarily in the areas of job promotion, health, education, safety, public services, and infrastructure.

> in opposition not only to a centrally planned and directed economy, but also to a laissez faire economy, where the state cannot and must not interfere in economic processes. (STC 0008-2003-AI/TC: 16)

We thus agree with Landa's assertion that the scenario in which economic freedoms play out consists of three elements that must be considered jointly: general social wellbeing, the free market, and the role of the state, where this third element must seek to achieve a balance between subsidiarity and solidarity (Landa, 2015: 193). It is worth noting that interpretations of this constitutional provision must not champion the free market—or the maximization of competition as an expression thereof—as the component of greatest importance or normative force (López, 2011: 53 *ff.*), as some authors have argued. The mandate of the social market economy not only protects the space for the exchange of goods, but also stresses that this space must be suitable to guarantee the population's quality of life and respond to expectations for goods and services without excessive costs (STC 02093-2009-PA/TC).

According to the CC, this is the same framework within which free enterprise and free individual initiative must be exercised, subject to certain limits. With regard to free enterprise, the CC has argued that the recognition of this freedom in Section 59 of the Constitution[4] includes the power to choose the organization and develop the units for the production of goods or the provision of services, exercised within limits imposed by public order and the protection of fundamental rights, e.g., the right to health or personal integrity. In other words, free enterprise is exercised "subject to the law, with its basic limitations being those derived from safety, health, morality, or the preservation of the environment; and its exercise shall respect the different rights of a socioeconomic nature recognized in the Constitution" (STC 0008-2003-AI/TC: 26; STC 3330-2004-AA/TC: 32).

Along these same lines, the CC has maintained that the constitutional recognition of free individual initiative comprises free access to and continued participation in the market under equal conditions (STC 00051-2011-PA/TC: 20); and that this freedom is linked to Section 2, Subsection

---

[4] Political Constitution of Peru. Section 59: Economic Role of the State. The state stimulates the creation of wealth and guarantees the right to work and to free enterprise, commerce, and industry. The exercise of these freedoms shall not be injurious to public morale, health, or safety. The state provides opportunities for improvement to those sectors that suffer from any type of inequality, for which purpose it promotes small enterprises in all of their forms.

17 of the Constitution, which recognizes every person's right to participate, individually or collectively, in the different ambits of the country's life, including economic life. It must be understood, however, as a freedom that, when exercised, must not harm *"'the general interests of the community, which are protected by a plurality of norms contained in the juridical order,' i.e., by the Constitution, international conventions, and the laws on the matter"* (STC 0008-2003-AI/TC: 18).

In short, according to the jurisprudence of the CC, although the Constitution inarguably guarantees economic freedoms within the framework of a social market economy, it is essential to always bear in mind that *"business activity must be carried out with full respect for the fundamental rights of 'others' and subject to the norms regulating participation in the market"* (STC 0008-2003-AI/TC: 34)

The other aspect in the development of the process of constitutionalization of mercantile law involves consumer protection. With regard to this matter, the CC has gradually set forth an evolving line of jurisprudence. Initially, it considered the consumer *"as a mere final link in the production chain (objective notion of the act of consumption) [...], as just one more piece in the market,"* who had to be protected just like other market agents. Over time, its position shifted, however, concluding that the consumer is the weaker party in relations of consumption (Sosa, 2011: 146). This latter argument is based on the understanding that, within the framework of relations of consumption, consumers are human beings, and that, as such, their dignity and other fundamental rights must also be respected, protected, and guaranteed within this scope. Thus, from a constitutional standpoint, the standard of the average consumer holds that consumers act ordinarily in their relations of consumption, and not necessarily with particular diligence, such as *would* be demanded by the standard of a reasonable consumer. This position has been criticized, however, from an exclusively economic angle, under the argument that it fails to *"create incentives for responsible behaviour on the part of both suppliers and consumers, especially in those situations in which a culture of responsible consumption has not yet developed"* (Bullard, 2011: 188).

The protectionist stance that the CC has taken with regard to consumers is also expressed in the way it has interpreted and applied the mandate for protection set forth in Section 65 of the Constitution.[5] In the strictest sense,

[5] Political Constitution of Peru. Section 65: Consumer Protection. The state defends the interest of consumers and users. For such purpose, it guarantees the

this provision has an institutional facet, highlighting the state's obligation to protect consumers, while also identifying real subjective rights. This duty to protect may be interpreted as the objective facet of real fundamental rights, imposing upon the state the obligation to establish and adopt all measures necessary to preserve, protect, and materialize rights. In other words, it requires state bodies—acting within their competencies and duties, as established in the Constitution—to carry out actions to guarantee that these mandates are in fact achieved (Häberle, 1997: 189-192). This conclusion has also been reached by the CC (2003), in its argument that the special duty to protect *"requires the bodies of the state,* in suo ordine, *to establish or adopt all necessary and adequate measures aimed at preserving, protecting, and even repairing injuries to the different constitutionally protected rights"* (STC 0858-2003-AA/TC: 8).

In keeping with the foregoing, the CC has asserted that Section 65 of the Constitution establishes a twofold legal course to be followed: on the one hand, it establishes a guiding principle for the state's actions; while, on the other, it also sets forth a personal and subjective right. With regard to this second aspect, the CC holds that Section 65 of the Constitution implicitly recognizes the right to the defense of consumers and users in those cases where their legitimate interests—and thus, their right to gain access to goods and services in a competitive market—have been violated or ignored. This same section likewise expressly guarantees the right to information on the goods and services offered in the market, which involves access to "true, sufficient, appropriate, and easily available information"; and finally, people's right to health and safety as consumers (STC 3315-2004-AA/TC: 9; STC 7320-2005-PA/TC: 19-23).

The CC has also argued that the protection offered to consumers under the Constitution is based on a series of principles derived from the aforementioned Section 65, such as: i) the pro-consumer principle; ii) the principle of the prohibition of abuse of law; iii) the principle of real isonomy (equality); iv) the *restitutio in integrum* principle; v) the principle of transparency; vi) the principle of veracity; vii) the *in dubio pro consumer* principle; and viii) the pro-association principle (STC 3315-2004-AA/TC: 9), all of them with an essence that can be materialized in a subjective dimension able to be defended by consumers in both administrative and jurisdictional settings. In this regard, we coincide with Sosa, who states that *"the Constitution enshrines both a 'special duty of*

right to information on the goods and services at their disposal in the market. In particular, it safeguards the health and safety of the population.

protection,' as a mandate aimed primarily at the state; and a complex fundamental right 'to the protection of consumers' and users' interest,' which allows consumers to demand the protection of fundamental rights in their favour" (Sosa, 2011: 153).

Finally, in this overview of the most salient aspects of the process of constitutionalization in Peru, it is important to note three of the most important cases that have arisen with regard to labor law. The constitutional recovery of the protection of the fundamental right to work, deemed essential to social democratic states under the rule of law, requires that causality be respected and applied as a condition for the termination of the employment relationship (Villavicencio, 2013: 329-334). The Constitution of 1993 was drafted at a juncture marked by increasing economic flexibility, where certain forces sought to weaken the constitutional standards on labor, including the recognition of workers' rights and labor's status as a component part of the political and social system (Maestro, 2002: 3-8). Under these circumstances, note should be made of the CC's rationale in declaring itself competent to provide protection to the right to work, in those cases where this right is violated in connection to other fundamental rights, thus requiring the court to evaluate the termination of employment from a constitutional—and not merely a legal—standpoint. The court further asserts that, within the framework of a social and democratic state, the right to work as a constitutional right requires effective protection not only against arbitrary actions on the part of the employer, but also against violations by the legislative branch (STC 1124-2001-AA/TC: 2-3; STC 976-2001-AA/TC; STC 0206-2005-PA/TC: 7-25). Despite this progress in the protection of the right to work, the CC later qualified its stance—not without considerable criticism—with regard to government employees in STC 05057-2013-PA/TC, dated April 16, 2015.

Another of the constitutional aspects on which the CC has focused is the protection of the fundamental right to collective bargaining and the promotion of peaceful solutions to labor disputes, in accordance with Section 28 of the Constitution.[6] With the specific purpose of complying

---

[6] Political Constitution of Peru. Section 28: Workers' Collective Rights. The right to unionize, the right to collective bargaining, and the right to strike. The state recognizes the rights to unionize, engage in collective bargaining, and strike. In protection of the democratic exercise thereof:

1. It guarantees the right to unionize.
2. It encourages collective bargaining and promotes forms of peaceful solution to labor disputes. Collective bargaining agreements shall have binding force within the scope of the agreements reached.

with the mandate for the promotion of peaceful solutions to labor disputes, the CC has offered an interpretation of Section 45 of the Collective Labor Relations Act and its Regulations, approved by Supreme Executive Order (Decreto Supremo) 014-2011-TR. According to the CC, in the event of deceit or dishonesty in negotiations—negotiating in bad faith, for example—one of the parties is entitled to take the other to arbitration, even against the will of the latter party. In this case, the workers are the party with the standing to initiate arbitration; because their right to strike is also recognized by the Constitution, they must therefore choose between a measure of force and a mechanism for the peaceful solution of the dispute. This mechanism is known as voluntary arbitration, and has been addressed by the CC, in general terms, in the following judgments: STC 03561-2009-PA/TC; STC 2566-2012-PA/TC; and STC 3243-2012-PA/TC. Likewise, as part of a public interest action in which the court was required to evaluate the constitutionality of the voluntary arbitration mechanism established in Supreme Executive Order 014-2011-TR, the Standing Constitutional and Social Law Tribunal of the Peruvian Supreme Court upheld the constitutionality of this mechanism (Public Interest Action No. 5132-2014).

Finally, another area addressed by the CC in relation to the constitutionalization of labor law is the protection of the right to collective bargaining. Given that this has proved to be one of the most problematic cases in the process of the constitutionalization of Peruvian law, it will be discussed in its own section below.

IV. Tensions in the Process of Constitutionalization of the Peruvian Juridical Order: Two Cases for Further Reflection

By now, the constitutional court's contribution to the creation of law via interpretation has become quite evident, in Peru and elsewhere (Cappelletti, 1984: 628), especially with regard to the application of constitutional norms. It can thus be asserted that the constitutional judges, as part of their day-to-day work, must update the constitution and materialize its contents. This section will present two cases that demonstrate how the process of constitutionalization of the juridical order not only adds contemporary nuances to the tension and the debate between

3. It regulates the right to strike, so that it may be exercised in harmony with the social interest, establishing its exceptions and limitations.

the principle of democracy—on which the legitimacy of the state's legislative body is founded—and the principle of constitutionality—in defense of which the judges of the constitutional court seek to act; but also how the process of constitutionalization of the Peruvian juridical order is especially problematic when it comes to the relations between state bodies and their adherence to the mandates of the Constitution, as updated by the CC.

One of the cases examined here involves the protection that the CC has sought to guarantee, on up to three occasions, for the right to collective bargaining on the part of Peruvian government employees. With regard to this matter, the CC has pointed out the violation of government employees' fundamental right to collective bargaining by the legislature, on the one hand; while also addressing the lack of protection for the said right, given that no procedure for the approval of collective bargaining agreements has been established by law for those cases in which the state is the employer.

The other case addressed here involves the protection of congresspersons' right to freedom of thought against equally legitimate legislative measures intended to discourage—and, if necessary, punish—"defections" by members of congress.

a) Violation and Lack of Protection for Government Employees' Fundamental Right to Collective Bargaining

The first of these two cases is tied to the passage of Law 30057, known as the SERVIR Act. The purpose of this law is to establish a general normative framework that regulates the labor regimen, rights, and other aspects of the civil service or government employment. Critics challenged the constitutionality of this law, noting that it prohibited collective bargaining processes from addressing workers' remunerations, and restricted the subject matter of such bargaining to other employment conditions. In its first judgment, issued in May 2014, the CC stated that *"collective bargaining in the public sector poses certain difficulties, given that remunerations (...) are determined by the National Budget Act. This is not sufficient reason, however, to exclude union organisations formed by public officials from all participation in the establishment of their economic benefits, provided they respect the constitutional limits imposed by an equitable and balanced budget"* (STC 00018-2013-PI/TC: 74). However, the court was unable to adopt a ruling with regard to this aspect of the right to collective bargaining, because it lacked sufficient votes. As a result, the law remained in force, and the government employees' right to collective bargaining continued to be violated.

Later, in September 2015, the CC was charged with ruling on an action of unconstitutionality filed against Law 29812—the Public Sector Budget Act for 2012; and Law 29951—the Public Sector Budget Act for 2013. Both laws prohibited government entities and unions from engaging in collective bargaining and adopting agreements regarding pay raises, in addition to other unconstitutional defects that fall outside the scope of this text. On this occasion, the CC noted that prohibitions similar to those established in the challenged laws were also set forth, invariably, in previous and subsequent Public Sector Budget Acts, specifically those for 2006, 2008, 2009, 2010, 2011, 2014, and 2015 (STC 0003-2013-PI/TC, 0004-2013-PI/TC, 0023-2013-PI/TC: 92). Among other arguments, the court offered a joint interpretation of ILO Convention No. 151 and Sections 28 and 42[7] of the Peruvian Constitution, noting that the lack of any mention of government employees' right to collective bargaining in Section 42 cannot be interpreted as an exclusion of the right to bargain over remunerations. In any case, with a view to guaranteeing the right to equality and non-discrimination, it was necessary to apply the general protection provided for in Section 28 of the Constitution. The court went on to argue that although the right to collective bargaining is established by law, in view of the constitutional principles and other reality-based criteria that guide the formulation of the public budget (economic growth, the public debt, the evolution of economic cycles, etc.), it was not unconstitutional for the legislative branch to establish differentiated legal regimens for public and private employees in terms of the bargaining process (STC 0003-2013-PI/TC, 0004-2013-PI/TC, 0023-2013-PI/TC: 50-66). It did, however, deem it disproportionate—and thus unconstitutional—for the prohibition against salary raises through collective bargaining to be extended for such a long period of time, stating that "*although restrictions or prohibitions against bargaining for pay raises are not, in and of themselves, unconstitutional, it* is *unconstitutional for such prohibitions to exceed three years, which is the maximum period for which a measure of this nature can be extended*" (STC 0003-2013-PI/TC, 0004-2013-PI/TC, 0023-2013-PI/TC: 90).

[7] Political Constitution of Peru. Section 42: The Right to Unionize and the Right to Strike among Public Servants. Public servants have the right to unionize and the right to strike. This right does not include government officials with decision-making powers or those who hold positions of trust or management, nor members of the armed forces or the Peruvian National Police.

In the CC's opinion, Congress has violated the right to collective bargaining by extending the prohibition against bargaining, while also failing to fulfill its duty to protect—as derived from the constitutional recognition of government employees' right to collective bargaining—by ignoring its obligation to regulate such bargaining on a comprehensive basis, in relation to the state's budget capacities. As a result, the circumstances under which the bargaining process is carried out in the public administration, and the legal treatment of this issue, are incomplete and insufficient. Indeed, this represents a further violation of government employees' rights, since Congress has failed to sufficiently protect a fundamental right by leaving the regulations that would make such protection possible in an insufficient or defective state (Clérico, 2011: 179). This latter issue was highlighted by the CC, for example, when it pointed out that the SERVIR Act contains provisions that are not applicable to all public entities with regard to this matter (STC 0003-2013-PI/TC, 0004-2013-PI/TC, 0023-2013-PI/TC: 67-69).

In an effort to fix this issue, the CC called on the Congress of the Republic to act within the scope of its powers and approve regulations on collective bargaining by government employees, starting with the first ordinary legislative session for the 2016-2017 period, and for a term not to exceed one (1) year. In the meantime, the court declared a period of *vacatio sententiae* with regard to its ruling finding the prohibition against collective bargaining for pay raises by employees of the public administration—as contained in the appealed laws—to be unconstitutional. The court additionally urged Congress to include provisions in the new law establishing, among other aspects, the minimum amount of information that employees must have in their possession in order to initiate the bargaining process; the need for legislative approval of the collective bargaining agreement; and the specific bargaining process to be followed, as well as the level at which the bargaining is to be performed, in addition to other aspects pertaining to limits on pay raises.

In April 2016, the CC once again addressed the same subject, in response to new complaints of unconstitutionality filed against the SERVIR Act. On this occasion, the CC *did* find the prohibition against collective bargaining for pay raises by employees of the public administration to be unconstitutional. It further asserted that the principle of budgetary balance is not an absolute mandate, and repeated the criteria set forth in its ruling on the Public Budget Acts, once more urging the Congress of the Republic to act. Specifically, the court called on Congress to approve collective bargaining regulations, starting with the first ordinary legislative session for the 2016-2017 period, for a term not to exceed one (1) year, and again declaring a period of *vacatio sententiae* in the meantime (STC 0025-2013-PI/TC; 0003-2014-PI/TC, 0008-2014-PI/TC, 0017-2014-PI).

Nevertheless, as of December 2017, the Congress of the Republic has failed to heed the CC's call for action. None of the pertinent legislation has been passed, and the protection of government employees' fundamental right to collective bargaining continues—in violation of the Constitution—to be deficiently enforced.

b) Violation of Fundamental Rights and Failure to Comply with Constitutional Mandates: The Case of Congressional Regulations and "Defections"

On September 13, the CC issued a ruling on the partial unconstitutionality of the Regulations on the Congress of the Republic, amended in July 2017 by virtue of Legislative Resolution (Resolución Legislativa) 007-2017-2017-CR, with regard to the formation of parliamentary groups. In particular, we are concerned here with the provisions contained in Section 37.5 of these Regulations, which establish that:

> Parliamentary Groups are groups of Congresspersons who share common or similar ideas or interests, and are formed according to the following rules: (...)
>
> 5. Those congresspersons who withdraw, resign, or are separated or expulsed from the Parliamentary Group, political party, or electoral alliance with which they were elected cannot establish a new Parliamentary Group nor become a member of another, except in the case of electoral alliances, formed in accordance with law, that have decided to dissolve, in which case the members may form a Parliamentary Group.

As noted by the CC, parliamentary groups are organizations made up of congresspersons with common interests and ideas, which are formed by the political forces that have won representation in the Congress of the Republic. In most cases, it should be noted, these groups coincide with the programmatic foundations of each political organization. Their underlying objective is to organize Congress, making it possible to reach a consensus among different groups and thus more efficiently fulfill the constitutional mandates established for Congress. Without these parliamentary groups, Congress's work would be greatly hampered, to the point that it might be impossible to get anything done. It is important for members of Congress to belong to a parliamentary group, since this allows them, for example, to present bills, form part of commissions, run for leadership positions within

Congress, etc. In short, it enables them to comply with their congressional duties, as set forth in the Constitution (STC 0006-2017-PI/ TC: 107-108).

According to the CC, the Congress of the Republic is responsible for organizing its legislative work and establishing incentives, and even punishing those members of Congress who leave their parliamentary groups without justification, given that these cases of defection have a negative impact on governance and the legitimacy of the democratic system (STC 0006-2017-PI/ TC: 42-43). In doing so, however, Congress must strike a balance between its representative mandate and its ideological mandate, differentiating those cases in which a congressperson is justified in distancing himself or withdrawing from a political group, in the exercise of his right to freedom of thought. In other words, to comply with its constitutional mandates, Congress must differentiate between illegitimate and legitimate withdrawals and resignations—that is, illegitimate and legitimate defections—from parliamentary groups (STC 0006-2017-PI/ TC: 73-78). If no such differentiation is made, then the provisions set forth in Section 37 of the Regulations on Congress violate the fundamental right to freedom of thought, freedom of association, and the right to political participation, in the form of free disaffiliation from political parties. Additionally, this situation violates Section 93 of the Constitution, which prohibits congresspersons from being subjected to imperative mandates, as well as restricting their functional rights and parliamentary duties, as established by the Constitution.

The CC expressly notes that the Constitution prohibits "the legislature from restricting congresspersons from forming part of a parliamentary group after leaving their respective organization for valid reasons, and for such restrictions to result in a direct impairment of the parliamentary duties directly attributed to them by the Constitution" (STC 0006-2017-PI/TC: 78). Nevertheless, just two days after the court's judgment was published, the Congress of the Republic approved a provision similar to that declared unconstitutional, as shown in the following table:

Provision Declared Unconstitutional (September 13, 2017)	Provision Approved Subsequently by the Congress of the Republic (September 15, 2017)—Congressional Legislative Resolution No. 003-2017-2018-CR
Section 37: Parliamentary Groups are groups of Congresspersons who share common or similar ideas or interests, and are formed according to the following rules: (...) 5. Those congresspersons who withdraw, resign, or are separated or expulsed from the Parliamentary Group, political party, or electoral alliance with which they were elected cannot establish a new Parliamentary Group nor become a member of another, except in the case of electoral alliances, formed in accordance with law, that have decided to dissolve, in which case the members may form a Parliamentary Group (...)	Section 37: Parliamentary Groups are groups of Congresspersons who share common or similar ideas or interests, and are formed according to the following rules: (…) 5. Those congresspersons who resign, or are separated or expulsed from the Parliamentary Group, political party, or electoral alliance with which they were elected cannot establish a new Parliamentary Group nor become a member of another, except in the case of electoral alliances, formed in accordance with law, that have decided to dissolve, in which case the members may form a Parliamentary Group (…). This prohibition does not apply to those Congresspersons who resign from their Parliamentary Group due to a violation of the guarantee of due process or the rights established in the internal regulations of each Parliamentary Group. In which case they may file an appeal, in the first instance, with the Parliamentary Group, and in the second and final instance, with the Steering Committee. 6. Those Congresspersons who have resigned in accordance with Section 5, Paragraph 2, or those whose expulsion has been overturned or annulled in accordance with the provisions established in Section 4, may join another parliamentary group or become members of the Mixed Parliamentary Group.

Prepared by the author.

This situation raises troubling questions regarding the advances made in the process of the constitutionalization of the Peruvian juridical order.

V. Conclusions for Discussion

Based on a quick and, at times, synoptic overview of just some of the strengths of the process of constitutionalization of the different areas of Peruvian law, it is clear that this process revolves around the protection of the fundamental rights recognized in the Constitution and their normative force. The Constitution is interpreted and applied directly in defining the institutions and categories inherent to private law, family law, labor law, and others. While the CC has played a leading role in this process, other actors in the judicial branch have also had a hand in it.

It would be naive, however, to assert that we are dealing with a linear process, free of nuances or even setbacks. The resistance displayed by the Congress of the Republic to the mandates of the Constitution, as interpreted by the CC within the scope of its constitutional competencies, can be observed in response to the court's judgments urging Congress to act, or even the court's ruling overturning the legislation passed by Congress. It is precisely this situation that is the gravest of all, leading us as it does to ask difficult questions: How effective is the protection given to fundamental rights, when it comes to the relations and decisions of political bodies? Does the system of weights and counterweights inherent to constitutional thought function effectively when faced with congressional majorities that scorn court orders, or—even worse—rebel against the constitutional design of the duties and competencies of constitutional bodies, such as the CC?

The process of constitutionalization lays bare the ways in which constitutional jurisdiction participates in the political life of states and updates the *conflict* between the political and the juridical. As we have noted, critics argue that the actions of the constitutional courts have upset the fragile balance between the juridical and the political within the state—where both variables coexist more or less harmoniously, yet always in tension—effectively politicizing justice, since it is impossible for the juridical to submit completely to power. Nevertheless, the constitutional jurisdiction remains necessary and legitimate, especially given that the constitutionalization of the juridical order occurs through the resolution of disputes—even political disputes—based on legal arguments, rationally constructed within the framework of jurisdictional proceedings. And that, above all, is the guarantee of its legitimacy.

Bibliography

AGUILÓ, J. (2007). "Positivismo y postpositivismo. Dos paradigmas jurídicos en pocas palabras." *Doxa. Cuadernos de Filosofía del Derecho* (30), Universidad de Alicante, pp. 665-675.

AJA, E. (ed.) (1998). *Las tensiones entre el tribunal constitucional y el legislador en la Europa actual*. Barcelona: Ariel.

BALDASSARRE, A. (1994). "Constitución y teoría de los valores." *Revista de las Cortes Generales* (32): 7-34.

BASTIDA, J., et al. (2004). *Teoría general de los derechos fundamentales en la Constitución Española de 1978*. Madrid: Tecnos.

BULLARD, A. (2011). "¿Es el consumidor un idiota? el falso dilema entre el consumidor razonable y el consumidor ordinario." In: SÚMAR, O., *Ensayos sobre protección al consumidor en el Perú*. Lima: Universidad del Pacífico. Available at: <http://repositorio.up.edu.pe/bitstream/handle/11354/186/SumarOscar2011.pdf?sequence=1> (last retrieved on October 30, 2017).

CAPPELLETTI, M. (1984). "Necesidad y legitimidad de la justicia constitucional." In: *Tribunales constitucionales europeos y derechos fundamentales*. Madrid: CEC.

CARBONELL, M., and SÁNCHEZ, R. (2011). "¿Qué es la constitucionalización del Derecho?" *Quid Iuris* (15): 33-55. Available at: <http://historico.juridicas.unam.mx/publica/librev/rev/qdiuris/cont/15/cnt/cnt3.pdf> (last retrieved on October 30, 2017).

DE CABO, C. (2000). *Sobre el concepto de ley*. Madrid: Trotta. (1997). *Contra el consenso. Estudios sobre el Estado constitucional y el constitucionalismo del Estado social*. Mexico: UNAM.

DE OTTO, I. (1999). *Derecho constitucional. Sistema de fuentes*. 2nd ed. Barcelona: Ariel.

DE VEGA, P. (2002). "La eficacia frente a particulares de los derechos fundamentales (La problemática de la drittwirkung der grundrechte)." In: CARBONELL, M. (coord.), *Derechos fundamentales y Estado. Memoria del VII Congreso Iberoamericano de Derecho Constitucional*. Mexico, UNAM, pp. 687-707. Available at: <https://archivos.juridicas.unam.mx/www/bjv/libros/1/340/32.pdf> (last retrieved on December 6, 2017).

FAVOREU, L. (2001). "La constitucionalización del Derecho." *Revista de Derecho* Vol. 12, No. 1: 31-46. Universidad Austral de Chile.

FIORAVANTI, M. (2004). "Estado y constitución." In: *El Estado moderno en Europa*. Madrid: Trotta.

GARCÍA VILLEGAS, M. (2012). “Constitucionalismo aspiracional: Derecho, democracia y cambio social en América Latina.” *Análisis Político* (75): 89-110. Universidad Nacional de Colombia.

GOMES CANOTILHO, J. (2003). “Teoría de la constitución.” *Cuadernos “Bartolomé de las Casas”* No. 31. Madrid: Dykinson-Instituto de Derechos Humanos “Bartolomé de las Casas” de la Universidad Carlos III.

GUASTINI, R. (2009). “La ‘constitucionalización’ del ordenamiento jurídico: el caso italiano.” In: CARBONELL, M., *Neoconstitucionalismo(s)*. Madrid: Trotta.

GUASTINI, R. (2000). “La Constitución como límite a la actividad legislativa.” *Derechos y libertades.* Year V (8): 241-252.

HÄBERLE, P. (2017). *Tiempo y constitución. Ámbito político y jurisdicción constitucional*. Lima: Palestra.

HÄBERLE, P. (2003). *El Estado Constitucional*. Lima: UNAM-Fondo Editorial de la PUCP.

HÄBERLE, P. (2002). *Pluralismo y constitución. Estudios de teoría constitucional de la sociedad abierta*. Madrid: Tecnos.

HÄBERLE, P. (1997). *La libertad fundamental en el Estado Constitucional*. Lima: Fondo Editorial de la PUCP—Master’s Thesis in Constitutional Law.

HART ELY, J. (1997). *Democracia y desconfianza*. Bogota: Siglo del hombre.

HELLER, H. (1974). *Teoría del Estado*. Mexico, 7th printing. Fondo de Cultura Económica.

HESSE, K. (1992). *Escritos de derecho constitucional*, 2nd ed. Madrid: CEC.

HESSE, K. (2001). *Derecho Constitucional y Derecho Privado*. Madrid: Civitas.

LANDA, C. (2013). “La constitucionalización del Derecho Peruano.” *Revista Derecho PUCP* (71): 13-36.

LANDA, C. (2014). “La constitucionalización del derecho civil: el derecho fundamental a la libertad contractual, sus alcances y sus límites.” *THĒMIS-Revista de Derecho* (66): 309-327.

LANDA, C. (2015). “Constitucionalización del Derecho Mercantil.” *THĒMIS-Revista de Derecho* (67): 191-204.

LÓPEZ, P. (2011). “La ciudadanía económica en el Perú: el consumidor.” In: Súmar, O., *Ensayos sobre protección al consumidor en el Perú*. Lima, Universidad del Pacífico. Available at: <http://repositorio.up.edu.pe/bitstream/handle/11354/186/SumarOscar2011.pdf?sequence=1> (last retrieved on October 30, 2017).

MAESTRO, G. (2002). *La constitución del trabajo en el Estado social.* Granada: Comares.

MENDOZA, M. (2009). *Derechos fundamentales y derecho privado. Eficacia de los derechos fundamentales entre particulares y su protección procesal.* Lima: Grijley.

MONTILLA, J. (2002). *Minoría política y Tribunal constitucional.* Madrid: Trotta.

PERUVIAN CONSTITUTIONAL COURT

- Constitutional Court Judgment (STC) 0858-2003-AA/TC. Available at: <http://www.tc.gob.pe/jurisprudencia/2004/00858-2003-AA.html> (last retrieved on December 3, 2017).
- Constitutional Court Judgment (STC) 06730-2006-PA/TC. Available at: <https://tc.gob.pe/jurisprudencia/2008/06730-2006-AA.pdf> (last retrieved on December 3, 2017).
- Constitutional Court Judgment (STC) 00607-2009-PA/TC. Available at: <http://www.tc.gob.pe/jurisprudencia/2010/00607-2009-AA.html> (last retrieved on December 3, 2017).
- Constitutional Court Judgment (STC) 4972-2006-PA/TC. Available at: <http://tc.gob.pe/jurisprudencia/2007/04972-2006-AA.pdf> (last retrieved on December 3, 2017).
- Constitutional Court Judgment (STC) 6167-2005-PHC/TC. Available at: <http://www.justiciaviva.org.pe/nuevos/2006/marzo/16/sentenciatc.htm> (last retrieved on December 2, 2017).
- Constitutional Court Judgment (STC) 00142-2011-PA/TC. Available at: <http://www.tc.gob.pe/jurisprudencia/2011/00142-2011-AA.html> (last retrieved on December 2, 2017).
- Constitutional Court Judgment (STC) 3541-2004-AA/TC. Available at: <http://tc.gob.pe/jurisprudencia/2006/03541-2004-AA.pdf> (last retrieved on December 2, 2017).
- Constitutional Court Judgment (STC) 0729-2003-AA/TC. Available at: <http://www.tc.gob.pe/jurisprudencia/2003/00720-2003-AA%20 Resolucion.pdf> (last retrieved on December 2, 2017).
- Constitutional Court Judgment (STC) 0362-2002-HC/TC. Available at: <https://tc.gob.pe/jurisprudencia/2002/00362-2002-HC.html> (last retrieved on December 2, 2017).
- Constitutional Court Judgment (STC) 00481-2000-AA. Available at: <http://www.tc.gob.pe/jurisprudencia/2002/00481-2000-AA.pdf> (last retrieved on December 2, 2017).

- Constitutional Court Judgment (STC) 03605-2005-AA/TC. Available at: <https://tc.gob.pe/jurisprudencia/2007/03605-2005-AA.pdf> (last retrieved on December 2, 2017).
- Constitutional Court Judgment (STC) 09708-2006-PA/TC. Available at: <https://tc.gob.pe/jurisprudencia/2007/09708-2006-AA.pdf> (last retrieved on December 2, 2017).
- Constitutional Court Judgment (STC) 06572-2006-PA/TC. Available at: <https://tc.gob.pe/jurisprudencia/2008/06572-2006-AA.pdf> (last retrieved on December 2, 2017).
- Constitutional Court Judgment (STC) 09332-2006-PA/TC. Available at: <http://www.tc.gob.pe/jurisprudencia/2008/09332-2006-AA.pdf> (last retrieved on December 2, 2017).
- Constitutional Court Judgment (STC) 0008-2003-AI/TC. Available at: <http://www.tc.gob.pe/jurisprudencia/2003/00008-2003-AI.html> (last retrieved on December 2, 2017).
- Constitutional Court Judgment (STC) 3330-2004-AA/TC. Available at: <http://www.justiciaviva.org.pe/jurispu/otras/3330-2004-aa.htm> (last retrieved on December 2, 2017).
- Constitutional Court Judgment (STC) 00051-2011-PA/TC. Available at: <http://www.tc.gob.pe/jurisprudencia/2011/00051-2011-AA.html> (last retrieved on December 2, 2017).
- Constitutional Court Judgment (STC) 0858-2003-AA/TC. Available at: <http://www.tc.gob.pe/jurisprudencia/2004/00858-2003-AA.html> (last retrieved on December 2, 2017).
- Constitutional Court Judgment (STC) 3315-2004-AA/TC. Available at: <http://www.tc.gob.pe/jurisprudencia/2005/03315-2004-AA.html> (last retrieved on December 2, 2017).
- Constitutional Court Judgment (STC) 7320-2005-PA/TC. Available at: <http://www.justiciaviva.org.pe/nuevos/2006/marzo/02/06_07320-2005-AA.htm> (last retrieved on December 2, 2017).
- Constitutional Court Judgment (STC) 1124-2001-AA/TC. Available at: <http://www.tc.gob.pe/jurisprudencia/2002/01124-2001-AA.html> (last retrieved on December 3, 2017).
- Constitutional Court Judgment (STC) 976-2001-AA/TC. Available at: <http://tc.gob.pe/jurisprudencia/2003/00976-2001-AA.pdf> (last retrieved on December 3, 2017).
- Constitutional Court Judgment (STC) 05057-2013-PA/TC. Available at: <http://www.tc.gob.pe/jurisprudencia/2015/05057-2013-AA.pdf> (last retrieved on December 3, 2017).

- Constitutional Court Judgment (STC) 03561-2009-PA/TC. Available at: <http://www.tc.gob.pe/jurisprudencia/2009/03561-2009-AA.pdf> (last retrieved on December 3, 2017).
- Constitutional Court Judgment (STC) 2566-2012-PA/TC. Available at: <http://www.tc.gob.pe/jurisprudencia/2013/02566-2012-AA.html> (last retrieved on December 3, 2017).
- Constitutional Court Judgment (STC) 3243-2012-PA/TC. Available at: <https://tc.gob.pe/jurisprudencia/2016/03361-2013-AA.pdf> (last retrieved on December 3, 2017).
- Constitutional Court Judgment (STC) 00018-2013-PI/TC. Available at: <http://www.tc.gob.pe/jurisprudencia/2014/00018-2013-AI.pdf> (last retrieved on December 3, 2017).
- Constitutional Court Judgments (STC) 0003-2013-PI/TC, 0004-2013-PI/TC, 0023-2013-PI/TC. Available at: <http://www.tc.gob.pe/jurisprudencia/2015/00003-2013-AI%2000004-2013-AI%2000023-2013-AI.pdf> (last retrieved on December 3, 2017).
- Constitutional Court Judgments (STC) 0025-2013-PI/TC; 0003-2014-PI/TC, 0008-2014-PI/TC, 0017-2014-PI/TC. Available at: <http://spij.minjus.gob.pe/content/noticia/pdf/LEY30057.pdf> (last retrieved on December 3, 2017).
- Constitutional Court Judgment (STC) 0006-2017-PI/TC. Available at: <https://tc.gob.pe/jurisprudencia/2017/00006-2017-AI.pdf> (last retrieved on December 3, 2017).

PERUVIAN SUPREME COURT. Standing Constitutional and Social Law Tribunal. Public Interest Action, File 5132-2014. Available at: <file:///C:/Users/eleal/Downloads/PC20160618.pdf> (last retrieved on October 30, 2017).

PRIETO SANCHÍS, L. (2004). "El constitucionalismo de los derechos." *Revista Española de Derecho Constitucional,* Year 24, (71): 47-72.

ROUSSEAU, D. (1992). *La justice constitucionelle en Europe*. Paris: Clefs.

SALARZAR, P. (2008). *La democracia constitucional. Una radiografía teórica*. Mexico: UNAM—Fondo de Cultura Económica.

SCHNEIDER, H. (1991). *Democracia y constitución*. Madrid: CEC.

SMEND, R. (1985). *Constitución y derecho constitucional*. Madrid: CEC.

SOSA, J. (2011). "Una mirada constitucional a la defensa del consumidor." In: Súmar, O., *Ensayos sobre protección al consumidor en el Perú*. Lima, Universidad del Pacífico. Available at: <http://repositorio.up.edu.pe/bitstream/handle/11354/186/SumarOscar2011.pdf?sequence=1> (last retrieved on October 30, 2017).

SUPERIOR COURT IN AND FOR LIMA. Seventh Constitutional Tribunal. Judgment kept in File 22863-2012-0-1801-JR-CI-08, dated December 21, 2016. Available at: <http://conexionvida.net.pe/wp-content/uploads/2017/01/336110538-Sentencia-Oscar-Ugarteche-Matrimonio-Igualitario.pdf> (last retrieved on October 30, 2017).

VILLAVICENCIO, A. (2013). "El derecho al trabajo: en tránsito del despido libre al derecho constitucional garantizado." *Revista Derecho PUCP* (71): 309-339.

ZAGREBELSKY, G. *El Derecho dúctil. Ley, derechos, justicia*, 4th ed. Madrid: Trotta.

INDEX